BONUS! - Heighte[...]
Mediumistic Abilities To Obtain The
Most Out Of Life

Dragonstar's Occult
Science Series

Command Others
Through
Thought Transference

Command Others

Through

Thought Transference

Inner Light/Global Communications

Command Others Through Thought Transference

By Dragonstar and Master Yogi Ramacharaka

Please address any questions about this book to:
mrufo8@hotmail.com

Timothy Green Beckley: Editorial Director

Carol Ann Rodriguez: Publishers Assistant

Tim R. Swartz: Editor

Sean Casteel: Associate Editor

William Kern: Associate Editor

Cover Graphics: © Vlue | Dreamstime.com

For Free Subscription to The Conspiracy Journal Write:

Tim Beckley/Global Communications

Box 753, New Brunswick, NJ 08903

Email: mrufo8@hotmail.com

www.ConspiracyJournal.Com

CONTENTS

THE BEGINNING

The Power of Enchantment to Command Others to Do Your Bidding

THERE are a lot of things in life that we simply do not have control over. With all of the factors that go into everything that happens around us and affect our lives we simply cannot have an impact on most of them. One thing that so many people think is far outside of their sphere of influence is getting people to do what they want them to. Everyone has free will, so if they are not willing, it is impossible to have any real influence over others. But just exactly how true is this?

What would you think if you were told that you could silently and subtly influence the people around you to give you what you want?

What would you think if you were told that just through the way that you think and the things that you day during a conversation you can get people to think and act the way you want them to by guiding their thoughts. This can make major changes in your lives, and you can use it to help others overcome difficulties in their own lives as well.

Impossible! Unimaginable? Unrealistic?

Well think again, because it is possible, and in this book you will be taught the amazing techniques to command others to do your bidding through thought transference, conversational influence and other secret methods that have been used throughout time by the world's movers and shakers.

Mind power is one of the strongest and most useful powers you possess. This power consists of your thoughts. The thoughts that pass through your mind are responsible for everything that happens in your life. Your predominant thoughts influence your behavior and attitude and control your actions and reactions. As your thoughts are, so is your life.

This is true for everyone. So to be able to influence and command others, you must first recognize how your own thoughts influence your reality. Thoughts have a natural tendency to grow and manifest in your life. If you feed them with attention, interest and enthusiasm your thoughts will become your reality. If your thoughts constantly dwell on the negative, your reality will manifest negatively. The same goes with positive thoughts. It may sound cliché, but happy thoughts will manifest a happy reality.

Your thoughts pass from your conscious mind to your subconscious mind, which in turn, influences your actions in accordance with these thoughts. Your thoughts also pass to other minds, and consequently, people who are in a position to help you, might offer you their help, sometimes, without even knowing why.

The power of your mind is part of the creative power of the Universe, which means that your thoughts work together with it. You are a manifestation of the Universal mind. When you repeat the same thought over and again, in one way or another, this mighty power helps you make your thoughts come true. This is true whether you have positive or negative thoughts. This is why it is important to learn how to control those negative influences.

Negative Thoughts Get in the Way

In order to be able to get people to do what you want them to do, you must first focus on controlling negative thoughts. Negative thinking is one of the most difficult things to control but it is an important factor of living a happier, more positive life. The average person has thousands of thoughts every second, some of which are conscious self-inflicted ideas, and others that play silently in the background of our subconscious mind. Many of these thoughts are immersed in negativity, whether we are conscious of it or not.

The problem with negative thoughts is that they tend to be difficult to detect and often create a snowball effect that can quickly overcome our minds. Consider a frustrated moment when you felt bad about yourself, chances are this one negative emotion led to others that made things even more difficult. When we allow negative thoughts to enter our mind we run the risk of allowing them to overcome us and even consume us in mere moments.

The reason negative thinking is so dangerous to our lives is because many of these thoughts happen deep inside our mind where we are unable to read, reach or even control them on a conscious level. Even though you will never be able to control every thought your mind processes, you do have the ability to choose and adjust the ones you think about consciously.

Conscious thoughts usually occur in reaction to some action. If you forget to do something during the day, your first reaction may be to think "I am such an idiot!" This routine reaction allows negativity to enter your mind get out of control. Instead of reacting negatively and blaming yourself, it is best to accept what happened and move on. Replace the negativity of the situation with a positive, purposeful thought instead.

Command Others Through Thought Transference

The key is to realize that reacting negatively is not going to change what happened. Remember that "this too shall pass," nothing lasts forever and each moment is an opportunity to learn something new. Look for the positive lesson in each situation and move on with your life. Don't dwell on the negative or you simply open the door for more negativity to enter your life.

One of the main sources of negative thinking stems from the words "I can't." I can't often originates from fear (fear of failure, rejection or judgment) and can be debilitating and harmful to your personal life. Fight fear with action and action oriented words. Instead of saying "I can't," just go ahead and give it a try. Not much is truly impossible; if you put your mind to it you "can" accomplish anything. Replace words like 'I can't" or 'I won't be able to' with 'I will' or 'I'll try' this simple act alone will change your outlook and greatly improve your level of happiness.

By learning to control those rampaging negative thoughts it will be a lot easier to influence others with your thoughts and commands. Negative thoughts actually act as a repellent. Positive thoughts are a whole lot easier to impress upon others to the point that people will want to do things for you.

Listening is also an important factor that has been largely ignored. People would rather talk than listen. You can use that to your advantage and let other people talk and tell you what they want and need. Freud pointed out that just the act of talking can provide healing. People tend to naturally do this in a supportive environment. By listening intently to what someone is saying you can hear what it is that they want and need. This is a great advantage for you as this makes it much easier to get people to do what YOU want them to.

The Laws of Enchantment

The Laws of Enchantment are in accord with the other laws of nature in recognizing the universal fact that there are various degrees of power, and that, all else being equal, the stronger power will prevail over the weaker. But, it is likewise true that the individual, by a superior knowledge of the art of science of defense and offense, may often triumph over a superior degree of strength in the other person. This fact is as true of Enchantment as it is of physical strength. The skilled enchanting individual may overcome his stronger adversary, just as the skilled boxer may overcome a stronger man, or a skilled fencer may disarm and defeat a much stronger opponent.

The conflict between the opposing enchantments of individuals is to be seen on all hands every day. In fact, it has been well said that two persons never meet but that there is at least a preliminary trial of enchanting strength. At any rate, no two persons ever meet, whose interests are in the least opposed, but that there occurs a little tilt of enchanting strength – sometimes a quite strenuous test, in fact. And in these tests there always is one triumphant and one defeated. It is true that the circumstances of the case sometimes affect the result, and the defeated today may be the victor tomorrow, but the fact remains, that for the time being, at least, there is always one on top and the other underneath at the finish of the enchanting duel, be it slight or serious. One has but to recall incidents in their own experience to recognize this fact.

Oliver Wendell Holmes recognized this powerful duel, in one of his books, when he speaks of "that deadly Indian hug in which men wrestle with their eyes, over in five seconds, but which breaks one of their two backs, and is good for three score years and ten, one trial enough – settles the whole matter – just as when two feathered songsters of the barnyard, game and dunghill, come together. After a jump or two, and a few sharp kicks, there is an end of it; and it is 'After you, monsieur' with the beaten party in all the social relations for all the rest of his days."

Dr. Fothergill, a well-known English Physician once wrote a little book upon the subject of the will..."The conflict of will, the power to command others, has been spoken of frequently. Yet what is this will power, which influences others? What is it that makes us accept, and adopt too, the advice of one person, while precisely the same advice from another has been rejected? Is it the weight or force of will, which insensibly influences us, the force of will behind the advice? That is what it is! The person who thus forces his or her advice upon us has no more power to enforce it than others; but all the same we do as requested. We accept from one what we reject from another. One person says of something contemplated, 'Oh, but you must not,' yet we do it all the same, though that person may be in a position to make us regret the rejection of that counsel. Another person says, 'Oh, but you mustn't,' and we desist, though we may, if so disposed, set this latter person's opinion t defiance with impunity. It is not the fear of consequences, nor of giving offence, which determines the adoption of the latter person's advice, while it has been rejected when given by the first. It depends upon the character or willpower of the individual advising whether we accept the advice, or reject it. This character often depends little, if at all, in some cases, upon the intellect, or even on the moral qualities, the goodness or badness, of the individual. It is itself an imponderable something; yet it carries weight with it.

"There may be abler men, cleverer men; but it is the one possessed of will who rises to the surface at these times – the one who can by some subtle power make other men obey him The will-struggle goes on universally. In the young aristocrat, who gets his tailor to make another advance in defiance of his conviction that he will never get his money back? It goes on between lawyer and client; betwixt doctor and patient; between banker and borrower; betwixt buyer and seller. It is not tact, which enables the person behind the counter to induce customers to buy what they did not intend to buy, and which when bought, gives them no satisfaction, though it is linked therewith for the effort to be successful.

"Whenever two persons meet in business, or in any other relation in life, up to lovemaking, there is this will-fight going on, commonly enough without any consciousness of the struggle. There is a dim consciousness of the result, but none of the processes. It often takes years of the intimacy of married life to find out with whom of the pair the mastery really lays. Often the far stronger character, to all appearances, has to yield; it is this will-element, which underlies the statement. 'The race is not always to the swift, nor the battle to the strong.' In 'Middlemarch' we find in Lydgate a grand aggregation of qualities, yet shallow, hard, selfish Rosamond masters him thoroughly in the end. He was not deficient in will power, possessed more than an average share of character; but in the fight he went down at last under the onslaught of the intense, stubborn will of his narrow-minded spouse. Their will-contest was the collision of a large, warm nature, like a capable human hand, with a hard, narrow, selfish nature, like a steel button; the hand only bruised itself while the button remained unaffected."

If you will substitute the term "Enchantment," for "will," "will power," etc., in the good doctor's words, you will see how perfectly he was in accord with the teachings contained in this book.

The student who has carefully studied the foregoing pages will have acquired sufficient knowledge of the theory and practice, the method and the technique, of enchantment, to be able to carry himself or herself though a "duel of the mind" with credit to himself or herself, and credit to myself, the teacher. But remember, that there is as much in adroitness, and skill, as there is in mere strength of enchantment. Carry in mind the tactics of the good boxer, or good fencer – try to reproduce (in the enchanting duel) the guards, the feints, the unexpected stroke, the rushes, the overpowering stroke, etc. It will not hurt you to purposely engage in some of these conflicts, as good practice preparing for the day of a real test of power on some important point. Assert your will a little, and strive to have your own way in small matters, particularly if you are opposed therein by others. The skill and practice, together with the self-confidence you will gain will prove useful to you in the hour or need.

In addition to the general and special instruction regarding the use of positive enchantment in relation to other persons, I now offer for your consideration the following special "flashes," for use on special occasions, especially in cases of the "enchanting duel." You will find these flashes of great use to you on such occasions, particularly (as is generally the case) where the opponent does not know the secret of his own natural power of enchantment, and is not versed in the art and science of using it. Study over these carefully – for they are valuable, and represent the result of years of experience and practice. Here follows the list just spoken of:

"My enchantment is stronger than yours – it is overpowering you."

"My enchantment is beating down your guard – you are weakening."

"I am more positive than you – you are negative and are beginning to retreat and give in to me."

"You are beginning to feel afraid of me, afraid, afraid, afraid of me."

"Retreat, retreat, retreat, I tell you – I am forcing you backward."

"I am scattering your forces – I am dissipating your energy – I am breaking your magnetism to bits, by the power of my own force."

"I am standing on the solid rock of power – your feet are on sand, and are slipping way from you."

"GET OUT OF MY WAY – I COMMAND YOU TO GET OUT!"

"I am crowding you back, off your feet; move back, I tell you - BACK, out of my way, I tell you!"

You may get the spirit of the above by carefully reading them, repeating them to your image in the mirror, throwing full fore into the words, and the expression into your eyes. Then you will be able to flash them out to others when the occasion arises, with ease, power and effect. You need not be bound by the precise words that I have given you, providing you catch the spirit behind them. You may use your own words – the very words that you would like to actually utter to the other person, if you prefer. The thing to do is to get the feeling and meaning into his mind.

"I am pouring into you a strong concentrated current of enchantment power which is overpowering you and conquering you, and bending you to my will. My enchantment is far stronger than is yours, and I know how to use it to better advantage than do you. I am overpowering you – I am conquering you – I am bending you to my will. I am MASTERING you, steadily and

completely. I shall command you to do as I will. You MUST do it, and do it now. Surrender, I tell you – surrender now – SURRENDER to me at once. You MUST, and you SHALL. I am breaking down your resistance. You are giving up – SURRENDER NOW – SURRENDER AT ONCE."

See Clearly What You Want

Another important aspect of learning to get others to do what you want is to first identify what it is that you actually want. A scattered mind leads to a scattered reality. If your thoughts are jumping all over the place, if you are not 100% certain what it is that you are after, then nothing is going to work and you will be left unsatisfied and full of doubt.

Visualization is one of the most important factors in controlling others. To "visualize" means to "see mentally"—that is, to form a mental image of a thing—to "see it in one's mind," etc., Visualization, along the lines of one's daily occupation is a most important thing, but one that is very poorly appreciated because little understood.

The best workmen, writers, inventors, composers, etc., are those who are able "to see the thing in the mind," and then reproduce it in materialized form. Sir Francis Galton, one of the best authorities upon the subject, has said: "The free action of a vivid visualizing faculty is of much importance in connection with the higher processes of generalized thought. A visual image is the most perfect form of mental representation wherever the shape, position, and relations of objects to space are concerned. The best workmen are those who visualize the whole of what they propose to do, before they take a tool in their hand.

"Strategists, artists of all denominations, physicists who contrive new experiments, and in short, all who do not follow routine, have need of it. A faculty that is of importance in all technical and artistic occupations; that gives accuracy to our perceptions, and justice to our generalizations ; is starved by lazy disuse, instead of being cultivated judiciously in such a way as will, on the whole, bring the best return. I believe that a serious study of the best means of developing and utilizing this faculty, without prejudice to the practice of abstract thought in symbols, is one of the many pressing desiderata in the yet unformed science of education."

And all that Sir Francis Galton has said above is equally true of the cultivation of the art of visualization in connection with Enchantment. The trouble with the majority of people is that they do not know just what they do want.

They are not able to form clear mental images of that which they wish to "create" or "materialize." The men who obtain the greatest and most wonderful results through mental influence, particularly in the form of enchantment, are those men who are able to "visualize" most clearly the things that they wish to "materialize"—who are able to form the mental image of the things they wish to manifest.

The secret of visualization lies in the occult and psychological principle that "as is the mental matrix, so is the mental form; and as is the mental form, so is the physical materialization."

In other words, the visualized mental image is the matrix or mold into which the enchantment is poured, and from which it takes form; and around this mental image the deposit of materialization forms—and thus does the ideal become the real.

If you wish to get the best effects from Enchantment you must create a mental image around which the material or physical materialization is formed—and the way to form the proper mental image is by visualization, which thus builds Tip the matrix or mold in which the Mind-Power pours. And as is the matrix so is the image, and as is the image so is the materialization.

Before you can draw to you the material needed for building up the things or conditions you desire you must form a clear mental image of just what you want to materialize—and before you can make this mental image, you must realize mentally just exactly what you do desire. And the process of this is called visualization. That is, you build up a mental matrix or mould, little by little, until you have it before you clearly—until it stands out clearly formed as a mental image, just as you would see it if it were actually materialized.

Then you must hold this mental image before you constantly, regarding it not as a mere imagination, but as a something real which you have created in your mind, and which will proceed to surround itself with the material necessary to give it material objectivity, or materialization.

If you cannot see the whole thing at first, as a mental image— that is, if you are not able to build up a complete matrix by visualization, then do the next best thing—which is the very best thing for the majority of people—and build a matrix of the first step toward the whole thing, that is, the first thing that is needed. Then concentrate upon this first thing until the mental image stands out sharp and clear and you will find that things have been started in motion.

Then, you may add little by little to your matrix, and build up your mental image a little larger and in greater detail. And here is an important thing. You must mentally see the thing as actually existing, right now, and not as "going to exist" later on. You must realize that the mental image exists right now, else it will lack clearness and effectiveness.

You must pour into that mental image a constant supply of strong, positive Desire-Force, and Willpower, all of which will spread out in the proper directions and affect the material needed to materialize your mental image. By so doing you impart to the Enchantment currents the necessary impetus and direction, and they will operate along these lines, and will proceed to materialize your mental image for you.

Things will come your way; people will appear who are necessary to your plans; information will come to you from strange sources, and in unexpected times and places; opportunities will open themselves up to you. But remember, you must be prepared to act upon these openings, and opportunities. You must be alert and watchful, and expectant. You will have to do the work, remember, yourself, although the forces you have started into operation will supply you with the material.

The door will be opened to you, but you must step in yourself; the tools and materials will be provided yon, but you must use them; the information will he laid before you, but you must make it your own. Even Enchantment will not avail the lazy man. You must learn to "do things" yourself.

Remember, always this rule—this Triple-Key of Attainment, as I have often called it:

(1) You must desire a thing most intensely;

(2) then you must earnestly expect it:

(3) then you must use your will in the direction of action tending to bring it about.

But first of all, as I have said, you must know just what you do want, and then proceed to create the mental matrix or mould by visualization—that is, you most proceed to mentally see it as already existing.

Enchanting the Mind

The pull of Mental Enchantment allows you to delve deep into the minds of others and allow your powerful enchanting energies to influence their thoughts and action in your favor. "Mental Suggestion" is the term used to designate this process of inducing or exciting mental states or ideas, by means of the imagination, by the agency of words of actions; outward appearances; or other physical symbols.

I divide the phenomena of Mental Suggestion into two general classes or phases, i.e., (1) Active Suggestion, and (2) Passive Suggestion, as follows:

By Active Suggestion I mean the induction or excitement of mental state or ideas in others by means of positive command, affirmation, statements, etc., bearing directly upon the desired mental state.

By Passive Suggestion I mean the induction or excitement of mental state or ideas by the subtle insinuation, introduction, or insertion of ideas into the minds of others, which insinuated ideas act in the direction of inducing the desired mental state. Active Suggestion is associated with the use of the motive-pole of the mind of the suggestor; and; Passive Suggestion is associated with the emotive-pole of the suggestor. One is the masculine method and the other the feminine. And here is a good place in which to direct your attention to a very important fact concerning the operation of suggestion in inducing mental states in others.

I allude to the fact that suggestion operates along the line of "emotional mentality," "feeling," or "imagination," and has nothing to do with judgment, reason, argument, proof, etc. It belongs clearly to the "feeling" side of the mind, rather than to the "thinking" side. One's reason may be appealed to by clever reasoning, argument, logic, proof, etc, and an effect gained—but this belongs to an entirely different phase of mental action.

The induction of mental states in others by means of suggestion has to do entirely with the "feeling" or "imaginative" phase of the mind. It deals with the production of "emotional mentality" rather than with "rational mentality." This is a most important point, and one that should be thoroughly understood by all students of the subject.

It is true that suggestion may accompany an appeal to the reason or judgment of the person influenced, and, indeed, is generally so used; but, strictly speaking, it constitutes an appeal to a part of the mind entirely removed from reasoning and judgment. It is emotional, and imaginative first, last, and all the time. And it operates along the same lines as the mental induction produced by Enchantment currents, as we shall see.

And now, with this preliminary understanding, let us pass on to a consideration of the meaning of the terms used. There is nothing like a clear understanding of the terms employed in treating of a subject. If one understands the "exact" meaning of the terms, he has progressed very far to an "exact" understanding of the subject itself, for the terms are the crystallized ideas involved in the subject.

Command Others Through Thought Transference

To understand the full and complete meaning of the terms of any subject is to know the whole subject thoroughly, for no one can understand a term thoroughly until he knows it in all of its relations—all that pertains to it.

Let us start with the word "suggestion" as used by the writers on mental suggestion. Some authorities give the broad, general definition of "anything that is impressed upon the mind through the senses," but this I consider entirely too sweeping, for this definition would make the term cover knowledge of all sort, no matter to what part of the mind it appealed, for all knowledge of the outward world is obtained through the senses.

Other authorities define the term as "anything insinuated into the mind, subtly, cautiously, and indirectly," this definition fitting nearly the one favored by the dictionaries in defining the word "suggestion" in its general sense, which is as follows: "a hint; a guarded mention; an intimation; something presented to the mind directly; an insinuation; etc."

But this last definition of mental suggestion does not fit all the phases of the subject. It fits admirably into the phase known as Passive Suggestion, which operates by direct, forceful command, statement, etc.

And so I must give my own definition of the term to fit my conception of and understanding of its meaning. I, therefore, here define my use of the term "a Mental Suggestion" as follows: A physical agency tending to induce or excite mental states or ideas through the imagination. This is a broad definition, which, I think, will cover all the observable phenomena of Mental Suggestion.

I use the word "physical" to distinguish suggestive agents from the "mental" agents inducing mental states by the operation of Enchantment currents. Of course this distinction will not please those who would claim all "mental" action as a form of the "physical," or vice versa.

But as I have to draw the line somewhere, I prefer to draw it between the "physical" agent and the "mental," and I think that the majority of my readers will approve of this position.

The word "agent" means, of course, "an acting power or cause," etc. The word "inducing," as I have used it, has been defined in the previous lesson. The word "excite" means "to call into activity in any way; to rouse to feeling; to kindle to strong emotions," The imagination is "that phase of mind which creates mental images, or objects, or sensation previously experienced."

In my use of the term "physical" in the above definition I include all words, spoken, written, or printed; mannerisms and physical actions of all kinds; physical; characteristics and appearances, etc., etc. All of these physical manifestations act as "agents" inducing mental states under favorable circumstances.

By "mental states" I mean "states of feeling or emotion." By "ideas," I mean "images of objects conceived of by the mind."
It may be urged that the use of "words, spoken, written or printed," may be employed, and are employed, in every appeal to the mind of another, whether the appeal be along the lines of suggestion or argument, reason, etc. Certainly!

And in that sense they act as suggestions. Arguments appeal to judgment and reason—but not to feeling, emotion or imagination which are, on the contrary, excited or induced by suggestions or other forms of emotional induction.

Command Others Through Thought Transference

One may present an idea to the mind of another, in a bold, forcible, logical manner, accompanied by argument or proof, but this is an appeal to reason and judgment, not to "feeling or emotion," which belong to an entirely different field of the mind. Then again, many personal appeals, which are apparently made to reason, are really made to the emotional side.

One may subtly insinuate into an argument or conversation an appeal to the feelings or emotion of the hearer, in the shape of an idea in the nature of a hint, or indirect mention. Such idea will be "felt" by the listener, who will accept it into his mind, and before long he will regard it as one of his own thoughts—he will make it his own. He will think that he "thought" it, whereas, really, he simply "feels" it, and the "feeling" is induced. This is a case of "suggestion."

In ordinary social intercourse you will find that women are adepts in this subtle form of insinuative suggestion, as compared to men. Men will blurt out statements and ideas, and attempt to "prove" them, but the woman will gently "insinuate" the idea into the mind of the other person, so that, "without having proven a fact, she will have managed to create a definite idea of feeling in the mind of the other by "suggestion." I think I need not give examples of this fact—it is apparent to all who have mingled with people.

And really this "suggestion" resembles the mental suggestion of the psychologists very much. It is true that the practitioner of mental suggestion, in his "treatments," often makes use of direct, forceful statements, such as: "You are strong, cheerful, well and happy," but you will notice even here that he does not "argue the point," or attempt to "prove" his statements.

He simply affirms and asserts the fact, and by constantly repeated suggestions he finally causes the mind of the other person to accept the statement. So you see a "suggestion" may be either a subtle insinuation or a bold, positive statement—but it is never an argument, or process of proof.

The word "impression" is good, as applied to the effect of a suggestion, but I prefer to stick to my terms, and therefore I shall consider that the effect of mental suggestion is caused by induction. "What," you may say, "I thought that induction was a term used when a mental state was set up in one by mentative currents from the mind of another?"

Yes, this is true, but my last statement is true also. An induced mental state is one set up by outside influence of some kind, whether that outside influence be a mentative current or by suggestion through a word, a look, a sight or anything else. The word "induce," you know, means: "to lead; to influence; to prevail on; to effect; to cause," etc. And any mental state that is induced by an outside influence comes clearly under the term.

Any physical agent that tends to induce a feeling in the mind of another may be called a suggestion. Even the well-known instance mentioned in the textbooks on psychology comes under this rule.

In that instance it is related that a soldier was carrying some bundles and a pail to his barracks, when some practical joker yelled to him in an authoritative voice, "Attention!" Following the suggestion, which induced in him the "feeling" preceding certain habitual actions, he dropped his pail and bundles with a crash and stood at "attention," with eyes front, chin out, protruding breast, stomach drawn in, and bands at his sides with little fingers touching the seams of his trousers. That was a suggestion! Do you see the point?

The lives of all of us have been molded largely by induction through suggestion. We accepted this suggestion, or that one, and it changed the whole current of our lives. Certain things induced certain feelings—called into activity certain mental states—and action followed close upon the heels of feeling.

There are varying degrees of suggestive power just as there are varying degrees of what is called the "suggestibility" of persons—that is the tendency to accept suggestions. There are people who scarcely ever act from motives originating within themselves, but whose entire lives are lived out in obedience to the suggested ideas and feelings of others.

The development of the Will-Power regulates the degree of suggestibility. The man of the strong will is not so easily affected by a suggestion as is one whose will is weak, and who accepts without resistance the suggestions coming from all sides.

But note the apparent paradox, persons of weak will may have their wills so developed and strengthened by scientific suggestive treatment that they may become veritable giants of will.

The careful student may feel inclined to ask me, at this point, why I speak of suggested "ideas," when I have said that suggestion has to do with mental states of feeling and emotion. Are not "ideas," he asks, something connected with thought rather than with feeling? The question is a proper one, and I must meet it.

The word "idea" comes from the Greek word, meaning "to see." In its general use it means a mental image, or a general notion or conception held in the mind." An idea is "symbolic image held in the mind." It is a symbol of something thought or felt.

Ideas are not formed by thought alone—feeling contributes its share of these mental images. To tell the truth, the majority of people scarcely "think" at all, in the highest sense of the word. Their reasoning and logical faculties are very rudimentary. They accept their ideas at second hand or second-hundred hand—their thoughts must be pre-digested for them by others, and the handed-down "idea" is the result.

The majority of ideas held in the mind of the race arise from feeling and emotion. People may not understand things, but they have experienced feelings or emotions regarding them, and have consequently formed many ideas and "ideals" therefrom.

They do not know "just why" an idea is held by them—they know only that they "feel" it that way. And the majority of people are moved, swayed and act by reasons of induced "feelings," rather than by results of reasoning. I am not speaking of intuitional feelings now, but of the plain, everyday, emotional feeling of people.

Do you know what a feeling is? The word, used in this sense, means: a mental state; emotion; passion; sympathy; sentiment; susceptibility; etc. And "emotion" means an excitement of the feelings. Feelings belong to the instinctive side of our mind, rather than to the rational or reasoning side.

They spring up from the subconscious strata of the mind, in response to the exciting cause coming from without. The instinctive part of our minds are stored with the experiences, feelings, emotions and mental states of our long line of ancestors, reaching away back to the early beginnings of life. In that part of the mind are sleeping instincts, emotions and feelings, our inheritance from the past, which await but the inducing cause to call them into activity.

The reason or judgment, by means of the will, act as a restrainer, of course, according to the degree of development of the individual. And these outward agents, if of a "physical" nature, are suggestions of all kinds.

Look around you at the world of men and women. Then tell me whether they seem to be moved principally by reason or feeling. Are their actions based upon good judgment and correct and careful reasoning?

Or are they the results of feeling and emotion? Do people do things because the things are considered right in the light of reason, or do they do them "because they feel like it?"

Which produces the greatest motive force—an appeal to the reason of a number of people, or an appeal to their feelings and emotion? Which sways a gathering of people; the votes of a people; the actions of a mob— reason or feeling? Which moves even you, good student, reason or feeling? Answer the questions honestly, and you will have the key of suggestive influence.

The Power of Seduction

This section explains the little-known method for seducing another person using Enchantment. Providing you follow the steps clearly and patiently, these techniques will open you up to a hidden world around you and give you a peek at just how easily you can influence others.

Command Others Through Thought Transference

This ability must be used with great caution and discretion. Even though this ability can lead to a lot of pleasant and even profitable ventures, it can also lead to a lot of pain and suffering to all involved. Remember, just because you can use this power on others, doesn't mean that you should. You should always use wisdom with the use of this power.

As human adults, we are already well versed in the experience of mind manifestation. When you look around you in your everyday life, you will see countless examples of a human's ability to manifest "stuff" from thought.

All manmade things first began in the thoughts of a person, or a group of people. Imagination plays a key role. The idea/concept is first birthed in the mind. Then the idea is discussed, either with oneself or with others. There is more mental work done to paint a final manifested picture in the mind(s). Finally, the idea is taken into aspects of physical processes which start the manifestation process, bringing the original mind-birthed idea into full manifestation in the physical world.

Even how you arrange your furniture is an example of thought-to-manifestation, whereby your plans/ideas are first created in the mind then you do the physical process (like moving your furniture around the room) to completely manifest your intended redecorating idea (thought).

Looking at the physical things around you are not examples of obvious or redundant things. They are all examples of mind/thought manifestation. When you begin to view your mental abilities in this light, you will begin to realize that you are well advanced in mind power already. On a subconscious level, your mind is a highly advanced machine: Just to name a few...it stores information, processes data, allows you to communicate with your spoken language, and also maintains regulation of all your bodily functions (advanced systems in themselves) without your conscious mind needing to do the work.

Keep these things in mind when you begin to enter the world of Enchantment, for really, you are not a beginner at all. Your mind is truly amazing and you can already create physical things stemming from a single thought (idea). It is your inner attitude (belief) which offers that magic substance which will eventually open you up to even higher levels of Enchantment and mind manifestation.

What is Enchantment-Seduction?

The Enchantment-Seduction of others' is the ability to erotically or sexually arouse another person using only the silent powers of Enchantment. When you apply these techniques on someone, that person will feel deeply attracted and sexually drawn to you. Most often, a condition of "falling in love" begins to take place upon the person you want to seduce. No communication with the person is needed. It need not even be someone you know. However, eventual communication will happen and should happen, for the obvious reasons, for it will provide you with valuable feedback as to the effectiveness of your Enchantment-Seduction.

The methods presented here are, without a doubt, very powerful. Do not start this technique if you are not positive about the person whose attention you desire. If you have any doubts, do not apply these powerful techniques. The effect begins instantly, however there will be a certain degree of lag time before you physically see results. Instant and automatic sexual influence is a mental skill that takes time. Like any skill, you need to develop it through effective and regular practice. You must maintain patience and calm rather than trying to hurry the process up.

As your skill increases, manifestation will come quicker. If you are new to these techniques, then expect anywhere from a couple of weeks to a few months for results to be seen. Results are directly influenced by the amount of time you involve yourself in this, at least during these beginner stages. Patience and calm pays off though, for you will begin to see your influence taking effect and molding into manifestation on a physical level; that person will become so drawn to you that eventually they will want to be with you.

Getting Started

Let's start out by calling the person you would like to seduce your "target." Your target is your goal, your intention. To reach your intention, you must first decide upon which individual you want to influence. Most people have their eye on someone already; someone whom they want to be with. You need not have had prior or current communications with your target. They can be someone with whom you have never spoken. It is preferable though, especially during these "beginner" stages, that it is someone you see frequently, like someone you work with. Later, as you progress in this art, you do not even have to be in the same city as your target.

For now, find someone close to you, someone you will see often, so you can glean feedback. Being able to observe the person during the period you are influencing them offers you valuable feedback. Feedback is a tool which not only helps you progress with your skill at mind power influence, but it can steer you in the right direction when you are working on a target project.

Remember, you are not only using your mind to manipulate thought and feelings of another person, but also to manipulate events and circumstances; all this for the final goal to eventually

31

manifest your initial intent. Monitoring your target (gaining feedback) allows you to better assess a situation or follow the progress of a series of events. With careful observation and planning, you can learn to best gear your influence in the most appropriate way or frequency of practice.

Once you have found your target, you should keep a notebook or something akin to that to keep track of all your observations. Keeping notes is a valuable tool which will increase your overall Enchantment influence skill level.

The Enchantment Influence

When you begin to use Enchantment-Seduction to influence another person, a vast array of things will happen. Some of these things are observable (and should be recorded) and some not so apparent. People react in different ways to Enchantment-Seduction influence. Some submit easily, others with resistance. But all of the reactions point to one inevitable occurrence: The target will become very, very drawn and attracted to you. The feelings will be deep and strong, and resemble "falling in love" emotions.

At no point will the person feel like they being forced or influenced. Even if the feelings might feel strong (which is common) or confusing (which is rare), the target will only feel like it is themselves that are starting to be drawn to you. Then the target will eventually reach out to start communicating with you more.

It is advisable to not flirt in any way at first with the person you want to influence. Just focus on being friendly and funny (making the other person smile/happy) and allow your seduction influence to do its work. Often a target will put up mental walls of sorts if they know that someone is just trying to hit on them. People have a sense about them when thought energy is being directed at them. So don't push too hard at first as this will make getting through even harder. Act friend-like only, while your influences are making them more drawn to you.

Don't jump the gun if you get a good sign that they now have erotic feelings towards you. Be patient and allow the conscious mind of the person to feel good towards you. All the while you are programming their subconscious mind with your intent.

Your Daily Routine

The first thing you need to do is set up a daily routine. These are the techniques which you will be putting into gear towards your goal of Enchantment-Seduction. First, find one hour a day. The hour is split in two Enchantment-Seduction sessions: Thus you will be doing a half hour session at one time in a day, and another session at a later time in the same day.

If need be, reduce each session by 15 minutes, but it is preferable to do half hour sessions. Serious Enchantment-Seduction adventurers may even find the desire to do longer sessions, perhaps two or more hours a day. Keeping notes of your sessions is also advisable.

The process of mental seduction is done through specific visualization methods. Your thoughts have an uncanny ability to manipulate your surroundings; effectuating change within the physical world. If you are seeing something within your mind's eye (via imagination, visualization, etc.), providing it is done in a patient, confident, and repetitive manner...it will begin to manipulate the ether around you and have pronounced effect upon the events and people in your life.

Calming the Mind

It is crucial that your session begins with a calming of your mind. In other words, you need to be in a comfortable relaxed state to do your sessions. As your mind relaxes, your electrical brainwave patterns lower in their frequency. These brainwaves then become more in sync with the natural frequency pulse of the planet (7.85 cycles per second) and thus facilitate a resonance between your mind and the physical world around you. Relaxing the mind also enables you to visualize easier and your bodily functions are kept to a minimum.

It is important to maintain a calm mind in order for these techniques to work properly. Allow a comfortable and relaxed state of mind to occur and your visualizations will be effective. Over time, you can train yourself to go into deeper states of relaxation. Too often, beginners worry or focus on issues such as just how relaxed to be, or whether or not their visualizations are clear. The most important thing to remember is that practice brings skill, and this will develop over time. One should not worry or obsess over issues of mental clarity or precise relaxation methods, but rather one should focus more on doing the actual seduction visualization techniques on a frequent basis, allowing the skill level to improve naturally over time.

Without this frame of thinking, one can easily spend more time worrying about technicalities or theory data, rather than actually working with the specific visualization methods. Too often, people embarking on a spiritual quest tend to get lost in the vast array of information out there and spend less time on actual personal application of the spiritual teachings they are investigating.

You can spend years reading the books and arming yourself with facts, theory, and information. Then you find out you do not spend much time doing personal experimentation and action. This is why so few actually attain a high level of personal power, although they may have every book on the subject. So when relaxing your mind and beginning your sessions, don't worry if you are relaxed enough or if you are doing the methods properly...just do the work and the skill and technicalities will improve and become refined over time.

Influencing Your Target

Your half hour session should include the following two forms of visualization. 20 minutes should be used to erotically "touch" (in your mind) the other person. The last 10 minutes should involve "scenario building." Let's go into more details. For the sake of simplification, visualization can be viewed simply as imagining, as if daydreaming. Simply allow yourself to imagine. Whether or not you can see things clearly in your imagination is not important. Visualization clarity develops over time through practice.

For the first twenty minutes you need to imagine yourself touching the target in a sexual/erotic way. Focus more on the touch itself and the effect that the touch is having on the other person, not on the situation or scene that you are in. Keep your touches gentle and erotic, not rushed or aggressive. In your mind's eye (imagination) focus more on the feeling of touch, rather than seeing yourself touching.

For some practice on feeling (touching) things in your mind, imagine yourself touching cotton balls, or touching a pen, or touching some rocks. Take your time and caress these objects in your mind, feeling the hardness or softness, etc. But these practice sessions are separate from your seduction sessions.

Erotically caressing someone involves some knowledge or experience in sexual intimacy. If you have had some prior sexual experiences, then you already can come up with ways to erotically touch someone. If you have no experience prior, then just use your imagination as best as you can.

Erotic touches and caresses should be focused on typical erogenous areas of the target's body, such as the nipples and genital areas as well as other tender areas of the body such as the neck or face. As you touch that person in your mind, feel (as best as possible) the reaction the other person should experience, such as wetness (if the target is a woman) or hardness (if the target is a man). You want to slowly erotically touch the person and feel their reaction building in your mind, eventually driving them to a sexual frenzy. Take your time and don't try to rush over the touches, trying to cover all sensual parts of their body. Different areas can be explored in different sessions. Once again, the target's "turned on" feeling as a result of your mental touches should be prominent in these visualizations.

The final 10 minutes of your half hour session should be visualizing you and your target together in scenarios. If you are trying to instill a feeling of "falling in love" within your target, then imagine (visualize) you and your target hanging out, holding hands, cuddling on the couch, etc. If you want a strictly sexual relationship, visualize you and your target having intense sexual encounters in exciting locations and situations. Imagine how you and your target feel the excitement, tension and intense fulfillment when you finally come together in pleasure.

Find one thing to focus on and keep that scenario for the entire 10 minutes. In these scenario sub-sessions, try to encompass as much emotion and senses as possible. You can see the target, touch the target, hear their voice, see the surroundings of where you are, etc.

Most important to visualized scenarios is the feeling of "now." You want to experience the scene in your imagination as if it was happening in the present moment. Not later, not then...but NOW.

To add that extra dosage of belief into the process, when you are doing your session you should hold yourself with an inner smile...an inner knowing that your efforts are working and have come to fruition. Even if you feel doubtful, fake the feeling. It will eventually become your feeling. The feeling is that confident holding of oneself with that unbreakable faith that your Enchantment is highly effective and powerful.

With that inner confident feeling, you also instill patience, seriousness, and calm...which are all emotions (energy) which work in conjunction with your visualization sessions (thoughts) to eventually manipulate and change the physical world around you (e.g. making events happen).

This describes the half hour session you must do. 20 minutes of mentally and erotically touching someone, and their deep arousal/reaction to it. Then 10 minutes of situation scenarios. This total session should be done twice a day preferably. Be patient and have faith, and don't be in a rush to see results immediately. Even if an outward response takes a couple of weeks, you are not wasting any time whatsoever by doing the daily sessions. On the contrary, you are training yourself in new mental efforts, you are training yourself to have patience (which means confidence that things WILL manifest as you are commanding), and you are continually charging up the influences upon the other person.

Your Influence

Your influences are having an effect upon your target. The visualizations (thought commands) are seeping deeply into your target's subconscious mind. And they are starting to have erotic or loving feelings towards you. In most cases, the target usually tries to not show these feelings...just like you are not revealing all your emotions as you carry on your daily life around others. But in time you will see signs.

Your target is beginning to think about you. And soon they will begin to have erotic feelings towards you. They will find themselves becoming more and more drawn to you. When they are alone, they may find the need to fantasize about you, especially after you have done numerous days of sessions upon them. They will probably occasionally dream about you as well, while they sleep.

During this time, purposeful monitoring of the other person's reactions is vital. In your notebook, keep careful notes of their behavior around you not matter how trivial it may seem. Even if you are not in communication with the target, you can merely observe them when you see them.

If you talk or know the target, then monitor signs when you are talking to them. And remember what was mentioned above. If you are communication with the target, just offer yourself to them in a friendly and enjoyable (perhaps funny) manner...not in a flirty way. If the other person senses that you are trying to flirt with them...then emotional walls on their part may go up. This is an annoying wall to break down with your Enchantment.

Taking an interest in the target, asking questions about them, this is another great way to break down walls. Just act as if you are a safe and fun friend or acquaintance, and you provide a clear path for effective thought transmission.

As you start to get feedback from the person, you can study the trend of the behavior; watch how it grows and weans, or goes up and down, or obvious to discreet. Don't feel silly to write down in your notebook, "Target made eye contact with me, and looked at me with a smile."

Monitoring feedback also offers another way of helping to mold events to your favor. For example, if you start to sense that the person is becoming friendlier to you...you can initiate more interaction with them.

Be faithful with the methods, and keep notes of your efforts and your target's reactions. That person is now erotically driven to be with you. Without doubt, it will happen.

Practice, Practice, Practice

Always be confident in your powers and enjoy the process of learning to advance these skills. Experimentation is vital but don't go way off into your own methods until you have gained repetitive results with the methods presented here.

Keep up with your practice. If you do daily sessions, a year from now your skill will be of a surely higher level. Never give up on a target. Even if you choose a new target, you can still work on the previous one at the same time (extra sessions). Be sure and think about the ethics of the issue prior to venturing off into mind control methods.

If your intentions are positive and not harmful, then you will be fine. If you wish to use your powers to hurt or be violent to others, then you are the proud winner of a collection of negative forces which will seek to guide you down a darker wider path.

Don't tell the person you are trying to influence them, for obvious reasons. Don't tell anyone you are using methods on someone else (others' doubt can add resistance to your efforts). By using your Enchantment-Seduction Powers, you can soon learn how to influence and manifest the events you want. As time goes by, you will learn to develop methods on your own, based on experimentation and practice.

Remember, the one who develops the skill with Enchantment-Seduction, is the one who is master at controlling others and master at preventing being controlled by others.

Attract A New Lover With Enchantment

Enchantment can be used as a one-way telepathic communication. According to Caitlin MacKenna, it can be directed to a particular person, or it can be broadcast like a radio or television signal. One use for Enchantment is to attract a new lover with particular qualities that you want, or to attract a particular person. Using Enchantment-Seduction to attract a new lover is a simple process. You don't have to believe in it; you just have to do it.

First, start by creating a thought-form of your ideal lover, or of the particular person whom you are trying to attract. Close your eyes and imagine the body of your lover life sized in three dimensions. Take as much time as you need to do this step. The more vivid your mental image, the more effective your mental influence will be. Second, in your mind, begin making love with your lovers thought-form. Be as realistic as you can. Involve all of your senses. You must actually feel the thought-form body when you touch it.

Third, while making love with your lover thought-form, think about his or her qualities. Say to yourself, "I love your hair color, eye color, the softness of your skin, etc. Continue with this type of inner dialogue during the lovemaking. Picture the qualities of your lover as vapor inside his or her body.

Fourth, when you feel ready, transfer your Enchantment energies to your lovers thought-form. Picture your energy in the form of a vapor flowing from your penis or vagina and filling the thought-form.

Fifth, you can repeat step 3 and 4 as long as you want though spending 15-30 minutes on your Enchantment-Seduction influence session is about right. When you are finished, don't think about it anymore. If you keep thinking about your objective, your thought-form stays attached to you. You have to release your thought-form, so it can reach its target.

The sixth step requires that you repeat the steps 1-5 daily until you achieve results, which could take from a few hours to a few weeks. If you don't get results within a month, there are three possible problems: 1. your mental imagery is not vivid enough to create a viable thought-form; 2. you are obsessing about your objective, and, thereby, not allowing your thought-form to reach its target; or 3. you are not getting out or going anywhere that you could meet your new lover.

Some say that using Enchantment-Seduction to attract a particular person is wrong because it "violates free will." Magical traditions all over the world disagree with that viewpoint, and I personally don't see how mental influence is different from the other methods people use to attract new lovers, such as sexy clothes, perfume or cologne, music, etc. However, if you do think that it is wrong, don't do it. Just use Enchantment-Seduction techniques to attract your ideal lover, leaving it to the universe to send the right person.

When using Enchantment-Seduction techniques, some people meet with resistance from their target. Signs of resistance show you that your Enchantment-Seduction is starting to work. It does not mean that your efforts will not work. All it means is that it will take longer for the programming to be successful.

Overcome Resistance

Caitlin MacKenna has also pointed out that when using Enchantment-Seduction techniques, some people meet with resistance from their target. Your prospective lover may be cold, rude, or even hostile towards you. Though it may be hard to believe, that's a good thing, not a bad thing. Signs of resistance show you that your mental influence is starting to work. It does not mean that your efforts will not work. All it means is that it will take longer for the programming to be successful.

Here are five ways to overcome resistance to Enchantment-Seduction.

1. You can apply longer and more intense visualizing until the person's resistance breaks down. This will increase your influence even if the person is suppressing their feelings or ignoring you. They will learn that resisting you will cause more visualizing on your part (of course, this is all on an subconscious level since they don't consciously know that you are using mental influence techniques on them.)

2. You can make a U-turn and visualize them very much attracted to you while, at the same time in your visualizing, you give them the cold shoulder. When you visualize, make them want you and

be very eager to please you while you brush them off and reject them. This can break the person's resistance completely because their mind cannot understand this influence or how to resist it, and, therefore, the person is defenseless. As well, nothing attracts a person more than thinking that they can't have you.

3. You can stop doing your Enchantment-Seduction sessions for a few days and then start again with more force. Continue this stopping and starting if the person still resists. These pauses can be very effective because, when you are holding off on your techniques for a few days, the subconscious mind of the person feels that the pressure is off, and the person begins to let down their defenses. When the defenses go down, all your visualizing begins to creep into the person's mind. When your mental images are blocked, they don't fade away. They just "hang around" until an opening is found into the person's mind. If the person is resisting, the visualizing you have done just waits and accumulates until there is a clear opening into the mind (such as when their defenses are down).

4. If the person is showing signs of being fearful about the new sexual feelings you are creating in them, use your visualizing to slow down the passion. It's sometimes best to begin with a gentle approach, and then later you can slowly build up to intense, erotic scenarios. Visualize being friends at first and doing friend-type things (non-threatening) and then work up to sexual things after a few weeks. This technique is especially important if you are trying to get a person to fall in love with you. You first visualize the person being happy and comfortable with you; maybe laughing and playing, and then put in the sexual scenarios when you have fully instilled the "safe" scenarios.

5. If their unconscious mind can't handle the load of your influence, the person may even try getting away from you. This

can occur even if they don't know you, but are resisting subconsciously. It doesn't matter how far the distance (the farther the better) since their defenses will go down. You can continue to do your work, and your influence will gain entry into their mind much more easily. If you continue your mental influence after they move, they will begin to miss you terribly. The only problem is that you won't be able to monitor their reactions or signs of changed behavior, but that's no problem because sparks should fly the next time they see you.

If the person you are working is resisting to some extent, then work with one or all of these techniques. Be very alert of their signs so that you can use the best technique. Some people get ill from energy/strength loss when trying to wrestle against your influence. Sooner or later, their subconscious mind will give up if you keep up the work. With Enchantment-Seduction, they will become yours.

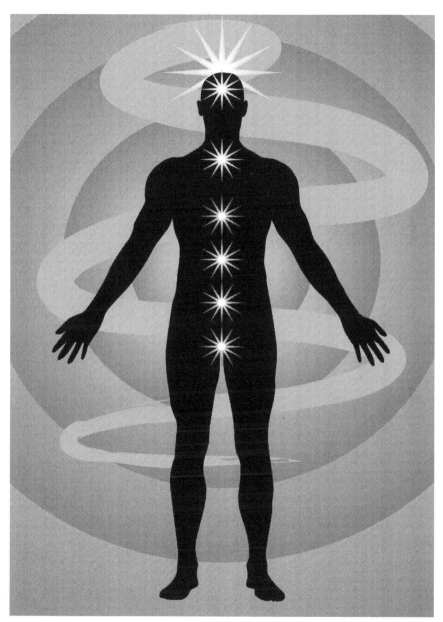

Mind power is one of the strongest and most useful powers you possess. This power consists of your thoughts. The thoughts that pass through your mind are responsible for everything that happens in your life.

PART I

NATURE'S FINER FORCES

ONE of the most common mistaken conceptions of the average student of the occult sciences, and of so-called "psychic phenomena" in general, is that which may be expressed by the term "supernatural." This term, as you know, is used to express the idea of "that which is outside of the realm of Nature, and of Nature's laws."

Knowledge Versus Faith

As a matter of fact, as all the advanced students and teachers of the occult doctrine know full well, we have no direct knowledge whatsoever of anything that is "outside of the realm of nature, and of Nature's laws." It is true that we may, by an act of faith, profess to believe in powers and beings entirely apart from the great realm of Nature—in fact, most persons do believe in such powers and beings in connection with their formal religion—but their belief is entirely within the category of Faith, and is not even pretended to be based upon actual experience and phenomenal manifestation.

The moment that there appears any manifestation which is possible of being known to, or experienced by, the human senses, ordinary or extraordinary, that moment the phenomena and the immediate cause thereof must be regarded as being properly classed in the category of "natural." This is true not only of such phenomena as are perceived by means of our ordinary five senses, but also of those which are perceptible only to the highest powers of perception, or higher senses, which are latent in all 8human

46

beings but which are unfolded only in the case of a comparatively few individuals of the race.

It should be clearly understood by all students of occultism or psychic phenomena that man's knowledge and experience, normal or supernormal, is confined to the realm of Nature. There is a "ring pass-not" around the boundaries of the Kingdom of Nature which mortals cannot pass, no matter how high may be their degree of development and advancement. Even those great mystics whose writings are filled with the startling revelations of "union with the Divine," and of "At-one-ment with Deity," are under no illusion concerning this fact they know full well that only in so far as Deity involves itself in Nature—wraps itself up in the garments of Nature—can it be directly experienced by man, and thus actually known by him.

Supernormal, Not Supernatural

Perhaps a clearer understanding of this important subject will be had if we but substitute the term "supernormal" for that of "supernatural." The term "supernormal" is not commonly employed, and but few know that such a word is to be found in the dictionaries, much less know its meaning; but a study of its meaning, and its adoption in our thinking, will serve to give us a clearer conception of the true nature of many strange phases of experience of which we have become conscious, either by reasons of their manifestation by ourselves, or else by the manifestation on the part of others. It will accordingly be well for us to carefully examine this term and its meaning.

"Subnormal" means: "Beyond, above, or exceeding that which is normal; extraordinary, inexplicable perhaps, but not supernatural." Now, the term "normal" means: "Conforming to a certain standard, rule, or type"; hence, anything that is "supernormal" is something that is above the usual pattern, rule, or type.

There is an important distinction to be noted here, to-wit: a thing may be outside of the usual pattern, rule, or type, in the sense of being inferior to or under the ordinary standard, and in this case is known as "abnormal," the latter term being employed as a term of depreciation. On the other hand, the "outside of the standard" quality may consist of a superiority to the prevailing standard, and accordingly is entitled to be classed in the category of the "supernormal"—the prefix "super" meaning "above, over, higher, etc."

It is important that the distinction be made clearly between the use and meaning of these two terms, "abnormal" and "supernormal," respectively. The first named denotes inferiority, and the latter denotes superiority. This distinction may be more clearly apprehended by means of a concrete example, as follows:

On our own plane of existence the senses of sight and hearing, respectively, are included in the usual standard, pattern, and type of sense normality—every normal person possesses these senses in a certain general degree of power; hence, on this plane of existence, a person born blind, or deaf, is spoken of as "abnormal," that is to say, such a person is deficient in regard to the sense powers.

On the contrary, let us imagine a plane of existence, in which the great majority of individuals lack the power of sight and hearing, respectively. On such a plane of existence, the occasional individual who was born possessed of the powers of sight and hearing, respectively, would be properly regarded as "supernormal," that is to say; such a person would be superior to the ordinary run of individuals—above them, in fact. The term "abnormal" means minus the ordinary standard quality; and the term "supernormal" means plus the ordinary standard quality.

And yet both the "plus" and the "minus" would be "outside" the normal type, though there is a difference as wide as that between the two poles, in this "outsideness."

Supernormal, Not Abnormal

The above important statement concerning the distinction between the "abnormal" and "supernormal" is not made merely for the purpose of academic differentiation and classification. On the other hand, it is made because there is a most pernicious tendency on the part of the ignorant and unthinking portions of the public to regard and to classify certain high phases of occult and psychic manifestation of power as "abnormal," hence below the standard; whereas, properly speaking, such manifestations of power are far above the standard, and, hence, clearly entitled to the term "supernormal."

The Prevailing Ignorance

The ignorant and unthinking attitude of certain portions of the general public toward this class of phenomena is akin to that of a community of blind and deaf persons, satisfied that their own "three sense" standard is the highest possible one attainable by living creatures and that all variation there from must be considered as "abnormal."

In such a community there would occasionally be born certain individuals possessed of the senses of sight and hearing, in addition to the common three senses possessed by the entire community. Judging by what we know of the tendency of human nature in such cases, we are warranted in conjuring that the ordinary run of persons in such a community would revile the seeing and hearing individuals as "abnormal," and their possessors therefore to be pitied, and perhaps shunned. Only the intelligent and thoughtful members of such a community would be able to grasp the fact that these exceptional individuals were really not only not "abnormal," and inferior to type, but that they were really "supernormal," and superior to type.

Prejudice Against the Unusual

Those to whom the above illustration may seem far-fetched, exaggerated, and unwarranted, are asked to carefully consider the ignorant and unthinking attitude which the great majority of the general public. But, what can be expected from those with closed minds? Fear is then displayed toward that most wonderful display of supernormal powers, known as "occult" or "psychic," made by the few highly developed individuals of the race who are able to manifest them to some degree.

These individuals are regarded as "queer," and "strange," "unnatural," and "abnormal" by their ignorant and unthinking neighbors and associates, just as the seeing and hearing exceptional individuals were likewise so regarded by their blind and deaf neighbors in the above illustration. And, here as in the illustration it is only the few intelligent and thinking individuals of the community who recognize that the departure from the standard type is in the direction of advancement and gain, rather than of retrogression and loss—a plus attribute, rather than a minus one. The illustration is startlingly true and in accordance with the facts of the case, as many thoughtful persons know only too well, and admit sadly.

But it would be unjust and unfair to the general public were we to fail to add to the above criticism the fact that there is underway a great change in the public opinion regarding this important matter. More and more persons are becoming interested in Nature's Finer Forces every day; more are becoming more familiar with the phenomena manifested by the gifted individuals possessing these wondrous powers; and more are coming to realize that these powers are really latent in all of the members of the human race, though lying dormant in the majority thereof, and may be unfolded and brought into active manifestation by scientific methods of training and development. But, even so, the student and teacher of this great subject should carefully bear in mind the important distinction above made between that which is "abnormal," and that which is "supernormal"; and such should lose no opportunity in pointing out this important distinction whenever the subject arises in conversation or argument—for the propaganda of truth should be earnestly and vigorously pursued, in order that the world may be liberated from its chains of error.

The Naturalness of the Occult Powers

Returning to the subject considered in the opening paragraphs of this book, namely, the naturalness of the occult and psychic higher powers and the manifestation thereof, we strongly advise all students of these subjects to acquire a working knowledge of the place in Nature occupied by these powers and their manifestations. A little scientific information on this subject will render the student better able to intelligently teach others concerning these matters, and also to successfully defend himself when the ignorant and unthinking seek to attack the things which are so dear to his heart, and so real and evident to himself. Many, by reason of their lack of scientific knowledge on these points, not only fail to make converts to their cause of truth, but often really drive away persons who might otherwise be interested. Many persons are really interested in and attracted to the manifestations of the higher occult and psychic powers, but are fearful of anything "unnatural" or "supernatural," and are disposed to be frightened off by any suspicion of such qualities in things.

These same persons, if shown that the phenomena have a perfectly valid scientific base in natural forces and laws, will throw aside their fears and will become earnest investigators and students of this great subject. Hence, as we have said, every teacher and student of this subject should know the true scientific natural basis thereof; and in the following few pages we shall endeavor to plainly, though briefly, present these to you.

The World of Vibrations

Modern science furnishes abundant testimony to support and substantiate the teachings of the ancient Hindu sages to the effect that everything in the Universe is in constant motion, which is manifested by varying rates, degrees, and modes of vibration. Everything moves, the Earth, the solar system, the galaxy, etc.

The modern scientists, alike with the ancient occultist, know that the differences between the things of the Universe arise mainly from the different rates, modes, and degrees of the vibrations manifested in the things themselves. If we change the vibration of a thing, we practically change the manifested nature of that thing. The difference between solid ice, liquid water, semi-gaseous vapor, and gaseous steam is simply the difference caused by various rates of vibration caused by heat. The difference between red and blue, green and violet, is simply that caused by varying rates of vibration. Light and heat, as well as sound, depend for the differences upon rates of vibration.

Moreover, as every text book on science informs us, there are sounds too low as well as those too high for the human ear to register, but which are registered by delicate instruments. Again, there are colors beyond the place of red, at one end of the visible spectrum; and others beyond the place of violet at the other end of that spectrum, which the human eye is unable to register and detect, but which our apparatus in the laboratory plainly register.

The ray of light which registers on the photographic plate, and which causes sunburn on our skin, is too high a rate of vibration for our eyes to perceive. Likewise the X-Rays, and many other of the finer rays of light known to science are imperceptible to the unaided human vision—they are actually "dark rays" so far as the human eye is concerned, though man has devised instruments by means of which they may be caught and registered.

The Higher Vibrations

The vibrations of magnetism and electricity are imperceptible to our sight, though they may be registered by the appropriate apparatus; and if we had the proper sense of apparatus to perceive them, these rays of vibratory force would open up a whole new world to us. Likewise, if we could increase our power of hearing-perception, we would seem to be living in a new world of sights and sounds now closed to us.

Reasoning along the same lines of thought, many great thinkers have held that there is no reason for doubting the possible existence of other world-planes of being, just as real and as actual as the one upon which we live, and move, and have our being, but which is forever invisible to the ordinary human sight and senses; the apparent nothingness of such worlds arising solely from the great difference in the rates of vibrations between the two planes of being.

Unseen Worlds

Listen to what careful thinkers have said concerning the possibility of entire worlds existing in the same space occupied by us, but of which we are unconscious by reason of our failure to sense their vibrations: One says, "All our sensations are due to the impact upon our sense-organs of vibrations in some form. Variations in the strength and rapidity of these vibrations constitute the difference in our perceptions. Our range of response is but a limited one. Some vibrations are too rapid and some too slow to affect our senses, and therefore we have called to our aid various mechanical contrivances which enable us to recognize existences which would otherwise remain unknown. But it is still conceivable that there may be, and doubtless are, conditions of vibratory energy that escape us, and which, if we could develop finer senses, would yield wonderful results and extensions of our power and knowledge. Today, indeed, we are coming into contact with forces, possibilities, and personalities which amount to a revelation of a new universe of things."

Interpenetrating Planes and Worlds

Another says: "It is true that 'things are not what they seem'; but everything seems to be 'thus and so' to us only because of its particular plane of being, and that plane of being is determined by its vibrations. On one plane there is a certain vibratory value or speed; on another plane, a different one; but a plane is not a place, but a state, and so it is possible that two utterly different planes of being might co-exist in the same place and be entirely unknown to one another. That may seem absurd, but it is a scientific truth, and many authorities have endorsed the same." Another says: "There may be, right here and now, passing through us and this world, some planet invisible to us, with mountains, oceans, lakes, rivers, cities, and inhabitants: and yet we know absolutely nothing of their existence." Another says: "Some students of the occult find it difficult to grasp the idea of a number of manifestations, each having its own rate of vibration, occupying the same point of space at the same time. A slight consideration of the phenomena of the physical world would perhaps aid such persons in assimilating the concept in question. For instance, as every student of physics knows, a single point of space may contain at the same time vibrations of heat, light of many shades, magnetism electricity, X-Rays, etc., each manifesting its own rate of vibration, land yet none interfering with the others."

Another says: "Every beam of sunlight contains many different colors, each with its own degree of vibration, and yet none crowding out the others. By the use of the proper forms of laboratory apparatus each kind of light may be separated from the others, and the ray thus split up. The difference in colors arises simply from the different rates of etheric vibrations. Again, it is possible to send many telegrams along the same wire, at the same time, by using senders and receivers of different vibratory keynotes. The same thing has its corresponding analogy in the case of the wireless telegraphy. So you see, even on the physical planes we find many forms of vibratory energy manifesting on, in, and at the same point of space at the same time, without interfering one with the other."

The ancient occult teachings have ever insisted upon the presence of numerous planes of existence, of which our own particular plane is but one. And all of these numerous planes are equally within the realms of Nature; none of them being supernatural. And there is always found to exist, a correspondence between these several planes of manifestation; and, under supernormal conditions, a certain degree of possible communication between them. Each of these planes has numerous subdivisions and subplanes, the divisions being according to the rule of "sevens," as follows: there are seven grand planes, and each of these are subdivided into seven secondary planes, and each of these into seven tertiary planes, and so on until the division has been made seven times.

Manifold Planes of Existence

The student of occultism, particularly at the beginning of his studies, experiences difficulty in comprehending just what is meant by the term "plane" as employed in the occult teachings. His first impression, usually encouraged by the use of the dictionary, is that each "plane" is one of a series of strata or layers, above and below which are present other layers or strata. Even after the student progresses in his understanding of the subject, this original picture of material layers and strata tends to persist in his thought on the subject. The error, of course, arises from his original conception of the planes, layers, or strata as being composed of gross material matter, whereas, as a matter of fact, only one of the many planes is so composed. When one stops to think that even the grossest form of matter is itself composed of vibrations of energy (for science teaches that all matter is but energy at the last); and that all other forms of material substance is likewise so composed of vibrations of energy; then one is on the road to the discovery of the real state of affairs. Then he begins to realize that instead of the planes of being rising one above the other in the scale of their fineness, they are graded according to their degree of vibratory energy, and each may actually occupy the same space as all the others. In short, the "planes" are not strata or layers of "matter" at all, but are simply different states of vibration of energy; and that which we know as "matter" is simply one (and a very low one) of the many forms of such vibrations.

From the above, it is seen that the various planes of being are not distinguished by spatial position; they are not one superimposed on the other, like layers or strata of matter. Instead, they interpenetrate each other in the same limits of space. A single point of space may accommodate the manifestations of each and all of the seven great planes of being, and all the subdivisions, and sub-divisions (sevenfold in division) at the same time. The old occultists impressed this and other facts upon the minds of their pupils by the oft-repeated aphorism: "A plane of being is not a place of being, but a state of being." And the "state of being" is simply a certain manifestation of vibratory energy. With these ideas firmly fixed in the mind, the student is less apt to wander astray from the facts of the case.

Planes and Vibrations

To those who may be disposed to regard the above statements concerning the "planes of being" as somewhat visionary, theoretical, or imaginary, we would say: "Go to modern science, and verify this statement." The following quotation from a writer on the subject will serve to illustrate this fact, viz.: "We are apt to think that we are familiar with every kind of matter in existence, but such is not the case. We are familiar with only a few forms of matter. Spectrum analysis shows us that on certain fixed stars there are forms of matter far different from matter as we know it on this planet. On some stars this unknown matter appears to be of a much lower form of vibration than that manifested by terrestrial matter; while on others, there appears to be a much higher vibratory rate than even that manifested by the most subtle forms of ultra-gaseous matter known to us here. Even on our own globe we can distinguish between several great class of matter. In addition to the forms called 'solid,' 'liquid,' and 'gaseous,' respectively, science now recognizes a fourth plane of matter known as 'ultra-gaseous' matter, and there are indications of several even finer states of matter, known under the general term of 'radiant matter.' In fact, modern science sees 'radiant matter' apparently fading away into 'radiant energy.'"

In view of the facts of modern science concerning the different planes of substance, matter and energy, it is mere stupidity that ventures to question the possibility of the existence of great plane of being and life beyond the range of the ordinary senses of man—planes surrounding us on all sides, occupying the same space as we do, yet unseen by us, and we largely unseen by those dwelling upon such planes.

The Higher Senses of Men

There are found persons who, while admitting the possibility of other and finer planes of being and life, yet question the possibility of communication between these planes of existence. They say, with apparently sound logic, "How is it possible for the human being, with his ordinary senses, to 'sense' things or being, dwelling on finer planes of being?" If this were all that there is to the question, we might well echo "How, indeed?" and agree with the critic. But, this is not all that there is to it—not even the beginning of the end of the tale.

For not only may things on the finer planes become perceptible to human beings by means of the lowering of the vibrations of these finer vibratory objects in certain ways, but human beings may develop and cultivate an increased power in their senses of sight and hearing, and thus raise their vibrations so as to "sense" the things of the higher vibrations; and, still more, human beings may, and often do, develop and cultivate certain latent powers of "sensing" which are inherent in every one of us, and thus directly "sense" the sights and sounds of the higher planes of existence, almost if not quite as clearly as they can sense the objects and events of their own plane of existence.

To understand how this can be, it is necessary to carefully consider the question of "sensing" in general, so as to understand just what enables us to "sense" anything at all. Once understanding this, it is but a step further to understand this supernormal sensing referred to. Let us then examine this matter of "sensing" in general.

The World of Sensation

The reports of our sense organs are called "sensations." A sensation is defined as "an impression, or the consciousness of an impression, made upon the mind through the medium of a nerve or one of the organs of sense. The term 'sense' is defined as 'a faculty possessed by animals of perceiving external objects by means of impressions made upon certain organs of the body, or of perceiving changes in the condition of the body.' Our senses have been well said to constitute 'the doors to the outside world.' Unless our attention is specially directed to the subject, few of us even begin to realize how completely we are dependent upon these 'doors' to the outside world" for our knowledge of that outside world. It is only when we stop to imagine how completely shut in, or shut out, we would be if all of our sense channels should be destroyed, that we can even begin to realize just how dependent we are upon our senses for our knowledge of the world in which we live, and move, and have our being.

A Senseless World

A writer on the subject has said: "Psychologists have pointed out to us the fact that if a human being were born without sense organs, no matter how perfect a brain he might have, his life would be little more than that of a plant. Such a person would exist merely in a dreamlike state, with only the very faintest manifestations of consciousness. His consciousness would not be able to react in response to the impact of sensations from the outside world, for there would be no such impact. And as consciousness depends almost entirely upon the impact of, or resistance to, outside impressions, his consciousness would be almost entirely inactive. He would be conscious of his own existence, but would probably never realize the fact fully, for he would have nothing else with which to compare himself and his self-consciousness would never be aroused by contact with things outside of himself. Such a person would not have even the memories of previous sensations or experiences to arouse or heighten his consciousness or thought, and consequently he would have no imagination to use.

"He would be, to all intents and purposes, a living corpse. Helen Keller has only two doors of sensation closed to her—the sense of sight and the sense of hearing. Touch, taste, and smell, however were left to her; and each was quickened and heightened in order to help so far as possible to perform the world of the defective senses. The reaching of the consciousness of this girl is considered by science to be akin to a miracle—yet only two senses were missing. To appreciate the full meaning of the importance of the senses, one has but to think of Helen Keller as having been also deprived of the sense of touch."

The Elemental Sense

Science informs us that all of the five senses of man, viz., the respective senses of touch, sight, hearing, taste, and smell are but modifications of one elementary sense namely the sense of touch; and that the other senses have been gradually evolved from that one elementary sense. This is seen to be the case when it is realized that the only way that we "sense" the presence of an outside object—be that object either a material substance, a vibration of the air, or an etheric vibration of light—is by that outside object coming in contact, directly or indirectly, with one or more of our sensory nerves, the latter conveying the report of the contact to the brain, which translates the sensation into what is called a "perception."

This is true of the sensations of touch, sight, hearing, taste, and smell, and of senses higher than these and which as yet are not recognized by science. Consequently, the consciousness of the presence of an outside thing arises from contact with that outside thing through the channel of the sense of touch, or of some of its more complex evolved phases.

The Raw Material of Thought

From what has been said, it is seen that we can know only those things concerning the outside world which are capable of being reported to us by means of sense impressions, simple or complex—all of our thought regarding the world is made up from "the raw materials of thought" which psychologists have termed sensations. Consequently, if an individual is deprived of one or more of his ordinary senses, his knowledge of the outside world is decreased to just that extent. And, likewise, if the individual were to be given one or more additional senses, his knowledge of the world would be increased in the same ratio. The same result, at least in a certain degree, would be attained if the existing senses of the individual were to be increased in power so as to register higher rates of vibration than they now consciously register and record.

This subject of increased sense-powers has always been a fascinating one for the psychologists, and much speculation has been indulged in concerning the increased consciousness of mankind were additional senses opened to it. We ask you to carefully consider the following quotations from psychologists possessing the "scientific imagination."

The Evolution of the Senses

A psychologist says: "All the senses have been evolved from the elementary sense of Touch. All of our senses are but modified, specialized, and more complex forms of the sense of Touch. The elementary life-forms possessed merely the sense of Touch; and that but faintly developed—but a faint sensitiveness to outside impressions.

Then developed the sense of Taste, from which later evolved the sense of Smell, the latter even now being closely associated with the former. Then evolved the sense of Hearing, or the consciousness of the contact of air vibrations called 'sound.'

Then evolved the sense of sight, or the consciousness of contact with the light waves of the other. And it is not impossible, or even improbable, that the human race will eventually develop other and more complex senses—in fact, many even now claim that the development of extra senses is now under way in the race, and that the same are now manifesting the presence and their powers in exceptional cases."

The same writer continues as follows: "Even as it is man is able to perceive only a limited number of sound vibrations—there are many sound vibrations above and below his scale, and which he is unable to perceive, but which are registered by delicate instruments. Likewise, man is able to perceive only a limited range of light vibrations, there being enormous fields of such vibrations above and below his range. Again, man is unable to sense electrical waves, or magnetic waves—though, theoretically, he should be able to sense these as well as light waves, the difference between these respective fields of etheric vibrations being simply different rates of vibration. Imagine what a new world would be opened to man if he could sense the waves of electricity. In that case he could 'see' things as far away from him as the waves of electricity could travel, and even though solid objects intervened, as in the case of the X-Rays. In such a case a man might actually 'see' things at the other side of the world, by means of 'wireless electrical waves.' Theoretically these things are possible, providing that man's optical nerves are rendered more sensitive, or provided that he evolves a new set of sensory nerves and instruments of impression."

Discovery of New Worlds

Another psychologist says: "If a new sense or two were added to the present normal number in man, that which is now the phenomenal world for all of us might, for all that we know, burst into something amazingly different and wider, in consequence of the additional revelations of these new senses." Another authority has said: "It does not seem at all improbable that there are properties of matter of which none of our senses can take immediate cognizance, and which other beings might be able to see in the same manner that we are sensible to light, sound, etc." Another writer has said: "We know that our sensory nerves are capable of transmitting to the brain only a part of the phenomena of the universe. Our senses give us only a section of the world's phenomena. Our senses usher only certain phenomena into the presence of our minds. If we had three or four new senses added, this might appear like a new world to us; we might become conscious of a vast number of phenomena which at present never have any effect upon our nervous system. It is not possible to imagine a race of beings whose senses do not resemble ours, inhabiting other worlds."

Transcendental Senses

Another writer has drawn an interesting picture, which is based upon a conjecture which is scientifically valid, as follows: "The late Professor James once suggested as a useful exercise for young students a consideration of the changes which would be worked in our ordinary world if the various branches of our receiving instruments happened to exchange duties; if, for instance, we heard all colors, and saw all sounds. All this is less mad than it seems. Music is but an interpretation of certain vibrations undertaken by the ear; and color is but an interpretation of other vibrations undertaken by the eye. Were such an alteration of our senses to take place, the world would still be sending us the same messages, but we should be interpreting them differently. Beauty would still be ours, though speaking in another tongue. The birds' song would then strike our retina as pageant of color; we should see all the magical tones of the wind, hear as a great fugue the repeated and harmonized greens of the forest, the cadences of stormy skies. Did we realize how slight an adjustment of our own organs is needed to initiate us into such a world, we should perhaps be less contemptuous of those mystics who tell us in moments of transcendental consciousness they 'heard flowers that sounded, and saw notes that shone'; or that they have experienced rare moments of consciousness in which the senses were fused organs is needed to initiate us into such a world into a single and ineffable act of perception, in which color and sound were known as aspects of the same thing."

We Sense Only Vibratory Motion

In assimilating the strange and wonderful conceptions of the psychologists above quoted, concerning the possibility of a new world of sensation arising from the possession of new channels of sense impression, we must never lose sight of the basic fact that all sensations result from contact with vibratory motion. An eminent scientific authority has said regarding this: "The only way the external world affects the nervous system is by means of vibratory motion. Light is vibratory motion; Sound is vibratory motion; Heat is vibratory motion; Touch is vibratory motion; Taste and Smell are vibratory motion. The world is known to us simply by virtue of, and in relation to, the vibratory motion of its particles.

Those vibratory motions are appreciated and continued by the nervous system, and by it brought at length to the mind's perception."

The Higher Planes of Nature

In view of the facts and principles above set forth and considered, we may begin to see that there is nothing "unnatural" in the hypothesis that there may be reports conveyed to the consciousness of man by means of higher vibrations than those of ordinary sound, or ordinary sight, providing that man has either (1) highly developed his ordinary senses of sight, hearing, or touch to a degree sufficiently high to register these higher vibrations; or else has evolved and unfolded into consciousness certain latent faculties of sense-impression which are lying dormant in the great masses of mankind.

In fact, the thoughtful person will be forced to admit that this new knowledge of the nature of sensations, and of its relation to vibratory motion, renders extremely probable the truth of the great body of reports of such so-called extra-conscious knowledge which the experience of the race has furnished from the beginning of human history down to the present time.

Such a person will see that it is not a sign of "credulity" for a person to accept such reports, so universally set forth; but that, rather, it is a sign of "credulity" for a person to accept blindly the dogmatic assertions of the materialistic skeptics to the effect that "there is no such thing possible in the natural world, under natural world, under natural laws—the whole thing is delusion or else deliberate fraud."

Such "know-it-all" persons are usually found to really "know much that is not true," and to lack knowledge of much that is true, regarding Nature, her realm and her laws.

An Appeal To Reason

Concluding these statements, let us say that the student of this book will find nothing contained within this book which is contrary to Nature's laws and principles. He will nowhere in it be asked to suspend the exercise of his reason, and to accept as facts things which violate all of Nature's laws. Instead, he will find at each point full natural explanations of even the most wonderful phenomena; and the appeal to accept same will be made always to his reason, and not to his blind faith or unreasoning belief. The student is urged to build his knowledge of this important subject upon this solid rock of natural law and fact, and not upon the shifting and sinking sands of mere dogmatic assertion and appeal to assumed authority ancient or modern.

Ancient occult Masters have taught about the presence of numerous planes of existence, of which our own particular plane, or reality is but one.

PART II

Mental Vibrations and Transmissions

IN the category of Nature's Finer Forces must be included that class of manifestations which are generally known as Telepathy, Thought Transference, Thought Force, etc., all of which are based upon the fact that there is present in all such mental states as Thought, Emotion, Desire, etc., a certain rate of vibratory motion, which motion is capable of being radiated from the mind of the person manifesting them in such power and force that they may be registered with more or less distinctness upon the minds of other persons are at a greater or less distance from the first person. In the more common forms of its manifestation, such mental force or power is known as Thought Force, Mental Influence, etc., and in its more pronounced and less common phases it is known as Telepathy, Thought Transference, etc., but the basic principle is precisely the same in all of such cases, simple or complex though their manifestations may be.

The Higher Forces

We may say here, frankly and plainly, however, that the advanced occultists regard this class of phenomena as comparatively simple and elementary, and therefore not fully entitled to be included in the same category with the higher phases of Nature's Finer Forces, such as, for instance, Clairvoyance, Psychometry, Communication with the Higher Planes, etc. But notwithstanding this, we are of the opinion that any and every one of the finer forces of nature, i.e., any of the forces which are over and above the plane upon which the ordinary senses of man, normally developed, ordinarily function and operate, should be placed in one general category of the Higher Forces of Nature, particularly in a work of this kind designed for the instruction of the general public upon these important subjects. Accordingly, these lesser manifestations of the finer forces in the natural world shall be carefully considered in this part of this book, so that the student may become acquainted with the scientific principles upon which they are based, and may be enabled to develop the power of manifesting such powers if he choose to do so; and that he may understand the nature of such forces and powers when they are manifested by other persons.

Chitta, or Mind Substance

The Hindu Teachings hold that that which we call "Mind" is not an intangible something different from anything else in Nature, but that, on the contrary, it forms a part of Nature's general manifestation, and is a substantial thing. The Hindus have given to this Mind Substance the name of Chitta. Without going into metaphysical discussion, or entering into technical details concerning this Mind Substance or Chitta, we may say that the Hindus believe it to be one phase of the great Manifestation which we call Nature—just as that which we call Matter is another phase of Manifestation—and, like Matter, having its own particular kind of force, or energy, its own rates of vibrations, and its own attribute of radiating its vibratory force or energy over space.

Chitta manifests its activity in creating Thought, Emotions, etc., and also in receiving impressions from the outside world which it translates into perceptions and ideals. Chitta, or Mind Substance, is not regarded by the Hindus as being identical with the Soul, or the Ego; but, on the contrary, they regard it as being an instrument for the expression of the activity of the Ego, or Soul, just as the Body is another kind of instrument. Both Body and Mind are regarded as being intended for the use of the Ego or Soul, and not as identical with the latter. We shall not discuss these distinctions further in this book, this subject being apart from the general field and scope of the present work.

What Modern Science Says

There are many to whom this conception of the vibration energy of Chitta or Mind Substance may seem strange. But such persons will be still more surprised, perhaps, when they are told that modern science has practically admitted the general truth contained in the Hindu teachings concerning the same, though modern science seems to cloak the facts of the case in technical terms so that the ordinary person is unable to comprehend the real facts dwelling beneath these terms. Science can never admit that ancient teachings could have any merit in the modern age. To this latter class we specially commend the following statement made by Professor Ochorowicz, the eminent European scientist, a few years ago. Professor Ochoriwicz says:

A Living Dynamic Focus

"Every living being is a dynamic focus. A dynamic focus tends ever to propagate the motion that is proper to it. Propagated motion becomes transformed according to the medium it traverses. Motion always tends to propagate itself. Therefore, when we see work of any kind—mechanical, electrical, nervic, or psychic— disappear without visible effort, then of two things, one happens, namely, either a transmission or a transformation. Where does the first end, and where does the second begin? In an identical medium there is only transmission; in a different medium there is transformation.

"You send an electric current through a thick wire. You have the current, but you do not perceive any other force. But cut that thick wire, and connect the ends by means of a fine wire, and this fine wire will grow hot—there will be a transformation of a part of the current into heat. Take a pretty strong current, and interpose a wire still more resistant, or a very thin carbon rod, and the carbon will emit light. A part of the current, then, is transformed into heat and light. The light acts in every direction around about, first visibly as light, then invisibly as heat and electric current. Hold a magnet near it. If the magnet is weak and movable, in the form of a magnetic needle, the beam of light will cause it to deviate; if it is strong and immovable, it will in turn cause the beam of light to deviate. And all this from a distance, without contact, without special conductors.

Dynamic Correlate of Thought

"A process that is at once chemical, physical and psychical, goes on in the brain. A complex action of this kind is propagated through the gray brain matter, as waves are propagated in water. Regarded on its physiological side, an idea is only a vibration, a vibration that is propagated, yet which does not pass out of the medium in which it can exist as such. It is propagated only as far as other vibrations allow. It is propagated more widely if it assumes the character which subjectively we call emotive. But it cannot go beyond without being transformed. Nevertheless, like force in general, it cannot remain in isolation, and it escapes in disguise.

"Thought stays at home, as the chemical action of a battery remains in the battery; it is represented by its dynamic correlate, called in the case of the battery a 'current,' and in the case of the brain, I know not what; but whatever its name may be, it is the dynamic correlate of thought. I have chosen the name 'dynamic correlate.' There is something more than that; the universe is neither dead nor void.

"A force that is transmitted meets other forces, and if it is transformed only little by little it usually limits itself to modifying another force at its own cost, though without suffering materially thereby. This is the case particularly with forces that are persistent, concentrated, well seconded by their medium. It is the case with the physiological equilibrium, nervic force, psychic force, ideas, emotions, tendencies. These modify environing forces, without themselves disappearing. They are imperceptibly transformed, and if the next man is of a nature exceptionally well adapted to them, they gain in inductive action."

Answer to Skeptical Critics

The two most likely objections advanced against this conception by skeptical critics are as follows: "(1) The mental vibratory motion, or vibratory waves, are not known to science, nor recorded on scientific instruments such as the galvanometer. What is the rate of such vibrations, and what is their general character? (2) Granted the existence of such vibratory energy, or thought-waves, how and by means of what channel does the second person receive them from the first person? How are they registered or recorded?" These objections are capable of being met in a scientific manner, to the satisfaction of any fair-minded critic or investigator. We shall now give you, briefly, the gist of the answer of science to the aforesaid objections.

The World of Vibrations

It is true that the scientific instruments of the laboratory, such as the galvanometer, do not record thought vibrations. This, because such instruments are capable of registering and recording on certain rates and modes of vibratory energy. Thought vibrations are registered only by their appropriate instruments, namely, the Chitta of Mind substance of living persons. As to the "general character and rate of vibration" of these waves of mental force, we can only say that their general character is that of "mental force" as opposed to "physical force."

As to their rate of vibration, we can only say that this is not precisely known, not having as yet been definitely ascertained; but it should be added that there is plenty room for these vibrations in the great field of vibratory energy. Read the following paragraphs, and decide this last matter for yourself.

Uncharted Seas of Vibration

The following quotations from eminent scientists will serve to give the student a general idea of the views of science upon the question of the possibility of the existence and presence of vibratory energy of kinds and characters as yet unknown to science:

The first scientist says: "There is much food for speculation in the thought that there exists sound waves that no human ear can hear, and color waves that no eye can see. The long, dark, soundless space between 40,000 and 400,000,000,000,000 vibrations per second, and the infinity of range beyond 700,000,000,000,000 vibrations per second, where light ceases, in the universe of motion, makes it possible to indulge in speculation." The second scientist says: "There is no gradation between the most rapid undulations or tremblings that produce our sensation of sound, and the lowest of those which give rise to our sensations of gentlest warmth. There is a huge gap between them, wide enough to include another world of motion, all lying between our world of sound and our world of heat and light. And there is no good reason whatever for supposing that matter is incapable of such intermediate activity or that such activity may not give rise to intermediate sensations, provided that there are organs for taking up and sensifying these movements."

The third scientist says: "The knowledge we gain by experiment brings home to us what a miserably imperfect piece of mechanism our bodies are. The ear can detect the slow-footed sound vibrations that come to us at the rate of between 40 and 40,000 a second. But the whole of space may be quivering and palpitating with waves at all sorts of varying speeds, and our senses will tell us nothing of them until we get them coming to us at the inconceivable speed of 400,000,000,000,000 a second, when again we respond to them and appreciate them in the form of light."

The fourth scientist says: "The first indications of warmth come to us when the vibrations reach the rate of 35,000,000,000,000 per second. When the vibrations reach 450,000,000,000,000 the lowest visible light rays manifest. Then come the orange rays, the golden yellow, the pure yellow, the greenish yellow, the pure green, the greenish blue, the ocean blue, the cyanic blue, the indigo, and finally the violet, the highest degree of light which the human eye can register, and which occurs when the vibrations reach the rate of 750,000,000,000 per second. Then come the ultra-violet rays, invisible to human sight but registered by chemical media. In this ultra-violet region lie the X-Rays, and the other recently discovered high degree rays; also the actinic rays which, while invisible to the eye, register on the photographic plate, sunburn one's face, blister one's nose, and even cause violent explosions in chemical substances exposed to them, as well as act upon the green leaves of plants, causing the chemical transformation of carbonic acid and water into sugar and starches. These forms of 'dark light,' that is, light too high in degree to be perceived by the human eye, are but faint indications of the existence of still higher and still finer vibrations of substance and energy."

The Human WiFi

Having seen that the first question of the skeptical critics is capable of being answered in the scientific spirit, and by ideas based upon scientific investigation, we now turn to the second question of the same critics, viz.: "Granted the existence of such vibratory energy, or thought-waves, how and by means of what channel does the second person receive these from the first person? How are they registered or recorded?"

This same question is also implied in the concluding sentence of one of the scientists above quoted, viz.: "There is no good reason whatever for supposing that matter is incapable of such intermediate activity, or that such activity may not give rise to intermediate sensations, provided that there are organs for taking up and sensifying these movements."

Let us see what science has to tell us regarding the provision of Nature for the reception and "sensing" of this class of vibratory energy. And the easiest way to ascertain the report of science regarding this important matter is to consider carefully what representative leading scientists have said concerning the same in their writings or public addresses. We call your attention to the following quotations from such sources.

Let us begin with that great master of modern science, Sir William Crookes, the inventor of the celebrated "Crookes' Tubes," without which the discovery of the X-Ray and Radio-Activity would have been impossible. Several years ago, this eminent scientist, addressing the Royal Society, at Bristol, England,—a gathering made up of distinguished scientists from all over the world, most of the members being extremely skeptical concerning occult phenomena—said to the brilliant gathering: "Were I now introducing for the first time these inquiries in the world of science, I should choose a starting point different from that of old (where we formerly began). It would be well to begin with Telepathy; with that fundamental law, as I believe it to be, that thoughts and images may be transferred from one mind to another without the agency of the recognized organs of sense— that knowledge may enter the human mind without being communicated in any hitherto known or recognized ways. * * * If Telepathy takes place we have two physical facts, viz., (a) the physical change in the brain of A, the transmitter, and the analogous physical change in the brain of B, the recipient of the transmitted impression. Between these two physical events there must exist a train of physical causes. * * * It is unscientific to call in the aid of mysterious agencies, when with every fresh advance in knowledge it is shown that ether vibrations have powers and attributes abundantly able to meet any demand—even the transmission of thought.

"It is supposed by some physiologists that the essential cells of nerves do not actually touch, but are separated by a narrow gap which widens in sleep while it narrows almost to extinction during mental activity. This condition is so singularly like a Branly or Lodge coherer [a device which led to the discovery of wireless telegraphy] as to suggest a further analogy. The structure of brain and nerve being similar, it is conceivable that there may be present masses of such nerve coherers in the brain, whose special function it may be to receive impulses brought from without, through the connecting sequence of ether waves of appropriate order of magnitude. Roentgen has familiarized us with an order of vibrations of extreme minuteness as compared with the smallest waves with which we have hitherto been acquainted; and there is no reason to suppose that we have here reached the limit of frequency. It is known that the action of thought is accompanied by certain molecular movements in the brain, and here we have physical vibrations capable from their extreme minuteness of acting direct upon individual molecules, while their rapidity approaches that of internal and external movements of the atoms themselves. A formidable range of phenomena must be scientifically sifted before we effectually grasp a faculty so strange, so bewildering, and for ages so inscrutable, as the direct action of mind upon mind."

Human Electro-Magnetism

Professor Bain, another eminent authority, tells us: "The structure of the nervous substances, and the experiments made upon the nerves and nerve-centres, establish beyond a doubt certain peculiarities as belonging to the force that is exercised by the brain. This force is of a current nature; that is to say, a power generated at one part of the structure is conveyed along an intervening substance and discharged at some other part. The different forms of electricity and magnetism have made us familiar with this kind of action."

Professor Draper, another eminent authority, says: "I find that the cerebrum is absolutely analogous to in construction to any other nervous arc. It is composed of centripetal and centrifugal fibres, having also registering ganglia. If in other nervous arcs the structure is merely automatic, and can display no phenomena of itself, but requires the influence of an external agent—the optical apparatus inert save under the influence of light, the auditory save under the impression of sound—the cerebrum, being precisely analogous in its elementary structure, presupposes the existence of some agent to act through it."

Prof. M. P. Hatfield has said: "The arrangement of the nerve-envelopes is so like that of the best constructed electrical cables that we cannot help thinking that both were constructed to conduct something very much alike. I know that there are those who stoutly maintain that nerve force is not electricity, and it is not in the senses that an electrical battery is not the same thing as a live man; but, nevertheless, nerve-force is closely allied to that wonderful thing that for want of a better and clearer understanding we agree to call 'electricity.'"

Human Etheric Force

Professor Haddock, a popular writer along the lines of scientific psychology and kindred subjects, in a part of his work in which he was considering the idea that thought may be communicated by means of ether-vibrations, forcibly says: "The ether is accepted by science as a reality, and as a medium for light, heat, electricity, magnetism, etc. The nervous system is certainly comparable to an electric battery with connecting wires. Communications of thought and feeling without the mediation of sense-perceptions as commonly understood is now established. Inanimate objects exert, now and then, 'strange influences.' People certainly carry with them a personal atmosphere. The representation of the condition of these facts by a psychic field, compared to the magnetic or electric field, becomes, therefore, if not plausible, at least convenient. As such a 'field' exists surrounding the sun, so may a 'field' be assumed as surrounding each human individual. 'We have already strong grounds for believing that we live in a medium which conveys to-and-fro movements to us from the sun, and that these movements are electro-magnetic, and that all the transformation of light and heat, and indeed the phenomena of life, are due to the electrical energy which comes to us across the vacuum which exists between us and the sun—a vacuum which is pervaded by the ether, which is a fit medium for the transmission of electro-magnetic waves.' By means, then, of a similar theory applied to mind and brain and body, we may find reasonable explanations of many otherwise insoluble mysteries of life, and, which is of more importance, deduce certain suggestions for the practical regulation of life in the greatest individual interest."

The Brain-Battery

The same writer says: "All states of body and mind involve constant molecular and chemical change. The suggestion arises that the brain, with its millions of cells and its inconceivable changes in substance, may be regarded as a transmitting and receiving battery. The brain being a kind of battery, and the nerves being conductors of released stored-up energy to different parts of the body, by a kind of action similar to the actions of electricity and magnetism, it is suggested that, either by means of the ether, or of some still finer form of matter, discharges of brain energy may be conducted beyond the limits of the body.

If the nerve-track corresponds to wires, this refined medium may correspond to the ether-field supposed to be employed in wireless telegraphy. As electrical movements are conducted without wires, or other visible media, so could brain-discharges be conveyed beyond the mechanism of the battery, without the intervention of nerves—except as they may constitute a part of the battery. Generally speaking, such discharges would originate in two ways, viz., by direct mental action, or by mental or physical states—perhaps by a combination."

A Peculiar Organ

So much for the conceptions of modern western science, which agree in the main with those of the ancient oriental occultists, although of course different names and terms are employed. But, we think it worthwhile to call your attention to the fact that the western scientists have failed to note the significant presence of a peculiar organ in the human body, which is regarded as most important in its functions and offices by the oriental teachers, and which we believe has a very close connection to the subject just discussed by the western scientists. We refer to that strange organ or gland known to western science as the Pineal Gland. Let us see just what this is.

The Pineal Gland

The Pineal Gland is a mass of nervous substance which is found located in the human brain in a position near the middle of the skull, almost directly above the extreme top of the spinal column. It is shaped like a small cone, and is of a reddish-gray color. It lies in front of the cerebellum, and is attached to the third ventricle of the brain. It contains a small quantity of peculiar particles of a gritty, sand-like substance, which is commonly known as "brain sand." It derives its scientific name from its shape, which resembles a pine-cone. Western physiologists are at sea regarding the function and office of this interesting organ, or gland, and the text books generally content themselves with stating that "the functions of the Pineal Gland are not understood." The oriental occultists, on the other hand, claim that the Pineal Gland, with its peculiar arrangement of nerve-cell corpuscles, and its tiny grains of "brain-sand," is intimately associated with certain forms of the transmission and reception of waves of mental vibrations. Western students of occultism have been struck with the remarkable resemblance between the Pineal Gland and a certain part of the receiving apparatus employed in wireless telegraphy, the latter also containing small particles which bear a close resemblance to the "brain-sand" of the Pineal Gland; and this fact is often urged by them to substantiate the theory of the oriental occultists concerning the function and office of this interesting organ of the human body which is located in the brain of man.

Transmission of Thought

Many other facts set forth by modern western science could be cited in our consideration of the question of the existence of any possible organ for the reception of thought vibrations, but it is thought that sufficient evidence of this kind has already been submitted to your attention—sufficient to remove any reasonable doubts, and to give the student at least a clear and open mind on the subject. Summing up such evidence, we may say that modern science is fast approaching the position which is so well expressed by Camille Flammarion, the eminent French scientist, as follows: "The action of one mind upon another at a distance—the transmission of thought, mental suggestion, communication at a distance—all these are not more extraordinary than the action of the magnet on iron, the influence of the moon on the sea, the transportation of the human voice by electricity, the revolution of the chemical constituents of a star by the analysis of its light, or, indeed, all the wonders of contemporary science. Only these psychic communications are of a more elevated kind, and may serve to put us on the track of a knowledge of human nature. What is certain is this: That Telepathy can and ought to be henceforth considered by Science as an incontestible reality; that minds are able to act upon each other without the intervention of the senses; that psychic force exists, though its nature is yet unknown."

A General Principle

At this point we wish to impress upon the minds of the students of this book that what has been above said regarding that class of mental communications generally classed under the head of Telepathy also applies to many much higher phases of occult phenomena and psychic manifestations. In fact, this is one of the reasons why we have paid such close attention to the scientific evidence substantiating this class of phenomena.

It is not too much to say that in what has been said in the foregoing pages there is to be found a scientific basis for the phenomenon of "spirit communication," at least in many of its phases. It is but a step in thought—and a natural and easy step at that—from the matter of the communication of thought from the mind of one person or the material plane of life to another person on the same plane, on to the matter of the communication of thought from the mind of an individual entity on a higher plane of life to a second person who is abiding on the lower material plane occupied by us at this stage of our existence. It is seen that the difference consists largely in the matter of the degree and rate of vibratory energy employed, and the preparation of a proper receiving instrument for the reception and translation of such messages. This phase of the subject will be considered in fuller detail in a subsequent portion of this book.

Transformation of Vibrations

One of the things which seem to greatly puzzle the average student of the subject of mental vibrations, and thought-transference, is that which may be called "thought waves." The student is unable to conceive of a wave of "thought" being projected into the air, and then traveling along until it reaches the mind of other persons. The difficulty, upon analysis, is seen to consist of the inability to conceive of "thought" as being a material substance capable of traveling in "waves." It is no wonder that the student finds this conception difficult, for there is no such thing as "thought" traveling in this way. The phenomenon of thought transference is accounted for scientifically in quite another manner, as we shall see in a moment. The student is advised to carefully note this distinction, for upon its understanding depends greatly the intelligent comprehension of the entire subject of thought vibrations and thought-transference.

Example of Electric Light

Perhaps this matter may be best explained by means of illustrations of the operation of electricity and light—electric vibrations and light vibrations. In both cases the secret of the transmission of the vibrations or waves of vibratory energy may be summed up in the word "transformation." For instance, when we transmit electric vibrations over a fine wire or thread of carbon, the electric vibrations are transformed into light vibrations and manifest as "electric light." In another form of transmission the electric vibrations are transformed into "electric heat."

However, this is merely one phase of the transformation; consider carefully the more complex phases, as follows: We speak into the receiver of a telephone and the sound vibrations produced by our voice are transformed into electrical vibrations and in that form travel over the telephone wire; arriving at the other end of the wire, these electric vibrations enter into the receiver, and are there transformed into sound vibrations, and as such are heard by the person holding the receiver. Now note this: the sound vibrations do not travel at all; instead, they are transformed into electric waves, which in turn are transformed at the receiving end of the line into sound vibrations once more. And unless the receiving apparatus be present, and properly adjusted, there is no second transformation at all; and in such case the electric vibrations remain such.

Example of WiFi

Likewise, in the case of WiFi, the electric energy produced by the sending instrument is transformed into subtle and finer etheric waves, which travel to the receiving instrument, and are there transformed into electric waves, the latter producing physical changes in the receiving apparatus which enable them to be read by the observer. In the case of WiFi there is still more complex process of transformation, as follows: the speaker conveys sound vibrations into the instrument; these are transformed into electric vibrations; and the latter into the etheric vibrations which travel through space to the receiver. Reaching the receiver, the etheric vibrations are transformed into ordinary electric vibrations, and these in turn into sound waves capable of being sensed by the listener.

Example of Light Waves

The same process is detected in the transmission of what we call light waves. The activities manifested by the substance of the sun set up certain vibrations which we call "light vibrations." These are communicated to the ether in the form of so-called "light waves" but which are merely etheric waves of a certain rate of vibration. These waves travel through space and are transformed into "light" only when they reach some material substance capable of receiving and reflecting their vibrations. Science tells us that empty space is perfectly dark, and that light manifests only when the etheric light vibrations come in contact with material substance and are there transformed into "light." Light, as "light" does not travel from the sun—what we know as "light" is simply the result of the transformation of certain etheric waves into "light" by reason of their contact with material substances.

Transformation of Mental Vibrations

Now for the analogy. Mental vibrations are so only when they remain in their own uninterrupted medium of channel of activity, i.e., the brain and the nervous system of the individual. Many hold that they are able to leap over the barrier of flesh separating two persons when such persons are in immediate physical contact, and the conditions are of a certain kind; but as a rule they do not do so.

But, as all investigators know, mental vibrations are capable of being transformed into some subtle form of etheric vibrations, and the latter when coming in contact with the nervous system of other persons may be again transformed, this time into mental vibrations which produced thoughts, feelings and mental images in the minds of the second persons or persons, corresponding with these mental states in the first person. Think over this carefully, until you grasp the idea fully.

Vibrational Attunement

And here we find another startling correspondence between the phenomena of wireless telegraphy and that of thought transference or transmission of mental vibrations. We allude to the fact that while a wireless telegraphic sending instrument may be sending forth vibrations of the strongest power, its messages are capable of being received or "picked up" only by those instruments which are "in tune" with the sending instrument to at least a certain degree; to all other instruments, those which are not "in tune" with the sending instrument, there is no message perceptible. Precisely this same state of affairs is found to prevail in the realm of mental vibrations and thought transmission.

The individual receives only such messages as emanate from instruments with which he is "in tune"—to all the rest he is deaf and unconscious. But once "in tune" with the higher vibrations of the mental realm, he will receive every message traveling on that particular plane at that particular time, unless he deliberately shut them out. We shall see how this works out in ordinary life, when we consider the general subject of Telepathy and Thought Transference in the succeeding chapter.

But, in connection with the above statement of the "in tune" law or rule of manifestation, we wish to call to the attention of the student the important fact that the same law prevails in the case of communications from the higher planes of existence—the so-called "spirit communications" and other messages of this kind reaching individuals on our own plane of existence. It is only when the individual on the "earth plane" becomes "in tune" with the sending mental instrument of the entity abiding on a higher plane of existence, that it is able to "pick up" the message being sent to earth. Even the same individual is often unable to "catch" the messages at one time, while at other times he experiences no difficulty whatsoever. An understanding of this fact—this law or rule of manifestation—will throw a great light over many dark places of misunderstanding and perplexity concerning certain phases of occult and psychic phenomena. This feature of such phenomena will be considered in detail in subsequent parts of this book.

The Two Key-Words

Concluding our consideration of the "just how" of the transmission of thoughts, messages, and "psychograms" between two minds, be they both on earth plane, or one of the two on the higher planes, we would say: "Always remember the two Key-Words, namely Transformation and Attunement." These two Key-Words will enable you to unlock many doors of thought on these subjects—doors which otherwise will remain closed to you.

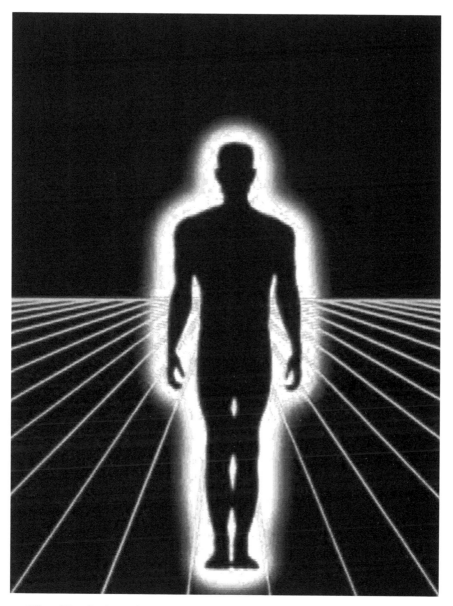

The Hindu Teachings say that the "Mind" is not intangible, somehow different from everything else in Nature, but that, on the contrary, it forms a part of Nature's general manifestation, and is a substantial thing.

PART III

THOUGHT TRANSFERENCE

THE most elementary and simple form in which mental vibrations are transmitted is that which may be called Thought Transference. In the category of Thought Transference may be included two quite general classes, as follows: (1) Involuntary Transmission of Mental Vibrations, and (2) Voluntary Transmission of Mental Vibrations, commonly known as Telepathy. In this part of this book both of these general classes of Thought Transference shall be considered in some detail.

Involuntary Transmission of Mental Vibrations

Mental vibrations emanating from the brain of the individual take on the form of wave-like movements in the ether, which are accordingly known as "thought-waves." These thought-waves are constantly being sent forth from the brains of all persons, and after being sent forth they spread in space from the immediate neighborhood of the person originating them, to a distance proportioned to the strength and power energizing the original mental state. These thought-waves have the power of awakening and arousing into activity corresponding mental states in other persons coming within their field of force, according to the laws of Mental Induction. It should be noted here that the activity aroused in the mind of the receiving person is accomplished by the setting into vibratory motion the Chitta or Mind-substance of that person, just as the receiving diaphragm of the telephone is set vibrating at the same rate as that of the sending instrument, and thus the original sound-waves are reproduced.

Thought Waves

Thought-waves are manifested in various forms, modes, and phases, and in different degrees of power. Some are emanated without any clearly defined desire or intent to accomplish certain ends, while others are charged with strong desire focused to a definite point by clear-cut ideas of ends sought to be accomplished. The latter, however, are usually entitled to be classed among the "involuntary" phases of Thought Transference, because the senders are generally unaware that thought-waves have an actual effect upon the minds of other persons; their thoughts and mental states arising in accordance with their feelings, desires, and general aims. Where the individual has learned that thought is an active power, he may deliberately send forth his thought-waves directed toward the person or persons whom he wishes to affect and influence.

The student must remember, however, that there is a great difference in the power and effective activity between thought-waves sent forth under different circumstances. Some are sent forth idly, and with no focused power or energy of desire and feeling, and such naturally are weak in effect upon others. Others are sent forth vitalized with strong desire and feeling, and focused with a clear ideal and mental picture, and, consequently, exert a far greater degree of effect upon the minds of others with whom they come in contact.

The analogy of the waves of electricity holds good here, for just as the electric power may be strong or weak, as the case may be, so may the mental force be strong or weak under different circumstances, and in different individuals.

Vibratory Thought Force

The vibratory force of thought-waves persist for some time after their original emanation. Here, also we have analogies on the physical plane, as follows: The heat of a room continues for some time after the fire which originally caused it has ceased to burn. Likewise, the air of a room may manifest the perfume of a flower, or extract, long after the latter has been removed from the room. Again, rays of light persist in existence long after the star manifesting them has been blotted out of existence. In the same way thought-vibrations continue to manifest in a place, large or small though its space may be, long after the original sender has passed from that plane—perhaps even long after he has passed from earth life.

Mental Atmospheres

A well known American writer on this subject has said concerning this point: "There are many places today filled with the thought-vibrations of minds long since passed out of the body. There are places filled with the strong vibrations of tragedies long since enacted there. Every place has a mental atmosphere of its own, the same arising from the thought-vibrations set in motion by the various persons who have inhabited or occupied them. Every city has its own mental atmosphere which has its effect upon persons moving into them. Some are lively, some dull, some progressive, some old-fogyish, some moral, some immoral—the result of the character of the early settlers and leading spirits, of the place in question. Persons moving into these towns are affected by the mental atmospheres thereof, and either sink to the general level, or else, if strong enough, help to change the mental tone of the place. Sometimes a change in conditions brings a large influx of new people, to a town, and the mental waves of the newcomers tend to bring about a marked change in the local mental atmosphere. These facts have been noticed by many observing people who often have not been familiar with the principles underlying and producing the facts which the observers have so clearly discerned."

The Contagion of Thought

The same writer says, along the same general lines: "Many have of course noticed the differing mental atmospheres of stores, offices, and other places of business. Some of such places give one an air of confidence and trust; others create a feeling of suspicion and distrust; some convey an impression of active, wide awake management, while others impress one as being behind the times, and suffering from a want of alert, active management. These differing mental atmospheres are caused by the different prevailing mental attitudes of the owners of the respective establishments. The managers of business places send forth thought-waves of their own, and their employees naturally falling into the pace set for them also send forth similar vibrations, and before long the whole place is vibrating on a certain scale. A change of management soon produces a marked change in the entire mental atmosphere of the place. In the same way, we notice the mental atmospheres of the houses we happen to visit; in this way we become conscious of an entire mental scale of many notes, the notes being sounded unconsciously by the minds of the occupants of the houses. From some thresholds radiate harmony, while others breathe the spirit of inharmony. Some radiate emotional warmth, while others chill one like an iceberg, by reason of the emotional coldness of the dwellers therein. Likewise, the low quarters of our cities, the dens of vice, and the haunts of dissipation vibrate with the character of the thought and feeling of those inhabiting them. And, often, the weak-willed visitor is thus tempted. In the same way, certain other places are charged with the vibrations of strong, helpful, elevating mental states, which tend to lift up and elevate, energize and stimulate the minds and feelings of those visiting these places. Thought and feeling are contagious, by reason of the laws of mental vibration and mental induction."

Mental Whirlpools

The contagion of thought-vibrations is manifested by such vibrations coming into contact with the minds of other persons within the field of mental induction of the first person, and there setting up similar vibrations. We know orators, actors, preachers and others addressing audiences of persons, send forth strong mental currents which tend to awaken corresponding vibrations in the minds of their hearers. We weep, smile, grow angry and feel happy, according to the character of the thought-waves, of the person on the platform or the stage, providing that we accept the same. And, according to the same principle, persons scattered over large areas are influenced and affected in the same way by whirlpools of mental vibrations set into original motion by some strong, masterful public man. A writer has said concerning this point:

"We know how great waves of feeling spread over a town, city, or county, sweeping people off their feet, and causing them to lose their balance. Great waves of political enthusiasm, or war-spirit or prejudice for or against certain people, or groups of people, sweep over places and cause men to act in a manner which they afterward often regret when they come to themselves and consider the matter in the light of cold reason. People are swayed by demagogues or magnetic leaders who wish to capture their votes or patronage; and they are often led into acts of mob violence, or similar atrocities, by yielding to these waves of contagious thought. On the other hand, we know equally well how great waves of religious emotion spread out over the community upon the occasion of some great 'revival' excitement or religious fervor."

Immunity to Thought Influences

Persons becoming acquainted for the first time with the above recited facts of mental vibrations, mental currents, mental waves, and mental contagion, frequently raise the objection that if all this be true, why are we not constantly swept off of our feet by these great waves of mental vibrations, whereas, in fact, we are seldom or never aware of them? The question is a natural one, and is capable of a satisfactory answer.

In the first place, many of these mental currents neutralize each other, and thus both cease to exert any marked effect. And again, most persons are really "immune" to most of the thought waves reaching them, this by reason of the protective resistive power bestowed by Nature, and acquired during the evolution of the race.

To understand this, we have but to think of our immunity to the great majority of sounds and sights on the streets of a busy city. On a busy street corner, we are assailed by an infinitude of sounds and sights—but we hear but few of these, and see still fewer. The rest of these impressions are lost to us, although we have ears to hear and eyes to see. We hear and see only those impressions which are strong enough to awaken our attention. In the same way we fail to perceive the numerous thought vibrations and mental currents constantly surrounding us, and our attention is attracted and awakened by those sufficiently strong and vigorous to awaken our attention. The analogy is a very close one, and the understanding of one set of phenomena gives us the key to the other.

Mental Attunement

It should not fail to be noticed, moreover, that we habitually receive and accept more readily those thought vibrations which are in harmony with our own average habitual mental states; and, according to the same general principle, we tend to habitually reject and fail to receive those vibrations which are inharmonious to us for the same reason. Here, you will notice, we have an illustration of the principle of "attunement" which, as we have informed you, is operative on the plane of thought and mental vibrations as well as on that of wireless telegraphy.

Just as it is a psychological fact that we tend to see and to hear those things which are in harmony with our beliefs and opinions, and our interest, so is it a metaphysical fact that we tend to accept and absorb the mental vibrations which are in harmony with our opinions, beliefs, and interest, and to reject those which are opposed thereto.

Moreover, the person who acquaints himself with the law of mental vibrations and thought-transference acquires a practical knowledge which enables him to render himself immune to objectionable and undesirable mental currents or thought-waves. We are not necessarily open to the influence of every stray current of thought or feeling that happens to be in our immediate vicinity. Instead, by the proper methods, consciously or unconsciously practiced and manifested, we may, and often do, insulate ourselves so that these undesirable mental influences fail utterly to affect us; and, likewise, we may actually attract to ourselves the desirable mental currents.

These principles and methods will be given later in this part of this book; they are mentioned here merely to acquaint you with the fact that they are existent and known to those familiar with this subject.

Voluntary Transmission of Mental Vibrations

Under the head of Voluntary Transmission of Mental Vibrations may be placed the following two general classes of phenomena, viz., (1) Voluntary Efforts to Exert Mental Influence upon Others; and (2) Voluntary Efforts to Produce the Phenomena of Telepathy, along Scientific Lines. Each of these general classes of phenomena will now be presented for your inspection and consideration.

Voluntary Mental Influence

Under the category of Voluntary Mental Influence we find much of the phenomena formerly classed as "Magic"—and by this we mean both White Magic, or efforts to produce results beneficial to the person influenced, and Black Magic, or efforts to produce results beneficial to the person exerting the influence, and often to the positive detriment of the person influenced.

White Magic

Under the category of White Magic may be placed all those efforts of mental healing, and similar phases of metaphysical therapeutics; and the accompanying efforts directed toward the general happiness and welfare of the person "treated." The word "treatment" has sprung into use in this connection, in America and Europe, by reason of its employment by the numerous metaphysical cults and schools flourishing there. We hear on all hands of persons being "treated" for Health, Happiness, and Prosperity in this way. While in some cases, the "magic" is worked on higher planes than those of thought-vibrations, it is nevertheless true that in most instances the entire process is that of mental induction, along the lines described in the preceding pages of this book. In such cases the person influenced opens himself to the helpful thought of the person "treating" him, and

95

thus a co-operation and mental "team work" is secured, often with the most beneficial results. This phase of the subject is too well known to require lengthy consideration in this book, and is more properly the subject of the many books devoted to this special phase of mental power.

Black Magic

It has well been said that there are always two poles to everything in Nature, and continued experience and investigation seems to substantiate this statement. Whenever we find a force or power producing beneficial results, we may usually feel assured that the same force or power, turned in another direction, or possibly reversed in its action, will produce results of an opposite character. And so it is with this subject of "Magic" which we are now considering. While we would be very glad to pass over this phase of the subject, truth and duty to our readers compel us to state that White Magic has its opposite pole—that opposite pole known as Black Magic, or the use of psychic force for selfish and unworthy ends. There is no use trying to pursue the ostrich policy regarding these things—it is always better to face them boldly, and then to take means to avoid the evil contained in them.

Base Use of Mind Power

We prefer to quote from other writers on this subject, who have given this particular matter the most careful attention and investigation, and who have set forth simply and plainly the result of their investigations and discoveries. Here follow several quotations from authorities of this kind:

One writer says: "It is a fact known to all students of occultism that Black Magic has been frequently employed in all times to further the selfish, base ends of some people. And it is also known to advanced thinkers today that even in this enlightened age there are many who do not scruple to stoop to the use of this hateful practice in order to serve their own ends, notwithstanding the punishment that all true occultists know awaits such persons. The annals of history are full of records of various forms of witchcraft, conjuration, and similar forms of Black Magic. All the much talked of practice of 'putting spells' upon people are really forms of Black Magic, heightened by the fear and superstition of those affected. One has but to read the history of witchcraft to see that there was undoubtedly some force at work behind all of the appalling superstitions and ignorance shown by the people of those times. What they attributed to the influence of people 'in league with the devil' really arose from the use of Black Magic, or an unworthy use of Mental Influence, the two things being one at the last.

The Secret of Witchcraft

"An examination of the methods employed by these 'witches,' as shown by their confessions, give us a key to the mystery. These 'witches' would fix their minds upon other people, or their animals, and by holding a concentrated mental picture there, would send forth thought-waves affecting the welfare of the persons being 'adversely treated,' which would influence and disturb them, and often bring on sicknesses. Of course, the effect of those 'treatments' were greatly heightened by the extreme fear and superstition held by the masses of people at the time, for fear is ever a weakening factor in mental influence, and the superstitions and credulity of the people caused their minds to vibrate in such a manner as to render them extremely passive to the adverse influences being directed against them. It is well known that the Voodoos of Africa, and similar cults among other savage races, practice Black Magic among their people with great effect. Among the native of Hawaii there are certain men known as 'Kahunas' who pray people sick, or well, whichever way they are paid to do. These instances could be multiplied almost indefinitely, but the basic principle is ever the same in such cases.

Modern Black Magic

"In our own civilized lands there are many people who have learned the principles of mental influence, and who are using the same for unworthy purposes, seeking to injure others and to defeat their undertakings, or else trying to bring them around to their own (the treators') point of view and inclinations. The modern revival of occult knowledge has operated along two lines, and in opposite directions. On the one hand, we see and hear of the mighty power for good that mental influence is exerting over the race today, healing the sick, strengthening the weak, putting courage into the despondent, and transforming failures into successes. But, on the other hand, the hateful selfishness and greed of unprincipled persons is taking advantage of this mighty force of nature, and prostituting it to the hateful ends of such persons, without heed to the dictates of conscience or the teaching of religion or of ordinary morality. These people are sowing a baleful wind, which will result in their reaping a frightful whirlwind on the mental plane. They are bringing down upon themselves pain and misery in the future."

The Explanation of Sorcery

Another writer says: "In various stages of history we find the records of persons having been affected by the influences of witches, sorcerers, and other evil-minded, unprincipled persons. In most cases these so-called witches and sorcerers themselves were under the delusion that they were being assisted by the devil or some other supernatural being. They did not realize that they were simply using natural forces. Studying the history of witchcraft, sorcery, black magic, and the like, you will find that the devotees thereof usually employed some psychometric method. In other cases they would mould little figures of clay, or of wax, in the general shape and appearance of the person whom they wished to affect. It was thought that these little figures were endowed with some supernatural powers or attributes, but of course this was mere superstition. The whole power of the little figures arose from the fact that they aided the imagination of the spell-worker in forming a mental image of the person sought to be influenced; and thus established a strong mental rapport condition. Added to this, you must remember that the fear and belief of the public greatly aided the spell-worker, and increased his power and influence over these poor persons."

The Power of Fear-Thought

The last-named writer explains the reference to "fear and belief" in the last sentence above quoted by the following very important statements, and these we ask every student of this book to firmly impress upon his mind, for a mighty truth is therein conveyed. The statements in question are as follows:

"Your attention is hereby called to a very important psychic principle involved in the manifestation of that class of phenomena in which is embraced the cases of witchcraft, sorcery, etc., with which the pages of history are filled. It is a well established fact that by denying the psychic power over you exerted by any person whatsoever, you practically neutralize the psychic power of such person, at least so far as its effect upon and power over yourself is concerned. The stronger and more positive is your mental attitude of immunity to such power, and your assertion and affirmation of that immunity, the greater is your own power of psychic resistance, and the less does his possible power over you become. The average person, not knowing this, is more or less passive to psychic influences of other persons, and may be affected by them to a greater or less extent, the degree depending upon the psychic development of the person seeking to influence him.

The Negative Pole

"At the extreme negative pole of susceptibility we find persons who believe firmly that other persons have psychic power over them, and who are consequently more or less afraid of such persons and of their influence. This belief and fear operates in the direction of making such persons peculiarly sensitive and impressionable to such influence, and thus easily affected by psychic induction. This is the reason that the so-called witches and sorcerers and others of evil repute have been often able to acquire such a power over their victims, and to cause them so much trouble. The secret is that the victims believed in the power of the other persons, and feared their power. The greater the belief in, and fear of, the power of the other persons, the greater the susceptibility to their influence; the greater the disbelief in such power, and the firm belief in one's own power of immunity and that of neutralizing the effect of the psychic influence of other persons, the less is one's degree of susceptibility, and the greater is one's degree of immunity and power. This is the rule in the case— keep it in mind!

Voodooism Explained

"Among the people of the South, in America, and among the Hawaiians, we find marked instances of this kind. The Voodoo men and women work Black Magic on those of their race who are superstitious and credulous, and who have a mortal fear of the

Voodoo. Travelers who have visited the countries have many interesting tales to recite of the terrible workings of these Voodoo black magicians. In some cases, sickness and even death is the result. But, mark you this! It is only those who believe in, and fear, the power of the Voodoos that are so affected. In Hawaii, the Kahunas or native magicians are renowned for their power to cause sickness and death to those who have offended them; or to those who have offended some client of the Kahuna, and who have hired the latter to 'pray' the enemy to sickness or death. The poor, native Hawaiians, believing implicitly in the power of the Kahunas, and being in deadly fear of them, are very susceptible to their psychic influence, and naturally fall easy victims to their vile arts, unless they buy off the Kahuna, or make peace with his client. Non-natives living in Hawaii are not affected by the Kahunas, for they do not believe in them, neither do they fear them. Unconsciously, but yet strongly, they 'deny' the power, and are immune. So you see the principle working out here, too. Once you have the master-key, you may unlock many doors of mystery which have heretofore been closed to you."

Self-Protection

The following quotations from writers on this special subject contain detailed directions for the use of those who may have reason to believe that some other person or persons are trying to use psychic force, or mental currents, upon them for selfish purposes, or otherwise. Of course the general mental attitude of disbelief, and assertion of one's one immunity is sufficient for the purposes of general psychic protection; but we have thought it proper to include the following special directions given by those who have made a close study of this subject.

One writer says: "When you come in contact with people who are seeking to influence you by psychic methods, either direct or indirect, you will find yourself able to defy their mental attacks by simply remembering the strength immanent in your Ego, or Spirit, aided by the statement or affirmation (made silently to yourself) 'I am an Immortal Spirit, using the power of my Ego, which renders me immune from all base psychic attacks or power.' With this mental attitude you may make powerful even the slightest mental effort in the direction of sending forth your own mental vibrations, and these will scatter the adverse influences in all directions; it will often be found that the other person will show signs of confusion in such a case, and will seek to get away from your presence. With this consciousness held in mind, your mental command to another, 'Let me alone—I cast off your influence by the power of my Spirit,' will operate so strongly that you will often actually see the effect at once. If the other person be stubborn, and determined to influence you by words of suggestion, coaxing, threatening, or similar methods, look him or her straight in the eye, saying mentally: 'I defy you—my inner power casts off your influence.' Try this the next time that any one attempts to influence you either verbally or by means of thought-waves, and see how strong and positive you will feel, and how the efforts of the other person will fail. This sounds simple, but the little secret is worth thousands of dollars to every individual who will put it into practice."

Repelling Adverse Influences

This writer continues: "Not only in the case of personal influence in the actual presence of the other person may be defeated in this way, but the same method will act equally well in the matter of repelling the mental influence of others directed against you in the form of 'absent treatments,' etc. If you feel yourself inclining toward doing something which in your heart you feel is not to your best interests, judged from a true viewpoint, you may know that, consciously or unconsciously, someone is seeking in influence you in this way. Then smile to yourself, and make the statements mentioned above, or some similar one, and holding the power of the Spirit within your soul, send forth a mental command just as you would in case the person were actually before you in person. You may also deny out of existence the influencing power, by asserting mentally: 'I deny your power to influence me; you have no such power over me; I am resting securely upon the Spirit within me; I deny out of existence any power over me asserted by you.' After repelling these absent influences you will at once experience a feeling of relief and strength, and will be able to smile at the thought of any such adverse influence affecting you in the slightest."

Neutralizing Psychic Influences

Another writer gives us the following most interesting information and advice for use in cases of this kind: "I wish to point out to you a means of protection against the use of psychic influence against yourself on the part of unscrupulous persons, or any other persons whomsoever, for that matter. One is fully justified in employing this method of protection against even the meddling influence of other persons, who are trying to influence you without your permission or consent.

The following is the method of self-protection or defense against this class of psychic influence: In the first place, you must, of course, refuse to admit to your mind any feeling of fear regarding the influence of other persons, for such fear opens the door to their influence, as all students of this subject know. If you have been, or are fearful of the psychic influence of any person, you must get to work and drive out that feeling by positive and vigorous denials. The denial, as all students know, is the positive neutralizer of the psychic influence of another person, providing you make it in full belief in its truth. You must take the mental position (which is really the true one) that you are absolutely immune to the psychic attack or influence. You should say, mentally, 'deny to any person the power to influence me psychically without my consent; I am positive to all such influences, and they are negative to me; I neutralize all such influences by this positive denial!'

It should encourage you to know that it requires far less force and power to repel and neutralize psychic influences of this kind, than is required to send forth the power; an ounce of denial and protection overcomes a pound of psychic attacking power. Nature gives you the means of protection, and gives you the 'best end of the stick'; and it is your own fault if you do not use it effectively. A word to the wise is sufficient."

Telepathic Phenomena

The second general class of phenomena in the general category of Voluntary Transmission of Mental Vibrations is that known as "Telepathic Phenomena." In a sense, of course, all phases of Thought Transmission, and particularly that of Voluntary Thought Transmission, may be considered as forms of Telepathy; but for the purpose of classification and distinction we have in this book classed as Telepathic Phenomena merely those forms and phases of Thought Transference in which there is an agreement between the telepathic sender and the telepathic receiver, and in which the experiments are conducted more or less along the lines of scientific investigation.

Scientific Investigators

Scientific observers, for a number of years past, have been conducting careful series of experiments in Telepathy, and many volumes of the reports of such investigations have been published by various psychic research societies. Among the eminent scientists who have devoted much attention to this subject are the following: Professor Henry Sidgewick, of Cambridge University; Professor Balfour Stewart, of the Royal Society of England; Rt. Hon. A. J. Balfour, the eminent English statesman and scientist; Professor William James, the eminent American psychologist; Sir William Crookes, the great English chemist, physicist, who invented the celebrated "Crookes' Tubes," without which the discovery of the X-Rays, Radio Activity, etc., would have been impossible; Frederick W. H. Myers, the celebrated investigator of Psychic Phenomena; and Sir Oliver Lodge, the eminent English scientist. All these men are of the highest international standing and reputation, and their acceptance of the phenomena of Telepathy places the same on a firm scientific basis.

How Experiments Are Conducted

The scientific experiments involving Telepathy, which have been conducted by numerous societies for psychical research and other bodies, have ranged from quite simple tests to those very complex. In all of these experiments there has been one person called the "sender," and another called the "receiver"—or names corresponding to these. The sender fixes in his mind a strong impression of the name or picture to be transmitted, and then makes a positive effort of the will to transmit the same to the receiver. The receiver assumes a passive receptive mental attitude, and then reports the word or image that comes into his mind. The more complex tests embody these same simple features.

Some of the early reports of the Society for Psychical Research, of London, England, show results most amazing to those who have not made a personal investigation of these matters. In some of the tests, the receiver correctly reported seventeen cards in succession, the said cards having been shown the sender, but kept out of sight of the receiver, and no possible communication between the two being allowed.

In tests of naming small objects held by the sender, the receiver correctly named five out of six. In one complicated test, in which various objects, names, etc., were transmitted, the report shows a successful report of 202 out of a possible 382. Such results, of course, took the results entirely out of the operation of the law of averages. Other successful experiments showed a high percentage of results obtained from the reproduction by the sender of geometrical and other figures and designs exhibited to the sender.

Private Experiments

But, after all, the most convincing evidences of Telepathy are those which most of us have met with in our own experience. There are but few intelligent, observing persons who have not, at some time in their life, had experiences of this kind, in which the thoughts of others were perceived plainly by themselves. Many persons have established such a close rapport condition between themselves and friends or relatives that instances of remarkable thought-transmission between them are quite common and ordinary.

Development of Telepathic Power

Practically every person may develop a certain degree of telepathic power, sending, receiving, or both, by means of a moderate amount of regular and earnest practice and experiments. In developing sending power, the person should cultivate concentration, and the use of the will in the direction of projecting mental states; in the case of the desired development of the receiving power, the person should develop receptiveness and passivity, and a certain recognition of an actual telepathic impulse which is impossible to describe in words but which comes to every investigator, and which when once experienced is always recognized thereafter.

"Mind Reading"

Perhaps the best plan for the beginner is to practice the popular "mind reading" experiment or game, which is quite popular in some localities, and among persons interested in this line of thought. The experiments of this kind are performed, generally, about as follows: The receiver leaves the room, and during his or her absence the company in the room select some object, large or small, such as a chair or a small penknife, etc., and the same is shown and named to the sender. Then the receiver is called back into the room for the experiment, and is blindfolded securely. Then the receiver takes the right hand of the sender and places it in his (the receiver's) left hand, holding it firmly there.

The sender then concentrates his mind upon the object to be "found," and mentally wills that the receiver move toward it. The receiver then experiences a peculiar faint impulse in the direction of the object, and accordingly moves toward it. After considerable practice, the receiver acquires the faculty of not only finding large objects, but also is able to locate small objects, such as concealed rings, pins, etc. This class of experiments, while open to the objection that there may be more or less muscular direction consciously or unconsciously given by the sender, nevertheless tend to develop proficiency in both sender and receiver. In fact, such experiments are perhaps one of the very best methods of developing projecting or receiving power along the lines of occult or psychic forces. This because the persons become familiar with the psychic processes involved and their efficiency becomes increased by practice and experiment.

This plan is like that of teaching a child how to walk by means of holding its hand, allowing it to rest on chairs, etc. In practicing such experiments, the receiver will soon become conscious of receiving the thought message in what may be called a "wireless flash," instead of by the slower and less clear process of transmission through the physical body of the sender, and thence through his own nerves. When the sender begins to experience these flashes of consciousness, he is ready to proceed to the next stage.

The "Willing Game"

The second stage on telepathic development is much akin to that just described, with the difference that there is no physical contact between the sender and the receiver—no holding of hands, etc. A variation of this is found in the familiar "willing game" in which the whole roomful of persons concentrates upon the receiver, and "wills" that he find a selected object. On the whole, however, the private experiments conducted by the sender and the receiver, with perhaps a few intelligent and sympathetic spectators, are far better than the "willing game" plan, in which there are usually many triflers present ready to make a joke of the whole thing, and thus taking away that true concentration under which the best results may be obtained.

Formal Tests

The third step in telepathic development is that of conducting experiments similar to those originally conducted by the Society for Psychical Research, previously mentioned. That is to say, the sender may select cards from a pack, coins from a pile, small objects from a collection, etc., and then endeavor to transmit the impression of the same to the receiver—the latter then reporting his flashes of impression received. This may be rendered more complicated by having the sender in one place, and the receiver at another, the time having previously been agreed upon between them. In experiments conducted at long range, it has been generally found better for the receiver to write down the word, thought, or mental, picture which has been transmitted to him by the sender; and for the sender to write down the name or picture of the thing the idea of which he has transmitted. These memoranda serve not only as scientific proof of the experiment, but also serve as a barometer of progress being made during the experiments.

Automatic Writing

In this connection it may be stated that many investigators and experimentors along the lines of telepathic phenomena have met with considerable success in the direction of Automatic Writing from living persons, which of course is merely a special form of Telepathy. In some cases the communications received in this way were at first thought to be from disembodied entities, until later it was discovered that the thoughts were actually transmitted (in some cases unintentionally) by living persons. The late W. T. Stead, the London editor and famous investigator of psychic phenomena, who was lost on the "Titanic" several years ago, was remarkably successful along this special line of telepathic transmission, he being one of the most efficient receivers of this kind of which those familiar with the subject have any knowledge. His written records of these experiments are very interesting, and form a valuable contribution to this subject. In this class of experiments, the sender concentrates fixedly upon the thought—word for word—and wills that the recipient write down the word so transmitted; the receiver sit passively at the time agreed upon, and allows his arm and hand to be moved by means of the psychic currents beating upon him, and which are then unconsciously transformed into muscular action—the process being similar to that of ordinary writing, except that instead of the activity of the brain of the writer being behind the muscular motion, that of the sender performs that task.

Psychic Sensitiveness

The student of this book will find in the succeeding portions thereof, from time to time, certain general instructions regarding the cultivation of psychic receptivity and sensitiveness. These general instructions are also applicable to the cultivation of telepathic power, and may be properly applied to that end. There is really but one general principle involved in all the many forms of psychic receptivity, namely that of (1) shutting the senses to the ordinary impressions of the outside world, and (2) opening the higher channels of sense to the impressions coming in the form of vibrations of the higher forces and finer powers of Nature. At the last, it is simply a matter of "getting in tune," just as truly as in the case of the wireless telegraphy. These things are difficult to explain in ordinary words to one who has had no experience along these lines; but when one begins to actually experiment and practice, the way opens out gradually and steadily, and then the person can grasp the meaning of the little "hints" dropped by others who have traveled the same path. So, after all, it comes down to the matter of Practice, Experiment, and Learning by Trying!

Art By Carol Ann Rodriguez

Under the category of White Magic may be placed all those efforts of mental healing, and similar phases of metaphysical therapeutics; and the accompanying efforts directed toward the general happiness and welfare of the person "treated."

PART IV

CLAIRVOYANCE AND KINDRED PHENOMENA

A very large and very interesting class of occult or psychic phenomena is that known under the very general classification of "Clairvoyance," which term we have thought it advisable to employ in this sense in this book, notwithstanding the technical objections urged by some against such a general usage. The term "Clairvoyance" really means "clear seeing," or "clear sight," but its special meaning, established by long usage, is "A power of discerning objects not perceptible to the normal senses." When it comes to the technical use of the term by students and teachers of psychic research and occultism, however, there is found a confused meaning of the term, some employing it in one sense, and others in another one. Accordingly, it is perhaps as well to explain the particular usage adopted and followed in this book.

Clairvoyance Defined

The English Society for Psychical Research, in its glossary, defines the term as follows: "The faculty or act of perceiving, as though visually, with some coincidental truth, some distant scene; it is used sometimes, but hardly properly, for transcendental vision, or the perception of beings regarded as on another plane of existence." A distinguished investigator along psychic lines, in one of her reports to the English Society for Psychical Research, has given the following definition of this term as employed by her in her reports, viz., "The word 'clairvoyant' is often used very loosely,

112

and with widely different meanings. I denote by it a faculty of acquiring supernormally, but not by reading the minds of persons present, a knowledge of facts such as we normally acquire by the use of our senses. I do not limit it to knowledge that would normally be acquired by the sense of sight, nor do I limit it to a knowledge of present facts. A similar knowledge of the past, and if necessary, of future events, may be included. On the other hand, I exclude the mere faculty of seeing apparitions, which is sometimes called clairvoyance."

The last stated definition agrees almost perfectly with the views of the writer of the present book, and the term "Clairvoyance" is used here in the particular sense indicated by such definition. The student of this book, therefore, is asked to distinguish Clairvoyance, on the one hand, from the phenomena of Telepathy or Thought Transference, and, on the other hand, from the phenomena of communication with entities on other planes of existence, including the perception of apparitions.

The Phenomena of Clairvoyance

The phenomena of Clairvoyance may be subdivided (a) according to methods employed, and also (b) according to general distinctions. The said classifications follow:

Classification According to Methods. The classification of Clairvoyant Phenomena according to methods employed, proceeds as follows: (1) Psychometry, in which the clairvoyant becomes en rapport through the medium of some physical object connected with the person or scene which is the object of the en rapport connection; (2) Crystal Gazing, etc., in which the en rapport connection is established by means of a crystal, magic mirror, etc., into which the clairvoyant gazes; (3) Direct Clairvoyance, in which the clairvoyant directly establishes the en rapport connection by means of raising his or her psychic vibrations so as to become "in tune" with the finer vibrations of Nature, without the aid of physical objects.

Classification According to General Distinctions

The classification of Clairvoyant Phenomena according to general distinctions, proceeds as follows: (1) Present Clairvoyance, in which the objects perceived by the clairvoyant are present in Space and Time, although invisible to normal sight; (2) Space Clairvoyance, in which the clairvoyant vision includes objects and scenes removed in space from the immediate normal perception of the clairvoyant; (3) Time Clairvoyance, in which the clairvoyant perceives objects or scenes removed from him in past time, or future time. In order that the student may obtain a comprehensive understanding of the phenomena of Clairvoyance, we have thought it well to give you a brief, general outline of the particular phenomena fitting into these several classes, and to give you, also, a general idea of the principal methods employed to obtain the phenomenal manifestations in question. We begin by calling your attention to the three general classes of method employed to obtain the manifestation of clairvoyant phenomena, namely: Psychometry, Crystal Gazing, and Clairvoyant Psychic States, respectively.

Psychometry

In Psychometry, the clairvoyant establishes the en rapport connection with objects, persons or scenes, removed in space or in time, by means of some physical object associated with the distant object, person or scene; for instance, the physical objects may be a piece of clothing, a bit of stone, a coin, a bit of jewelry, etc., which has been closely associated with that which the clairvoyant desires to sense psychically. The distinctive feature of this class of clairvoyant phenomena is this connecting link of physical objects. A writer has cleverly compared this connecting link with the bit of clothing which the keen-scented bloodhound is given to sniff in order that he may then discover by scent the person sought, the latter having previously worn the bit of clothing presented to the dog's sense of smell.

The "Psychic Scent"

Occultists have elaborated a technical theory to account for the phenomena of Psychometry, or rather to account for the action of the "connecting link" of the physical object employed to establish the connection between clairvoyant and distant object, person, or scene. But we do not think it advisable to enter into a discussion of these elaborate, technical theories, which are apt to confuse the beginner, and to distract his attention from the important facts of the case.

We think it is sufficient to say that the "connecting link," or physical object, seems to carry along with it, in its inner substance or nature, the vibrations of its past environment; and that the clairvoyant, coming into receptive contact with such vibrations, is enabled with comparative ease to follow up the psychic "scent" until he establishes clairvoyant en rapport connection with the distant object, person, or scene associated with the physical object. When it is remembered that the physical "scent" of anything is merely a matter of the detection of certain vibrations, the illustration is seen to be not so very far out of the way after all.

Magnetic Affinity

A somewhat celebrated investigator of psychic and occult phenomena has said concerning this phases of Clairvoyance: "The untrained clairvoyant usually cannot find any particular astral picture when it is wanted, without some special link to put him en rapport with the subject required. Psychometry is an instance in point. It seems as though there were a sort of magnetic attachment or affinity between any particle of matter and the record which contains its history—an affinity which enables it to act as a kind of conductor between that record and the faculties of anyone who can read it.

For instance, I once brought from Stonehenge a tiny fragment of stone, not larger than a pin's head, and on putting this into an envelope and handing it to a psychometrist who had no idea what it was, she at once began to describe that wonderful ruin and the desolate country surrounding it, and then went on to picture vividly what were evidently scenes from its early history, showing that the infinitesimal fragment had been sufficient to put her into communication with the records connected with the spot from which it came. The scenes through which we pass in the course of our life seem to act in the same way upon the cells of our brain as did the history of Stonehenge upon that particle of stone. They establish a connection with those cells by means of which our mind is put en rapport with that particular portion of the records, and so we 'remember' what we have seen."

Distant En Rapport

One of the most familiar instances of the production of clairvoyant phenomena by means of Psychometry is that illustrated in the above quotation, namely the production of the en rapport relation with distant scenes by means of the connecting link of some small object which had at some time in the past been located at that point. In such cases the psychometrist usually presses the small object up to his or her head, and then induces a passive, receptive psychical condition; then, sooner or later, the clairvoyant experiences a "sensation," or a "dream picture" of the scene in question. Often, once the picture of the scene is obtained, the clairvoyant may manifest more marked past-time clairvoyance, in the direction of running back over the history of the scene itself.

The instance related in the above quotation is a case of this kind. Similar cases are frequently met with by the investigator along these lines, in which the clairvoyant is able to give the history of certain places in ancient Egypt, from the connecting link of a piece of mummy-cloth; or else to give a picture of certain events in antediluvian times, from the connecting link of a bit of fossil substance.

The history of Psychometry is filled with remarkable instances of this kind. Bullets gathered from battlefields also serve very effectively as such psychometric connecting links. Old furniture, old pictures, and old jewelry also are common objects serving to produce wonderful phenomena of this kind. Psychics have used Psychometry to solve perplexing murder cases. In fact, any physical object having past-time or far-distant space connections may be employed effectively in such experiments.

Psychic Underground Exploration

Psychometry is frequently employed to describe underground or "mine" conditions existing at the present time at the particular place from which a particular piece of ore or mineral has been taken, which ore or mineral has been handed the psychometrist to be used as the connecting link. As many practical miners know from actual experience, many valuable coal, zinc, lead, silver and gold mines have been successfully located in this way.

In such cases the psychometrist has been able to follow up the psychic "scent" given by the piece of mineral, and thus to describe the strata or veins of the mineral lying underground and unopened by the pick or drill.

Psychic Detective Work

Many cases are recorded by the investigators in which the psychometrist is able to "sense" a particular locality, a house, a room, a place of business, for instance, by means of the connecting link afforded by some physical object formerly associated with the said location. Some writers have called this class of psychometric phenomena "psychic spying" or "psychic detective work." One writer records a case in which he gave to a young psychometrist a penholder from the office of a lawyer, the latter being located about eight hundred miles away; the psychometrist then gave a perfect picture of the interior of the far-distant lawyer's office, the scene across the street visible from the office window, and certain events which were happening in the office and on the street at that particular time—all of which report was verified in detail by subsequent careful inquiry.

How to Psychometrize

The following general remarks concerning Psychometry, given by a writer on the subject, will be found interesting and instructive. The writer says: "There are no special directions to be given the student in psychometry. All that can be done is to suggest that each person should try the experiments for himself, in order to find out whether he has, or has not the psychometric power in some degree of development. He may be able to develop his psychometric powers by the general methods given for psychic development; but, in any event, he will find that actual practice and experiment will do much for him in the direction of experiment. Let the student take strange objects, and, sitting in a quiet room with the object held to his forehead, endeavor to shut out all thoughts coming from the outside world, and forget all his personal affairs. In a short time, if the conditions be right, he will begin to have flashes of scenes associated with the history of the object in question. At first these impressions may be somewhat disconnected and more or less confused, but before long there will be noticed a clearing away of the scene, and the mental picture will become quite plain. Practice will develop the power. The student should practice only when alone or when in the presence of some sympathetic friend or friends. He should always avoid discordant and inharmonious company while practicing his psychic power. Many of the best psychometrists keep their physical eyes closed when practicing this power, thus allowing the inner senses to function without distraction from the outer senses.

Developing Psychometry

"You have doubtless heard of the sensing of sealed letters spoken of as pure clairvoyance. But this phase of phenomena properly belongs to the realm of Psychometry. Letters frequently prove to be very excellent connecting links in psychometric experiments. I advise the student to begin with old letters. He will be surprised to discover how readily he will begin to receive psychic impressions from the letters—either from the person who wrote them, or from the place in which they were written, or from someone connected with their subsequent history. One of the most interesting experiments I ever witnessed in Psychometry was that in which a letter that had been forwarded from place to place, until it had gone completely around the globe, was psychometrized by a young Hindu maid. Although ignorant of the outside world of foreign lands, the young woman was able to picture the people and scenery of every part of the globe in which the letter had traveled. Her report was really an interesting 'travelogue' of a trip around the world, given in tabloid form. The student may obtain some interesting results in psychometrizing old letters—but let him always be conscientious about it, and be careful to refrain from divulging the secrets that will become his during the course of these experiments. Let him be honorable on the psychic plane as well as on the physical plane—more so, rather than less so, in fact."

Varieties of Psychometry

Another investigator along these lines gives the following instructive comments regarding the practice of psychometric power: "Persons of a highly-strung nervous organization, with large perceptive faculties make the best psychometrists. Phlegmatic people seldom psychometrize clearly, and usually lack receptivity to the finer forces. Letters, clothes, hair, coins, ornaments, or jewels—in fact, almost any article which has belonged to, or has been worn by, its possessor for any length of time, will suffice to enable the psychometrist to relate himself to, and glimpse impressions of, the personal sphere of that individual. Some psychometrists succeed better with certain kinds of objects than with others. Metals and minerals are not good 'conductors'— if we may use that term—to some operators; while they are very satisfactory to others. In the same way, some psychometrists are very good character readers, others are very successful in the diagnosis of diseases; some can read the book of Nature, while to others it is a sealed book, or nearly so, but they are able to gauge the mental qualifications of their visitors, while others realize their moral and spiritual states. Again, some read the Past, and enter into the Present states or condition of their clients, while others are successful in exercising prophetical prevision. These differences may be modified, and the boundaries of the perceptive power may be extended by self-study, experiment, and culture; but every psychic has his qualifications and his limitations; one will succeed where another may fail; hence it is well and wise for each one to discover what he can do best, what sphere he can best occupy, and then endeavor to fill it.

Psychometric "Getting in Touch"

"A psychometrist may, by holding a letter in his hand, or putting it to his forehead, be able to perceive and delineate the personal appearance of the writer thereof, and, in a way, to 'take on' his conditions, describe his feelings and thoughts to such an extent as to identify himself with him and to feel, for the time being, as if he, himself, were the writer; he may even tell what is written in the letter, although unable to see the writing. Human hair is found by some psychometrists to give them the best means of coming into touch with their subjects, and it is said that such hair should be cut from the head just behind the ears, as close to the scalp as possible. It not infrequently happens that a psychometrist gets started upon a false trail, so to speak, and especially so when the inquirer is suspicious, or where there is a mixture of psychic influences. A fan passed by a lady to a sitter in the front row at a meeting, and held in the hands of the latter for a few minutes while awaiting a chance to be handed to the psychic, has resulted in a blending of vibratory influences which has caused an imperfect or confused 'reading.' In one case the gentleman who held the fan said 'I fully recognize the part of the description which the lady does not admit—it applies to myself quite perfectly.' Hence the necessity for care in providing articles for psychometrists in a public meeting. A ring, for instance, which has been in the family for generations, and handed from one wearer to another in the course of years, may afford such a blending of psychic vibrations that the psychometrist may be unable to sense distinctly each distinct stratum of influence therein.

Psychometric Readings

"The person who sits for the psychometrist for a 'reading' should not be antagonistic nor frivolous, neither should he desire special information, nor concentrate his thought forces upon any given point, as otherwise he may dominate the psychic and thus mislead him into perceiving only a reflex of his own hopes or fears. He will do well to preserve an open mind, and an impartial though sympathetic mental attitude, and then await results. It is unwise to interrupt, explain, or question during the time that a delineation is being given, for by so doing the psychic sphere is disturbed and the thought projections caused to act like the breezes upon the surface of a lake, producing confused and distorted appearances. It is best to allow the descriptions to be given in its entirety before asking questions regarding any of its details; it is quite possible or probable that the very points upon which inquiries seem necessary will be more fully elucidated before the close of the reading. If a special reading and not a general one is required—say, for instance, a diagnosis of diseased conditions—a hint of what is desired at the outset should be sufficient."

Crystal Gazing, Etc

The second of the three general classes of the methods employed to obtain the manifestation of clairvoyant phenomena is that known as Crystal Gazing. In this class of methods the clairvoyant establishes the en rapport condition by means of a crystal, magic mirror, or similar object, which serves principally to concentrate the psychic visual powers to a focus, and thus to enable the psychic to raise his or her psychic vibrations at that concentrated focused point.

Crystals and Bright Objects

The use of crystals and other bright objects for this purpose has been common to occultists and psychics at all times, past and present, and at all places, oriental or occidental. The earlier races employed shining pieces of quartz or other clear crystal rock for this purpose. Later polished metals were used in the same way. The native soothsayers of barbaric lands employ clear water, glowing embers, or sparks, for this purpose. In some places the soothsayers hold drops of blood in the hollow of their hands for divining purposes. Others bore a hole in the ground, and fill it with water, and then gaze into it. Some tribes use dark polished stones. A writer on the subject has said: "They stare into a crystal ball, a cup, a mirror, a blot of ink, a drop of blood, a bowl of water, a pond, water in a glass bowl, or almost any polished surface, etc." In fact, it may be said that almost every object capable of presenting a polished surface has been employed by some race as an aid to psychic vision. In Europe and America, at the present day, quartz or glass crystals are so used; but others obtain quite satisfactory results from the use of watch crystals laid over a black cloth, preferably a piece of black velvet cloth. Others use highly polished bits of silver; while others content themselves with the use of a little pool of black ink lying on the bottom of a small saucer, while others have cups painted black on the inside, into which is poured water.

The Care of the Crystal

There is no particular virtue in any particular object used for this purpose, as such object acts merely to focus the psychic power of the person, as has been said. Certainly the student should not fall into the error of supposing that the crystal, or similar object, has any miraculous or supernatural power whatsoever, it is simply an instrument, like the microscope or telescope, nothing more or less. But, at the same time, it must be admitted that there is much truth in the claim of certain crystal gazers, to the effect that the use of a particular crystal seems to have the effect of polarizing its molecules so as to render it a more effective instrument in time. In fact, the phenomenon seems to bear a close relation to the well known case of a long-used violin becoming a more perfect instrument, and giving forth richer and fuller notes than a new instrument. The longer a gazing crystal is used, especially by the one person, the better does it seem to serve the purposes of that particular person. Experts in crystal gazing insist that the crystal gazer should keep his own crystal for his own particular use, and not allow it to be used indiscriminately, particularly in the case of strangers or of persons not sympathetic with psychic subjects. They claim that each crystal becomes polarized according to the individual character and needs of the person habitually using it, and that it is unwise to allow others to disturb this quality in it.

How to Use the Crystal

The best authorities on the subject of crystal-gazing insist that all experiments along the said lines should be conducted in a serious, earnest manner, and that all frivolity or trifling should be avoided if the best results are wished for. This, of course, is true concerning all phases of psychic investigation, as all true students of the subject know. All the authorities agree that the crystal gazer should sit with the light behind his back, and never in front of him. While an earnest steady gaze is desirable, there should be no straining of the eyes. As one writer has said: "Gaze calmly at the crystal, but do not strain your eyes. Do not try to avoid winking your eyes—there is a difference between 'gazing' and 'staring,' remember." Some authorities advise that the crystal gazer should make funnels of his hands, using them as he would a pair of opera-glasses.

The "Milky Mist"

While some experimenters obtain results almost from the time of the first trial, others find that it requires a number of sittings before they begin to obtain even faint results. The psychic picture in the crystal usually begins by the appearance of a cloudy "milky mist," succeeding the former transparent appearance of the crystal. The milky cloud becomes more dense, and finally there appears in its midst a faint form, outline, face, or scene of some kind. Some have compared this gradual emergence of the picture to the gradual development of the picture of the photographic plate when the latter is subjected to the action of the developing fluid.

Classes of Psychic Pictures

An English writer on the subject furnishes the following general classification of the psychic pictures manifested in the process of crystal gazing. The said authority might well have added that each and every form of clairvoyant picturing is possible in crystal gazing; for crystal gazing is merely one particular form or method of inducing clairvoyant or psychic vision, and is not a distinct branch of psychic phenomena in itself. The classification of the English authority, however, is as follows:

"1. Images of something unconsciously observed. New reproductions, voluntary or spontaneous, and bringing no fresh knowledge to the mind.

"2. Images of ideas unconsciously acquired from others. Some memory or imaginative effort which does not come from the gazer's ordinary self. Revivals of memory. Illustrations of thought.

"3. Images, clairvoyant or prophetic. Pictures giving information as to something past, present, or future, which the gazer has no other chance of knowing."

General Directions for Crystal Gazing

An old English authority on the subject of crystal gazing handed down to his students a certain set of general directions and rules to govern the conduct of their experiments. These rules and directions have never been improved upon by the later writers on the subject, according to the opinion of the best authorities; and such stand today as perhaps the simplest and best set of general rules and directions on this important subject. For this reason we have thought it advisable to include the same in this chapter, for the guidance of our own students. Here follow the said general rules and directions: "What is desired through the regular use of the translucent sphere is to cultivate a personal degree of clairvoyant power, so that visions of things or events, past, present, and future, may appear clearly in the interior vision, or eye of the soul. In the pursuit of this effort only, the crystal becomes at once a beautiful, interesting and harmless channel of pleasure and instruction, shorn of dangers, and rendered conducive to mental development. To the attainment of this desirable end, attention is asked to the following practical directions, which, if carefully followed, will lead to success:

Selection of Place, Etc.

"(1) Select a quiet room where you will be entirely undisturbed, taking care that it is as far as possible free from mirrors, ornaments, pictures, glaring colors, and the like, which may otherwise distract the attention. The room should be of comfortable temperature, in accordance with the time of year, neither hot nor cold. About 60 to 65 degrees is suitable in most cases, though allowance can be made where necessary for natural differences in the temperaments of various persons. Thus thin, nervous, delicately organized individuals, and those of lymphatic and soft, easy-going, passive types, require a slightly warmer apartment than the more positive class who are known by their dark eyes, hair and complexion, combined with prominent joints. Should a fire, or any form of artificial light be necessary, it should be screened off, so as to prevent the light rays from being reflected in, or in any other manner directly reaching the crystal. The room should not be pitch black, but rather shadowed, or charged with a dull or even red light, somewhat such as prevails on a cloudy or wet day.

Adjusting the Crystal

"(2) The crystal should be placed on its stand on a table, or it may rest on a black velvet cushion, but in either case it should be partially surrounded by a black silk or similar wrap or screen, so adjusted as to cut off any undesirable reflection that may be a distraction. Before beginning to experiment, remember that most frequently nothing will be seen on the first occasion, and possibly not for several sittings; though some sitters, if strongly gifted with psychic powers in a state of unconsciousness, and sometimes conscious degree of unfoldment, may be fortunate enough to obtain good results at the first trial. If, therefore, nothing is perceived during the first few attempts, do not despair or become impatient, or imagine that you will never see anything. Doubt and impatience is the enemy

There is a royal road to crystal vision, but it is open only to the combined passwords of Calmness, Patience, and Perseverance. Many will give up in frustration is they are not successful right away. If at the first attempt to ride a bicycle, failure ensues, the only way to learn is to pay attention to the necessary rules, and to persevere daily until the ability to ride comes naturally. Thus it is the same with the would-be seer. Persevere in accordance with these simple directions, don't give up and success will sooner or later crown your efforts.

Time of Sittings

"(3) Commence by sitting comfortably with the eyes fixed upon the crystal, not by a fixed stare, but with a steady, calm gaze, for ten minutes only, on the first occasion. In taking the time it is best to hang your watch at a distance, where, while the face is clearly visible, the ticking is rendered inaudible. When the time is up, carefully put the crystal away in its case, and keep it in a dark place, under lock and key, allowing no one but yourself to handle it. At the second sitting, which should be at the same place, in the same position, and at the same time, you may increase the length of the effort to fifteen minutes, and continue this period during the next five or six sittings, after which the time may be gradually increased, but should in no case exceed one hour. The precise order of repetition is always to be followed until the experimenter has developed an almost automatic ability to readily obtain results, when it need no longer be adhered to.

Other Persons Present

"(4) Any person, or persons, admitted to the room, and allowed to remain while you sit, should (a) keep absolute silence, and (b) remain seated at a distance from you. When you have developed your latent powers, questions may, of course, be put to you by one of those present, but even then in a very gentle, or low and slow tone of voice; never suddenly, or in a forceful manner.

Crystalline Vision

"(5) When you find the crystals begin to look dull or cloudy, with small pin-points of light glittering therein, like tiny stars, you may know that you are commencing to obtain that for which you seek, viz., crystalline vision. Therefore, persevere with confidence. This condition may, or may not, continue for several sittings, the crystal seeming at times to alternatively appear and disappear, as in a mist. By and by this hazy appearance, in its turn, will give way quite suddenly to a blindness of the senses to all else but a blue or bluish ocean of space, against which, as if it were a background, the vision will be clearly apparent.

Physical Requirements

"(6) The crystal should not be used soon after taking a meal, and care should be taken in matters of diet to partake only of digestible foods, and to avoid alcoholic beverages. Plain and nourishing food, and outdoor exercise, with contentment of mind, or love of simplicity of living, are great aids to success. Mental anxiety, or ill-health, are not conducive to the desired end. Attention to correct breathing is of importance.

Determining Time of Fulfillment

"(7) As regards the time at which events seen will come to pass, each seer is usually impressed with regard thereto; but, as a general rule, visions appearing in the extreme background indicate time more remote, either past or future, than those perceived nearer at hand; while those appearing in the foreground, or closer to the seer, denote the present or immediate future.

Two Classes of Visions

"(8) Two principal classes of vision will present themselves to the sitter, viz.: (a) the Symbolic, indicated by the appearance of symbols such as a flag, boat, knife, gold, etc., and (b) Actual Scenes and Personages, in action or otherwise. Persons of a positive type of organization, the more active, excitable, yet decided type, are most likely to perceive symbolically, or allegorically; while those of a passive nature usually receive direct or literal revelations. Both classes will find it necessary to carefully cultivate truthfulness, unselfishness, gratitude for what is shown, and absolute confidence in the love, wisdom, and guidance of God Himself."

Time and Space in Crystal Gazing

In the subsequent pages the student will perceive the different manifestations of clairvoyant vision classified according to the distinction of Time and Space. Clairvoyant vision may disclose objects, scenes, or persons either nearby in space, or far off in space; either existing in present time, in past time, or in future time. Inasmuch as the visions of crystal gazing are merely particular forms of clairvoyant vision, it follows that all of the several above named distinctive forms of vision are manifested in crystal gazing. The vision shown in the crystal may be that of something very near in space, or perhaps very far off in space, or removed in space only a moderate distance. Likewise such vision may be based upon things existing at the present time, or at some period of past time, or at some period of and visions of past, present, or future things, events, persons, scenes—each or all of these manifestations are possible to the clairvoyant vision of the crystal gazer, and pictured in the reflecting surface of the crystal or other shining surface employed by him in his experiments.

Direct Clairvoyance

The third of the three general classes of the methods employed to obtain the manifestation of clairvoyant phenomena is that known as Direct Clairvoyance. In this class of methods the clairvoyant directly establishes the en rapport connection with the past or present, near or distant, objects, persons, scenes, or events, by means of raising his or her psychic vibrations so as to become "in tune" with the finer vibrations of Nature, without the aid of the physical objects required in the methods of Psychometry and Crystal Gazing, respectively.

Trance Conditions

Many clairvoyants, manifesting their powers by means of the methods of Direct Clairvoyance, produce in themselves the condition of trance, or semi-trance condition. Many students believe that these conditions are absolutely necessary for the production of this kind of phenomena, but they neglect, or are actually unaware of, the fact that many of the highest forms of this class of clairvoyant phenomena are manifested by clairvoyants who are no more in a trance condition, or that of semi-trance, than those following the methods of Psychometry or Crystal Gazing, respectively. All that is required is that the clairvoyant maintain a quiescent mental attitude, shutting out the sounds, sights, and thoughts of the outside world, and concentrating the full attention upon the clairvoyant work before him or her. Some, it is true, pass easily into the semi-trance, or even the full trance condition, but the latter are not absolutely necessary states.

Clairvoyant Reverie

A writer on the subject of Clairvoyance says: "The best authorities instruct their pupils that the state of clairvoyant reverie may be safely and effectively induced by the practice of mental concentration alone. They advise positively against artificial methods. All that is needed is that the consciousness be focused to a single point—become 'one pointed' as the Hindu teachers call it. The intelligent practice of concentration accomplishes this without the necessity of any artificial methods of development, or the production of abnormal psychic states. You easily concentrate your full attention when you witness an interesting play, or listen to a beautiful rendition of some great masterpiece of musical composition, or gaze at some miracle of pictured or sculptured art. In these cases your attention is completely occupied with the interesting thing before you, so that you have almost completely shut out the outer world of sound, sight, and thought—but you are, nevertheless, perfectly wide awake and conscious. The same thing is true when you read a very interesting book—the world is shut out from your consciousness, and you are oblivious to the sights and sounds around you. We frequently witness the sight of two lovers to whom the outside world is non-existent for the time being, and to whom there is nothing in the world except themselves. Again, persons often fall into a 'brown study,' or 'day dream,' in which all consciousness of the outside world seems to be shut out, yet the person is fully conscious and wide awake. These mental states are very much akin to that of the trained clairvoyant, and is the state which should be sought after by all clairvoyants, whether they are following the methods of Psychometry, Crystal Gazing, or that of Direct Clairvoyance—for the principle is one and the same in all of such methods."

The Dawn of Clairvoyance

A well-known authority on the subject of Psychic Development says: "Occasional flashes of clairvoyance sometimes comes to the highly cultured and spiritual-minded man, even though he may never have heard of the possibility of training such a faculty. In his case such glimpses usually signify that he is approaching that stage in his evolution when these powers will naturally begin to manifest themselves. Their appearance should serve as an additional stimulus to him to strive to maintain that high standard of moral purity and mental balance without which clairvoyance is a curse and not a blessing to its possessor. Between those who are entirely unimpressionable and those who are in full possession of clairvoyant power, there are many intermediate stages. Students often ask how this clairvoyant faculty will first be manifested in themselves—how they may know when they have reached the stage at which its first faint foreshadowings are beginning to be visible. Cases differ so widely that it is impossible to give to this question any answer that will be universally applicable. Some people begin by a plunge, as it were, and under some unusual stimulus become able just for once to see some striking vision; and very often in such a case, because the experience does not repeat itself, the seer comes in time to believe that on that occasion he must have been the victim of hallucination. Others begin by becoming intermittently conscious of the brilliant colors and vibrations of the human aura; yet others find themselves with increasing frequency seeing and hearing something to which those around them are blind and deaf; others, again, see faces, landscapes, or colored clouds floating before their eyes in the dark, before they sink to rest; while perhaps the commonest experience of all is that of those who begin to recollect with greater and greater clearness what they have seen and heard on other planes during sleep."

Methods of Development

The same authority, after warning students against attempting to develop their psychic powers by unnatural and harmful practices, such as self-hypnotism, self-stupefication, etc., gives the following excellent advice concerning the normal development of clairvoyant and other high psychic powers and faculties: "There is one practice which if adopted carefully and reverently can do no harm to any human being, yet from which a very pure type of clairvoyance has sometimes been developed—and that is the practice of Meditation. Let a man choose a certain time every day—a time when he can rely upon being quiet and undisturbed, though preferably in the daytime rather than at night—and set himself at that time to keep his mind for a few minutes entirely free from all earthly thoughts of any kind whatsoever; and, when that is achieved, to direct the whole force of his being towards the highest ideal he happens to know. He will find that to gain perfect control of thought is enormously more difficult than he supposes, but when he attains it this cannot but be in every way more beneficial to him, and as he grows more and more able to elevate and concentrate his thoughts, he may gradually find that new worlds are opening before his sight. As a preliminary training towards the satisfactory achievement of such meditation, he will find it desirable to make a practice of concentration in the affairs of daily life—even in the smallest of them. If he writes a letter, let him think of nothing else but that letter until it is finished; if he reads a book, let him see to it that his thought is never allowed to wander away from his author's meaning. He must learn to hold his mind in check, and to be master of that also, as well as of his lower passions; he must patiently labor to acquire absolute control of his thoughts, so that he will always know exactly what he is thinking about, and why—so that he can use his mind, and turn it or hold it still, as a practiced swordsman turns his weapon where he will."

PART V

CLAIRVOYANCE: PAST, PRESENT AND FUTURE

AS we have said in the preceding chapter, in our consideration of the general subject of Clairvoyance, there is possible a general classification of clairvoyant phenomena according to general distinctions, as follows: (1) Present Clairvoyance, in which the objects perceived by the clairvoyant are present in time and in space, although invisible to normal sight; (2) Space Clairvoyance, in which the clairvoyant vision includes objects and scenes removed in space from the normal perception of the clairvoyant; and (3) Time Clairvoyance, in which the clairvoyant perceives objects or scenes removed from him in past time, or future time.

While the general methods of manifesting these various forms of clairvoyant power are practically the same, yet the nature of these several forms of phenomena vary considerably, as we shall see when we come to consider them in detail in the following pages: this is particularly true in the case of the distinction between past-time clairvoyant phenomena, and future-time clairvoyant phenomena—the difference between the perception of what has been, and what has not yet been.

Present Clairvoyance

In what is called Present Clairvoyance the objects perceived by the clairvoyant are present in time and in space, at the moment and place of the perception, although invisible to normal sight. It is seen at once that if the object seen clairvoyantly is present in time and in space to the clairvoyant, and yet is incapable of being perceived by the normal sight of the clairvoyant, then that object must be capable of being perceived only through vibrations above the normal range of the human senses. Perhaps the precise nature of this class of clairvoyant perceptions will be better understood by a more detailed description of the objects actually perceived by clairvoyant vision of this mode of manifestation.

The Human Aura

In the first place, this mode of clairvoyant vision discloses the interesting phenomena concerned with the human aura, or psychic atmosphere which surrounds the human body for a space of several feet, assuming an egg-shaped form. A writer says on this point: "The trained clairvoyant vision sees the human aura as a nebulous hazy substance, like a luminous cloud, surrounding the person for two or three feet on each side of his body, becoming more dense near the body, and gradually becoming less dense as it extends away from the body. It has a phosphorescent appearance, with a peculiar tremulous motion manifesting through its substance. The clairvoyant sees the human aura as composed of all the colors of the spectrum, the combination shifting with the changing mental and emotional states of the person. But, in a general way, it may be said that each person has his or her distinctive astral auric colors, depending upon his or her general character or personality. Each mental state, or emotional manifestation, has its own particular shade or combination of shades of auric coloring. This beautiful kaleidoscopic spectacle has its own meaning to the occultist with clairvoyant vision, for he is thus able to read the character and general mental states of the person by means of studying his auric colors. The human aura is not in a state of calm phosphorescence, however. On the contrary, it sometimes manifests great flames, like those of a fiery furnace, which shoot forth great tongues, and dart forth suddenly in certain directions toward the objects attracting them. Under great emotional excitement the auric flames move around in swift circling whirlpools, or else swirl away from a centre. Again, it seems to throw forth tiny glistening sparks of psychic vibrations, some of which travel for a great distance.

The Prana Aura

"The clairvoyant vision is also able to discern what is called the 'prana aura' of a person. By this term is indicated that peculiar emanation of vital force which surrounds the physical body of each and every person. In fact, many persons of but slight clairvoyant power, who cannot sense the auric colors, are able to perceive this prana aura without trouble. It is sometimes called the 'health aura,' or 'physical aura.' It is colorless, or rather about 108the shade of clear glass, diamond, or water. It is streaked with very minute, bristle-like lines. In a state of good health these fine lines are stiff like toothbrush bristles; while in the case of poor health these lines droop, curl, and present a fur like appearance. It is sometimes filled with minute sparkling particles, like tiny vibratory motion. To the clairvoyant vision the prana aura appears like the vibrating heated air arising from a fire, or stove, or from the heated earth in summertime. If the student will close his eyes partially, and peer through narrowed eyelids, he will in all probability be able to perceive this prana aura surrounding the body of some healthy, vigorous person—particularly if that person be standing in a dim light. Looking closely, he will see the peculiar vibratory motion, like heated air, at a distance of about two inches from the body of the person. It requires a little practice in order to acquire the knack of perceiving these vibrations—a little experimenting in order to get just the right light on the person—

but practice will bring success, and you will be repaid for your trouble. In the same way, the student may by practice acquire the faculty of perceiving his own prana aura. The simplest way to obtain this last mentioned result is to place your fingers (spread out into fan-shape) against a black background, in a dim light. Then gaze at the fingers through narrowed eyelids, and half-closed eyes. After a little practice, you will see a fine thin line surrounding your fingers on all sides—a semi-luminous border of prana aura. In most cases this border of aura is colorless, but sometimes a very pale yellowish hue is perceived. The stronger the vital force of the person, the stronger and brighter will this border of prana aura appear. The aura surrounding the fingers will appear very much like the semi-luminous radiance surrounding a gas-flame, or the flame of a candle, which is familiar to everyone."

The Auric Colors

Another writer says of the clairvoyant perception of the human aura: "As he looks, the clairvoyant will see himself surrounded by the luminous mist of the aura, flashing with all sorts of brilliant colors, and constantly changing hue and brilliancy with every variation of the person's thought and feelings. He will see this aura flooded with the beautiful rose-color of pure affection, the rich blue of devotional feeling, the hard, dull brown of selfishness, the deep scarlet of anger, the horrible lurid red of sensuality, the livid grey of fear, the black clouds of hatred and malice, or any of the other hundredfold indications so easily to be read in it by the practiced eye; and thus it will be impossible for any persons to conceal from his the real state of their feelings on any subject. Not only does the astral aura show him the temporary result of the emotion passing through it at the moment, but it also gives him, by an arrangement and proportion of its colors when in a condition of perfect rest, a clue to the general disposition and character of its owner."

Thought-forms

Another phase of clairvoyant phenomena of this class is that of the perception of "thought-forms," as they are called by occultists. As all students of occultism know, a strong thought or emotion manifests a certain high vibratory motion, and takes upon itself a vibratory "form" which is plainly perceptible to the trained clairvoyant vision. These thought-forms manifest a great variety in appearance and character. Some appear in a faint wave-like form, something like the tiny waves caused by the dropping of a pebble in a pond of water. Others take on a whirlpool form, rotating and whirling as they move through space. Others appear like whirling rings, similar in general form to the "ring" puffed forth from the mouth of a cigar smoker, or from the funnel of a locomotive. Others glow like great opals. Others appear like jets emitted from the spout of a teakettle. Others twist along like a corkscrew. Others appear like exploding bombs. Others branch out arms like a devil-fish, which wriggle in all directions, as if striving to attach themselves to some object upon which they wish to take hold.

The X-Ray Sense

Another phase of clairvoyant phenomena of this general class is that which may be called "the X-Ray Sense," for indeed it enables the clairvoyant to see through a brick wall, or other material obstacle, or through a sealed letter, etc. The higher psychic vibrations easily pass through the most solid object, just as do the X-Rays, and consequently the clairvoyant is able to see what is going on with the other side of a brick wall, or the walls of a house. Likewise, the clairvoyant vision is able to pierce through the dense earth, and to perceive veins of mineral or metal lying concealed beneath.

Microscopic Vision

Another phase of clairvoyant power of this general class, but one not nearly so common as those above mentioned, is described by a well-known occultist as follows: "Another strange power of which the clairvoyant may find himself in possession is that of magnifying at will the minutest physical particle to any desired size, as through a microscope—though no microscope ever made, or ever likely to be made, possesses even a thousandth part of this psychic magnifying power. By its means the hypothetical molecule and atom postulated by science becomes visible and living realities to the occult student, and on this closer examination he finds them to be much more complex in their structure than the scientific man has yet realized them to be. It also enables him to follow with the closest attention and the liveliest interest all kinds of electrical, magnetic, and other etheric action; and when some of the specialists in these branches of science are able to develop the power to see these things whereof they speak so facilely, some very wonderful and beautiful revelations may be expected."

Space Clairvoyance

In what is called Space Clairvoyance the objects, persons, scenes, or events perceived by the clairvoyant are removed in space from him—often being located at points in space thousands of miles distant, in fact. The pages of works upon occultism, and those devoted to the recording of proved instances gathered by the societies for psychical research, are filled with the most interesting cases of this form of clairvoyant vision. Instances are recorded, upon the very best possible authority, in which persons with clairvoyant powers have been perfectly cognizant of events occurring on the other side of the world, or across the Atlantic or Pacific Oceans. In fact, it would seem that distance and space are practically wiped out in this form of clairvoyant phenomena, and that it is just as easy to see clairvoyantly over the space of a thousand miles, as over that of a hundred feet—the principle involved being precisely the same.

The Psychic Telescope

Space Clairvoyance, or Distant Clairvoyance, is manifested in the form of Psychometry, Crystal Gazing, or Direct Clairvoyance, as we have said. We do not consider it necessary to record here any typical instances of this phase of phenomena, as the many books on this subject are chiefly devoted to a recital thereof, and every student is more or less acquainted with the same. The whole matter may be summed up by saying that in this form of clairvoyant vision, there is manifested what might be called a "psychic telescope with an X-Ray attachment," thus enabling one to see at any distance, and through any intervening objects. This gives you a mental picture of the process.

Radioactivity

In the theory of vibratory forces, as set forth in the earlier chapters of this book, we have the only scientific explanation of the phenomena of distant clairvoyance. Modern science, in its teachings regarding the radio-activity of physical objects, has thrown much additional light on this subject, and has corroborated the ancient occult teachings on the subject. These rays of higher vibratory power are like the rays of light or heat, although of a much higher rate of intensity and vibratory motion, and though the most delicate scientific instruments are able to register some of these, it is still practically admitted by science that the highest of these radio-active vibrations are beyond the scope and field of even the most sensitive instrument yet known to science. This is saying much when we remember that some of the delicate instruments of science are so sensitive that they are able to register the heat waves of a candle at the distance of one mile; while others are able to record the presence of certain chemical elements in the most distant of the visible stars, by means of the light waves carrying certain forms of vibration.

Sensing the Higher Vibrations

Under the radio-active theory it is quite reasonable to conceive of the clairvoyant sense being able to register and interpreting these higher vibrations which are beyond the power of even the most delicate instruments of science. It must be admitted that the existence of such vibrations being granted—and science tacitly admits their presence—then ordinary distances on earth would be no barrier at all to the action of clairvoyant vision capable of registering them. Moreover, in such case all intervening objects would be penetrated by these waves, and as a writer has well said, "they would be able to cross one another to infinity in all directions without entanglement, precisely as the vibrations of ordinary light do." Physical science and psychic science at last seem to have arrived at a common ground of understanding, and many of the most advanced scientists do not hesitate to admit this fact, though their more conservative brethren hesitate to do so.

Viewing Distant Scenes

A writer has said of this form of clairvoyant perception: "The view of a distant scene obtained in this way is in many ways not unlike that seen through a telescope. Human figures usually appear very small, like those upon a distant stage, but in spite of their diminutive size they are clear as though they were close by. Sometimes it is possible by this means to hear what is said as well as to see what is done; but as in the majority of cases this does not happen, we must consider it rather as the manifestation of an additional power than as a necessary corollary of the faculty of sight. It will be observed that in cases of this kind the clairvoyant does not actually leave his physical body at all—he simply manufactures for himself, and uses, a kind of psychic telescope. Consequently he has the use of his physical powers while he is examining the distant scene; for example, his voice usually describes what he sees even while he is in the act of making the observation."

Time Clairvoyance

In what is called Time Clairvoyance the clairvoyant is able to perceive objects, persons, scenes, and events removed from him in past time or future time. That is to say, the clairvoyant perceives things which have existed in the physical world in times long past, which things have long since vanished from physical existence; or, on the other hand, he perceives things which belong to future existence — this which have never as yet been in physical existence, and of course are not in such existence at the present time. The careful student will see at once that the principle of manifestation governing these two respective phases of clairvoyance must be quite different; and, accordingly, the two respective phases must be considered separately and apart from each other.

Past Time Clairvoyance

In what is known as Past Time Clairvoyance there is the manifestation of clairvoyant vision in the direction of scenes and

143

occurrences of the past. Here, the clairvoyant perceives the events and scenes of past time just as clearly and plainly as if such were present before him in time and in space. Just as in Distant Clairvoyance it is just as easy for the clairvoyant to see things at a great distance as those at a short distance, so in Past Time Clairvoyance it is just as easy for the clairvoyant to see things and events occurring five thousand years ago as it is to see things occurring one year ago, or one week ago for that matter. The principle involved is the same in either case. Modern Quantum physics theorizes that energy from the past still exists and is able to be perceived under the right mental conditions.

The Mystery of Seeing the Past

To persons investigating the phenomena of clairvoyance for the first time, however, there seems to be a much greater mystery attached to the phenomena of Past Clairvoyance than in the case of Distant Clairvoyance. To such persons it seems that while the perception of distant objects, scenes, and events is wonderful and mysterious, still at the last it is merely the perception of something now actually in existence—merely the extension of one's normal powers of vision so as to include objects beyond the range of the ordinary vision, but, still, actually in existence though at a distance.

The idea of the telescope enables the mind to grasp the naturalness of this kind of phenomena. But when it comes to the perception of things, scenes, and events which are no longer in existence—things which have passed entirely out of existence—the mystery seems to be increased, and incredulity becomes more insistent. But to the occultist there is really no more mystery in the one case than in the other—both sets of phenomena are seen to be perfectly reasonable and within the realms of Nature. Let us now see how and why the occultists view the matter in this light.

Analogies on the Physical Plane

We may find many correspondences on the physical plane to serve as illustrations of the phenomena of Past Time Clairvoyance, if we will but look for them. For instance, when we withdraw a heated stove from a room, the heat remains in the room. Likewise, though a woman bearing the odor of a certain perfume on her clothing may have passed from a house, the odor still lingers there. The wake of an ocean steamer is often visible for hours after the ship has passed from sight. As modern science expressed it: "Causes continue to exist in their Effects."

Thousand-Year-Old Light

But we have a much more striking illustration and correspondence in the case of the transmission of light from the distant stars, which we will do well to carefully consider. Light travels at the rate of 117186,000 miles per second. A "light-year," as known to astronomers, means the distance traversed by a light wave (at the stated rate of travel) during the period of one of our earth years. Some of the distant stars are estimated to be fully one thousand light-years distant from us; or, in other words, the light we now perceive as coming from them really is the light that left them one thousand years ago. If one of these stars were to be destroyed, observers on this earth would not become aware of it for a thousand years. The star whose light we may now perceive may actually have been destroyed nearly one thousand years ago. Other stars are only one hundred light-years removed from us in space; others only a few years; others only a few hours. But the principle is just the same in all cases, namely, that we see the stars not as they are at the present moment, but as they were when the light left them, perhaps many years ago. Thus, as you see, we may actually perceive events long after their happening.

Reading the Light Waves

Now, if our physical vision was sufficiently powerful to magnify objects on the stars, or if we had instruments to do this for us, we could actually witness scenes, objects, persons and events which had passed out of existence a thousand years ago. Their records are present in these light waves from the stars, and all that is needed is an eye or a telescope sufficiently strong to register them upon our mind. In a fanciful story written by Camille Flammarion, the French astronomer, many years ago, the principal character relates how, traveling in the astral body, he was able to witness the events of the French Revolution which had occurred many years before, by simply proceeding to the necessary distance from the earth and there perceiving the registered records in the earth's light-waves traveling through space at the rate of 186,000 miles a second. In fact, by getting at the right distance he was able to see even the events of his own childhood and youth, every event of his life, in fact, up to the moment of his leaving the earth. This story, fanciful as it is, nevertheless is based upon scientific facts, and its happenings would be quite possible for a being capable of traveling at a sufficiently rapid rate through space, and also possessed of the power of magnifying the records of light rays. In fact, a person on earth possessing the power of Distant Clairvoyance might be able to duplicate these feats, providing he were able to come in rapport contact with one of these light-waves bearing the past-time records. Think for a moment, and you will grasp the point of this statement.

The Akashic Plane

But this, however, is but an illustration of the correspondence on the ordinary physical plane of certain things on a higher plane of Nature. Past Time Clairvoyance is not dependent upon light-waves, or any other of the lesser phases of vibratory activity.

Instead, it depends entirely upon the phenomena and facts of a higher plane of Nature—a plane which occultists have called the Akashic Plane. Some occultists prefer the general term, "the Astral Plane," but the former term is a closer and more definite one. The Akashic Plane, as known to occultists, contains the impressions or "records" of all events that have happened on the earth plane during the present cycle of earth manifestation. The very subtle and tenuous substance of the Akashic Plane—the term "etheric" may best describe the nature of this substance—contains traces and impressions of all the happenings of the past of this earth; and such impressions may be read and seen by the clairvoyant who has developed sufficiently high powers of vision. These Akashic Records have well been called "the substantial memory of the earth." Upon the subtle etheric substance of the Akashic Plane are registered the records of every event, thing, object, happening, or activity of the earth which has existed or been manifested from the very beginning of the present cycle of the earth's existence. These records will, it is claimed, persist until the final ending of the present earth cycle.

The Akashic Records

The clairvoyant whose powers of Past Time Clairvoyance have been developed sufficiently, and who has mastered the art of concentration of his psychic attention, manages to come into more or less perfect en rapport condition contact with these Akashic Records, and is thus enabled to read from them what he sees there. To him it actually seems as if he were seeing the actions of things in present existence, and many excellent clairvoyants are ignorant of the existence of the Akashic Records, though they habitually read the contents thereof; these clairvoyants know simply that they "see" these past happenings—they have not the faintest conception of how they are able to see them. This is no more strange than would be the case of a man who witnessed a moving picture for the first time, and who was ignorant of the mechanism involved in the showing of the picture, the existence of the film, etc.,—such a man would simply know that he "saw" the things, and he might even believe that he was gazing upon an actual scene in real life.

Degrees of Clairvoyant Vision

There is, of course, many degrees of power and development among clairvoyants of this class; and as a result we have many varying degrees of correctness in their readings. Some have merely a glimpse, as through dim glasses; and some obtain merely distorted reflections similar to those of a scene reflected into the troubled waters of a lake. Others see far more clearly; but it is reserved for the trained occultist to read the records as he would read the scene before him on the physical plane. The clairvoyant does not become infallible simply by reason of the perhaps only faint awakening of his clairvoyant vision—he is not suddenly gifted with omniscience, as some seem to suppose. There are almost always elements of error or imperfect visioning, except among the advanced adepts of the occult world.

"The Memory of Nature"

A celebrated occultist says concerning the point just raised: "Comparatively few accounts of persons possessing this faculty of looking into the past are to be found in the literature of the subject, and it might therefore be supposed to be much less common than prevision, or future-time clairvoyance. I suspect, however, that the truth is rather that it is much less commonly recognized. It may easily happen that a person may see a picture of the past without recognizing it as such, unless there happens to be in it something which attracts special attention, such as a figure in armor, or in antique costume. It is probable that occasional glimpses of these reflections of the Akashic Records are commoner than the published accounts would lead us to believe. As usual, we find examples of all degrees of the power to see into this 'memory of Nature,' from the trained man who can consult the record for himself at will, down to the person who gets nothing but occasional vague glimpses, or has even perhaps had only one such glimpse. But even the man who possesses this faculty only partially and occasionally may still find it of the deepest interest.

Involuntary Clairvoyance

"The psychometrist, who needs an object physically connected with the past in order to bring it all into life again around him; and the crystal-gazer who can sometimes direct his less certain astral telescope to some historic scene of long ago, may both derive the greatest enjoyment from the exercise of their respective gifts, even though they may not always understand exactly how their results are produced, and may not have them fully under control under all circumstances.

In many cases of the lower manifestation of these powers we find that they are exercised unconsciously; many a crystal-gazer watches scenes from the past without ever realizing that he is in effect psychometrizing the various objects around him as he happens to touch them or stand near them. It would be well for all students to bear in mind that occultism is the apotheosis of common sense, and that every vision that comes to them is not necessarily a picture from the Akashic Records, nor every experience a revelation from on high. It is far better to err on the side of healthy skepticism than that of over-credulity; and it is an admirable rule never to hunt for an occult explanation of anything when a plain and obvious physical one is available. Our duty is to keep our balance always, and never to lose our self-control, but to take a reasonable, common-sense view of whatever may happen to us."

Future Time Clairvoyance

In what is known technically as Future Time Clairvoyance, we have the manifestation of the clairvoyant vision in the direction of scenes and events of the future. In this phase of clairvoyance the seer perceives the events and scenes of future time just as if they were present before him at that very moment. This phase of clairvoyance is far rarer and more uncommon than any of the other phases. In fact, it is so seldom met with in its perfection that its manifestation is a matter of greatest interest to those who make a study of the subject. It occasionally occurs in flashes, and cannot be produced at will by the ordinary clairvoyant. Unfortunately, its very rarity and uncommonness cause it to be counterfeited and imitated by unprincipled persons.

Seeing What Has Not Yet Happened

The student who reasons carefully and logically usually meets with what to him, at least at first, seems to be an insurmountable obstacle in the way of a rational explanation of Future Time Clairvoyance—when it comes to an understanding of how anyone can expect to see, or can really see, that which has never happened, he throws up his hands in despair. But, in this as in all the other phases of clairvoyant phenomena, there is found a reason and cause, although it requires some subtle thinking to find it, and to grasp it even when it is found. For many, it is too subtle, too esoteric to allow the mind to accept. Let us see what are the highest teachings on this subject, as announced by the careful thinkers along the lines for many centuries.

Simple Prevision

There is a phase of prevision, or prophecy of coming events, however, that is not true clairvoyance at all, but simply the subconscious workings of the mind along the lines of a supernormal perception of the laws of cause and effect. Give the active subconscious mental faculties the perception of a strong existing cause, and it will often reason out the probable effect (the almost certain effect, in fact) of that cause, even though that effect lies in the mist of the future. The subconscious mind works upon the principle that "coming events cast their shadows before." But this, at the best, is not true clairvoyance—it is merely the statement of "probable" results, and effects of existing causes, wonderfully exact and clear though the deduction may be in some cases. But a thousand-and-one unforeseen things may arise to completely upset the prediction, or deduction, for it is never actually true until it occurs. We must look further for real instances of Future Clairvoyance.

The Nature of Time

That eminent scientist, Sir Oliver Lodge, offers an ingenious and interesting, though very technical explanation of this class of clairvoyant phenomena as follows: "Time is but a relative mode of regarding things; we progress through phenomena at a certain definite pace, and this subjective advance we interpret in an objective manner, as if events moved necessarily in this order and at this precise rate. But that may be only one mode of regarding them. The events may be in some sort of existence always, both past and future, and it may be we who are arriving at them, not they which are happening. The analogy of a traveler in a railway train is useful; if he could never leave the train, nor alter its pace, he would probably consider the landscapes as necessarily successive, and be unable to conceive their co-existence. We perceive, therefore, a possible fourth dimensional aspect about time, the inexorableness of whose flow may be a natural part of our present limitations. And if we once grasp the idea that past and future may be actually existing, we can recognize that they may have a controlling influence on all present action, and the two together may constitute the 'higher plane' or totality of things after which, it seems to me, we are impelled to seek, in connection with the directing of form or determinism, and the action of human beings consciously directed to a definite and preconceived end."

Eastern Teaching

The Hindus, and other Asian peoples, however, have a clearly defined and positive explanation of the phenomena of Future Time Clairvoyance, which must be included in our consideration of the subject, even though it does involve certain metaphysical or philosophical conceptions which are apart from our present inquiry as conducted in this book. The Eastern theory is based upon that basic conception of the eastern philosophies which hold that the beginning, duration, and ending of any particular one of the infinitude of successive universes created by the Supreme Being, is to that Being but as a single moment of time; or, as the celebrated Hindu proverb runs: "The creation, duration, and destruction of a universe is but the time of the twinkling of an eye to Brahman." In other words, that to the Supreme Being, all the past, all the present, all the future of the universe, must be as but a single thought in a single moment of time—an instantaneous act of consciousness.

The Eternal Now

A writer on this subject has said: "Those occultists and metaphysicians who have thought long and deeply upon the ultimate facts and nature of the universe, have dared to think that there must exist some absolute consciousness—some absolute mind—which must perceive the past, present, and future of the universe as one happening; as simultaneously and actively present at one moment of absolute time. They reason that just as a man may see at one moment of his time some particular event which might appear as a year to some minute form of life and mind—the microscopic creatures in a drop of water, for instance—so that which seems as a year, or as a hundred years, to the mind of man, may appear as the happening of a single moment of a higher scale of time to some exalted Being, or form of consciousness on a higher plane."

Absolute Time

The daring flights of metaphysical fancy have resulted in the general acceptance, on the part of advanced metaphysicians, of the postulate of the existence of an Absolute Mind, independent of Time and Space, to which everything exists HERE and NOW. To such a mind the entire sequence of events in the life-history of a universe would appear as a single unit of conscious experience— an infinitesimal point of time in Eternity. The human imagination staggers at the idea, but logical thought finally posits it as an inescapable conclusion of extended thought. This, possibly, is the secret of Future Time Clairvoyance, Prevision, Second Sight, etc.

The Occult Hypothesis

But it must not be supposed that the oriental occultists hold for a moment the theory that the clairvoyant actually obtains access to the Divine Mind or Absolute Mind, when he experiences this vision of future events—their idea is very different from this. These occultists teach that the phenomena of each plane are reflected with more or less clearness upon the substance of the planes beneath it. This being so, it is readily seen that the seer who is able to contact with any of the higher planes of being might thereupon see the reflection, more or less clear, or more or less distorted, of that which is present in its completeness on the highest plane of all. This is a mere hint at the quite complicated occult teaching on this subject; but the capable thinker will be able to work out the full theory for himself in his own way.

The important fact is that Future Time Clairvoyance is a reality—that it is a matter of actual experience of the race, and one that has been authenticated by the investigations of such learned bodies as the Society for Psychical Research, of England, and other societies of the same kind in different lands. Future Time Clairvoyance, Second Sight, Prevision, etc., are facts as fully accepted by such societies as are the facts of telepathy.

"The Prophecy of Cazotte"

Students of history are familiar with the numerous recorded instances of marvelous prophecy of future events, wonderful predictions of events to come, which have been fully corroborated and verified by subsequent events. We lack the space in this book to record more than one of the most celebrated of these historical prophecies, namely the Prophecy of Cazotte. We have thought it advisable to reproduce the story of this celebrated prophecy, as told by La Harpe, the French writer, who was present upon the occasion. It may be mentioned that the fact of this prophecy, and its literal fulfillment, is a part of French history. The time was just previous to the French Revolution, and the tale as told by La Harpe is as follows:

"It appears as but yesterday, and yet, nevertheless, it was at the beginning of the year 1788. We were dining with one of the brethren at the Academy—a man of considerable wealth and genius. The conversation became serious; much admiration was expressed on the revolution of thought which Voltaire had started, and it was agreed that it was his first claim to the reputation he enjoyed. We concluded that the revolution must soon be consummated; that it was indispensable that superstition and fanaticism should give way to philosophy, and we began to calculate the probability of the period when this should be, and which of the present company should live to see it. The oldest complained that they could hardly flatter themselves with the hope; the younger rejoiced that they might entertain this very probable expectation; and they congratulated the Academy especially for having prepared this great work, and for having been the rallying point, the centre, and the prime mover of the liberty of thought.

The Illuminatus

"One only of the guests had not taken part in all the joyousness of this conversation, and had even gently and cheerfully checked our splendid enthusiasm. This was Cazotte, an amiable and original man, but unhappily infatuated with the reveries of the Illuminati. He spoke, and with the most serious tone, saying: 'Gentlemen, be satisfied; you will all see this great and sublime revolution, which you so much desire. You know that I am a little inclined to prophecy; I repeat, you will see it.'

"He was answered by the common rejoinder: 'One need not be a conjurer to see that.' He answered: 'Be it so; but perhaps one must be a little more than conjurer for what remains for me to tell you. Do you know what will be the consequences of this revolution—what will be the consequences to all of you, and what will be the immediate result—the well-established effect—the thoroughly recognized consequences to all of you who are here present?'

155

The Beginning of the Prophecy

"'Ah,' said Condorcet, with his insolent and half-suppressed smile, 'let us hear—a philosopher is not sorry to encounter a prophet—let us hear?' Cazotte replied: 'You, Monsieur de Condorcet—you will yield up your last breath on the floor of a dungeon; you will die from poison, which you will have taken in order to escape from execution—from poison which the happiness of that time will oblige you to carry around your person. You, Monsieur de Chamfort, you will open your veins with twenty-two cuts of a razor, and yet will not die till some months afterward.' These personages looked at each other, and laughed again. Cazotte continued: 'You, Monsieur Vicq d'Azir, you will not open your own veins, but you will cause yourself to be bled six times in one day, during the paroxysm of the gout, in order to make more sure of your end, and you will die in the night.'

The Shadow of the Guillotine

"Cazotte went on: 'You, Monsieur de Nicolai, you will die on the scaffold; you, Monsieur Bailly, on the scaffold; you, Monsieur de Malesherbes, on the scaffold.' 'Ah, God be thanked,' exclaimed Roucherm, 'and what of I?' Cazotte replied: 'You! you also will die on the scaffold.' 'Yes,' replied Chamfort, 'but when will all this happen?' Cazotte answered: 'Six years will not pass over, before all that I have said to you shall be accomplished.' Here I (La Harpe) spoke, saying: 'Here are some astonishing miracles, but you have not included me in your list.' Cazotte answered me, saying: 'But you will be there, as an equally extraordinary miracle; you will then be a Christian!' Vehement exclamations on all sides followed this startling assertion. 'Ah!' said Chamfort, 'I am comforted; for if we perish only when La Harpe shall be a Christian, we are immortal!'

The Fall of the Great

'"Then,' observed Madame la Duchesse de Grammont, 'as for that, we women, we are happy to be counted for nothing in this revolution; when I say for nothing, it is not that we do not always mix ourselves up with them a little; but it is a received maxim that they take no notice of us, and of our sex.' 'Your sex, ladies,' said Cazotte, 'your sex will not protect you this time; and you had far better meddle with nothing, for you will be treated entirely as men, without any difference whatever.' 'But what, then, are you really telling us of, Monsieur Cazotte? You are preaching to us the end of the world.' 'I know nothing on that subject; but what I do know is, that you, Madame la Duchesse, will be conducted to the scaffold, you and many other ladies with you, in the cart of the executioner, and with your hands tied behind your backs.' 'All! I hope that in that case I shall at least have a carriage hung in black.' 'No, Madame; higher ladies than yourself will go, like you, in the common car, with their hands tied behind them.' 'Higher ladies! what! the princesses of the blood?' 'Yea, and still more exalted personages!' replied Cazotte.

The Fate of Royalty

"Here a sensible emotion pervaded the whole company, and the countenance of the host was dark and lowering—they began to feel that the joke was becoming too serious. Madame de Grammont, in order to dissipate the cloud, took no notice of the last reply, and contented herself with saying in a careless tone: 'You see, he will not leave me even a confessor!' 'No, madame!' replied Cazotte, 'you will not have one—neither you, nor any one besides. The last victim to whom this favor will be afforded will be—' Here he stopped for a moment. 'Well, who then will be the happy mortal to whom this prerogative will be given?' Cazotte replied: 'It is the only one which he will have then retained—and that will be the

King of France!' This last startling prediction caused the company to disband in something like terror and dismay, for the mere mention of such things was akin to treason."

The Fulfillment of the Prophecy

To appreciate the startling nature of the Cazotte prophecy at the time when it was made, one needs but to be even slightly acquainted with the position and characteristics of the persons whose destinies were thus foretold. The amazing sequel to this wonderful prophecy is told by history—within six years every detail thereof was verified absolutely. The facts are known to all students of French history of that period, and may be verified by reference to the pages of any comprehensive history of those times.

Other Historical Instances

To mention but a few other celebrated instances of historic prophecy: George Fox, the pioneer Quaker Friend, had the clairvoyant faculty well developed, and numerous instances of its manifestation by him are recorded. For instance, he foretold the death of Cromwell, when he met him riding at Hampton Court; he said that he felt "a waft of death" around and about Cromwell— and Cromwell died shortly afterward. Fox also publicly foretold the dissolution of the Rump Parliament of England; the restoration of Charles II; and the Great Fire of London. These prophecies are all matters of history. For that matter, history contains many instances of this kind, as, for instance, the prophecy of Caesar's death, and its further prevision by his wife. The Bible prophecies and predictions, major and minor, give us semi-historical instances.

The Eternal Verities

As a writer has said concerning this phase of clairvoyant phenomena: "This phase of clairvoyance is very fascinating to the student and the investigator, and is one in which the highest psychic powers are called into play. There is a reflection here of something even higher than the psychic plane—there is a glimpse of regions infinitely higher and greater. The student here begins to realize at least something of the existence of that universal Consciousness 'in which we live, and move, and have our being'; and of the existence of the reality of the Eternal Now, in which past, present, and future are blended as one fact of infinite consciousness. He sees here the signboard pointing to the eternal verities!"

PART VI

MEDIUMSHIP

AMONG the higher categories of Nature's Finer Forces is included that which is popularly known as "mediumship." Although this term has suffered more or less by reason of its misappropriation by certain charlatans and the unprincipled exploiters of sincere investigators of the phenomena of the higher planes of existence, and also by reason of a certain prejudice against the term arising from misrepresentation and general misunderstanding, the term still remains a perfectly legitimate one and one clearly indicating the nature of the general class of phenomena sought to be embraced within its limits. Therefore there is no valid reason for its rejection in our consideration of the subject of Nature's Finer Forces in this book; and, accordingly, it is used here in a general way, although the more scientific term "higher plane communication," or similar terms, are employed herein in some cases.

What Is Mediumship?

Let us see just what is meant by the term "mediumship." The term "medium" is defined as: "That which lies in the middle, or between other things: hence, that through which anything is conveyed from one thing to another." In a special sense, a "medium" is "a person serving as the channel of communication between discarnate entities and human being still in the flesh," in "spiritualistic phenomena." The suffix "ship," of course, denotes state or office;

and in the case of "mediumship" it indicates that the designated person possesses the state or office of a "medium," the latter term being used in the special meaning above defined.

Of course, the term "mediumship," as above defined, lacks a clear meaning unless the term "spiritualistic," or "spiritualism" be defined. The term "spiritualism" (or as many of the best authorities prefer to state it, "spiritism") is applied to "a system of communication with the unseen world, or with the inhabitants thereof, the latter being usually known as 'spirits,' through persons called 'mediums,' which has attained popular favor in Europe and America since about 1850." Or, as another authority states it, "Spiritualism is a term employed to indicate the belief that not only does ones soul survive that great transition called death, but that these departed spirits are able and willing to communicate with those of us who are still here on the earthly sphere by means of psychical phenomena, commonly through a person of special susceptibility called a 'medium.'"

Ancient Mediumship

It is, of course, unnecessary to state in detail the fact that communication with discarnate entities has been known and practiced by the human race from the earliest days of recorded history, and probably long before that time, and is far from being a modern discovery. Moreover, such communication has been known and practiced by races of human beings other than those inhabiting Europe and America—particularly in the oriental countries. In the oriental lands such communication has been well established for many thousand years, and the most ancient records give evidences of it. The Hebrew Scriptures contain many instances of such communication, showing that the same was an accepted fact of the life of the race at the time and in the places at which these records were written.

161

Mediumship and Religious Belief

The careful student will of course notice that this communication with the higher planes of life and being—this so-called "mediumship"—does not depend upon any particular form of religious belief, or teaching, concerning the nature of the state or place of abode of the departed spirits of men; but, on the contrary, is common to all form of religion and to all phases of belief in the survival of the human soul. Therefore, a scientific consideration of the general subject does not necessitate the acceptance of any one particular phase of religious belief, or of any particular system of teaching concerning the nature or state of "life after death." All that is required of the person accepting the general fact of "higher plane communication" may be stated as follows: (1) Acceptance of the fact that the human soul persists after the death of the body, and independent of and removed from the dead body; (2) acceptance of the fact that the discarnate souls of human beings may, and do, establish communication with human beings still dwelling upon the earth-plane of existence.

We may state here that the term "discarnate" means "away from the physical body," or "out of the flesh;" the term being the opposite of "incarnate," meaning "clothed with flesh, or embodied in flesh." We may also state here that the teachings of most philosophies of the life after death hold that the discarnate human soul is not entirely devoid of a body, but rather occupies a body composed of some ethereal substance; this ethereal body being called the "astral body," or the "spiritual body."

The Ideals of Modern Spiritualism

A writer well expresses the ideals of modern western spiritualism as follows: "Through the gateway of mediumship for upwards of fifty years the world has been catching glimpses of the glory of the land immortal, and visitants from that 'bourne' from whence it has been erroneously said that 'no traveler returns' have made their presence known beyond all doubt or denial, thus proving the continued conscious existence of human beings and the sequential chapter of the life hereafter. Though the messages from the unseen have at times been imperfect and fragmentary, still they have been messages. If but telegraphic dispatches, so to speak, instead of voluminous letters; or like telephonic snatches of conversation rather than face-to-face outpourings of thought and feeling, still they have been greetings and comforting assurances of undying affection from the people living in the land 'beyond the veil.'

"Although many a sorrowing soul has longed for further revelation, and regretted the inability of the spirits to comply with the requests for fuller information, still the gates have been ajar, and sometimes it has truly seemed as though they had been flung wide open—so clear and consoling were the messages from the loved ones on the other side of death's valley of shadow. The manifestations of the presence of spirits and the evidences of their identity, which have been accumulating during all these years, have solved the 'great secret,' and we know that death is not a cul-de-sac, but a thoroughfare. The dread of death disappeared altogether with the mists of ignorance, as, through the gateway of mediumship, the shining presence of ministering spirits, 'our very own dear departed,' illumined the pathway which we must all tread to our great promotion.

Immortality Demonstrated Through Mediumship

"'Immortality demonstrated through mediumship' should be inscribed upon the banner of spiritualism, for the fact of life beyond the incident of death has been proved beyond all peradventure to millions of intelligent and enlightened people since the new spiritual era was inaugurated. To mediums—the

163

modern mediators—therefore belong the office and honor of rolling back the stone from the tomb and establishing faith upon the firm basis of knowledge (scientifically ascertained and proven) of the continued intelligent existence in the spiritual realms of those who went forth through the death change into light and liberty 'over there.'

"Mediums, as intermediaries, have enabled spirit people to comfort the sad and encourage the weak; to relieve the doubter and console the bereaved; to confirm the old-world traditions regarding bygone spirit intervention and revelation, and supplement our hopes and intuitions with proof palpable. Present day experiences of inspiration and spirit manifestation make credible and acceptable many things in ancient records which must otherwise have been discarded as superstitious and false. Spiritualism redeems the so-called 'supernatural' and 'miraculous' occurrences of the Bible, by explaining them and proving the naturalness. The capability claimed for old-time seers and prophets to see angels and hear voices is now known to be a natural faculty, which, in certain people, is perfectly normal while it can be induced in others by the influence of operators in or out of the body. It can also be cultivated to some degree by most people who care to study the necessary conditions for its development and exercise.

"The famine, 'not of bread, nor of water, but of hearing words from the Lord,' and the loss of 'open vision' of the spirit, which afflicted Christendom for so many years (because of the blind intolerance of zealots who, in their adherence to the 'letter,' crushed out the sensitives through whom the 'spirit' might have been revealed), that famine is rapidly passing away, and we are being fed with the living bread of spiritual inspiration, and are growing strong enough to welcome the messengers who come to us through the gateway of mediumship from their after-death home.

The Truth of Personal Survival

"When once there is established the conviction of the truth of personal survival of our loved ones, and the actual and satisfactory demonstrations thereof through mediumship (and we know of no means whereby such evidences can be obtained save through mediumship), we are thrilled and delighted; and when this conviction is borne upon us and driven home by the evidences, and the truth of spirit ministry has been realized, nothing can destroy it. The spiritualist stands upon firm ground—the impregnable rock of ascertained fact. He knows that intercourse between the two worlds is real, continuous; therefore he is proof against all speculations, denunciations, and adverse theories. Dogmatic condemnations, 'bogey' cries, charges of fraud against mediums, fail to move or frighten him. He can 'speak what he knows and testify to what he has seen;' his positive and affirmative experience and testimony outweigh all the opposition of 'doubting Thomases' who do not know.

The Gateway of Mediumship

"Through the gateway of mediumship the spirits make themselves known in a variety of ways. There are many phases of mediumistic phenomena, and the student will find that he must be patient, painstaking, and persevering if he would make sure of his facts. Careful investigation, possibly prolonged research, under many difficulties and with many discouragements, will be required, but 'success is certain if energy fail not,' and the results will adequately recompense him for all sacrifice and struggle! For in the light of the demonstrated fact of continued existence after death, it is clear that man is even now 'a spirit served by organs'—that consequently the basis of all religious experience and affirmation is the spiritual consciousness of mankind. There could be no revelation to man of spiritual truth or moral duty if he were not a spirit possessing the capabilities of receiving and comprehending, of interpreting and applying, the revelations and inspirations which appeal to and quicken the inner (and higher) self."

The Mediumistic Character

The following quotations from eminent modern spiritualists will further serve to illustrate the accepted general principles of "spirit communication" on the part of western spiritualism. E. W. Wallis says: "Spiritualism deals with a higher range and a wider field of supersensuous phenomena than mesmerism, hypnotism, telepathic psychometry, clairvoyance, etc., because the natural susceptibility of man in these directions is increased and intensified, and exercised upon a superior plane, when it is utilized by intelligent spirit operators. It is not true that sensitiveness is confined to those who are diseased, weak of will, neurotic, or hysterical. Those who are susceptible to psychic influence may be impulsive, warm-hearted, spontaneous, sociable, and not by any means, or of necessity, weak-minded or vicious."

Dr. Dean Clake says: "The word mediumship, as understood and used by spiritualists, technically speaking, means a susceptibility to the influence, and more or less control, of discarnated spirits. Physiologically, it means a peculiar nervous susceptibility to what may be termed the 'psychic force,' which spirits use to move the mind or body or both, of their mortal instrument. Psychologically, it signifies a passive or negative state of mind and body which renders a person subject to the positive will-power of spirits who influence him or her."

The spirit control who employed the hand of Stainton Moses, M.A., to write his thoughts, said: "The mediumistic peculiarity is one of spirit solely, and not of body, seeing that it occurs in all varieties of physical frames, in the male and in the female; in the magnetic and in the electric; in the stout and robust as well as in the puny and thin of body; in the old and in the young; in all conditions and under all circumstances. This alone would lead you to see that it is not a physical matter; and that conclusion is strengthened for you by the fact that the gift is perpetuated even after death of the earth body. Those who on your earth have been mediums retain the gift and use it with us. They are the most frequent visitors to your world; they communicate most readily; and it is through them that spirits who have not the gift are enabled to communicate with your earth."

Mediumistic Sensitivity

Emma Hardinge Britten said: "Whatever that force may be which constitutes the difference between a 'medium' and a non-medium, it is certainly of a mental and magnetic character—that is, a combination of the subtle elements of mind and magnetism, and therefore of a psychological and not of a purely physical character. Whilst the spiritualists of this generation have had no one to teach them either what spiritual gifts are, or how to use, or how to abuse them, experience has shown that the conditions under which spiritual phenomena are produced through mediums are not only helped or hindered by their mental states, but also by the will, magnetism, and mental states of those who surround them."

E. W. Wallis says: "The same laws govern the relations between the sensitive and the spirit operator as between the hypnotist and his subject. Therefore, mediumship is not necessarily spiritual; it may be of all kinds; there may be psychical relationship of a high grade and of a low one. There may be messages from beyond that prove the identity of spirits, and give evidence of the continuity of life, of the survival of mind, and yet they may not minister to spiritual growth, nor awaken any exalted desire to be of service to God and man. There may be psychical sympathy and not spiritual fellowship; there may be spirit intercourse and not that sweet spiritual communion which should be the goal of all who seek for evidences of life beyond the valley of death. It is no longer possible to regard mediumship as a supernatural endowment. It is, as regards the psychic susceptibility upon which it depends, the common property of the race, and is therefore as natural as are the 'gifts' of song or oratory, or the ability to paint or construct. But as certain gifts and graces are more developed in some individuals than in others, in like manner the sensitiveness which is called mediumship is more highly developed (or is capable of such development) in certain peculiarly constituted persons who may be regarded as supernormally gifted, yet as naturally so as are geniuses in other directions."

The Higher Vibratory Forces

The student who has carefully read what we have said in the earlier portions of the present book regarding the subject of Nature's Finer Forces, and those concerned with "vibrations," and "planes of being," will be able to harmonize the apparently somewhat conflicting opinions of those authorities above quoted concerning the nature of mediumship and spirit communication. In the first place, the student will remember that there exist planes of being higher and other than our own earth-plane, and that the rate of normal vibration on such planes is much higher than are those upon our own earth-plane. In the second place, he will remember that beings dwelling and manifesting on these higher planes are able to communicate only by means of their higher vibratory rate of manifestation. And, in the third place, he will remember that a person dwelling on the earth-plane will not ordinarily register and interpret these higher vibrations of communication; and that it is necessary for such a person to have originally, or else have developed, the capacity to raise his or her own vibrations to the key necessary to "catch" these higher vibrations. In short, we have here once more another instance of that "attunement" between sender and receiver the most common instance of which is the wireless telegraph.

Psychic Attunement

The entity, or spirit, dwelling on one of the many higher planes of being who wishes to communicate with persons on earth through a medium, must first select some person capable of raising his or her own vibratory rate of consciousness to become "in tune" with that of the spirit himself. Then he must learn to project his own mental vibrations with sufficient intensity and force to be "caught" by the sensitive perceptive organism of the medium. These things are beyond the understanding and accomplishment of many discarnate spirits, and unless they are taught by someone on their own plane of existence they are likely to fail in their attempts to communicate through a medium on the earth-plane. But at the present time, in view of the great interest being manifested "over there" in the communication with the earth-plane, an earnest, persevering spirit will usually have comparatively little difficulty in finding a proper instructor, and in acquiring the art of "earth-plane communication," as it is called on the spirit plane.

The Development of Mediumship

As regards the acquirement of mediumship qualities, information and scientific instruction is much needed, particularly at the present time. In this book we shall endeavor to throw much light upon this particular matter, and to give such instruction and information in a plain, practical form. We may begin by reminding the candidate for mediumship that the methods of development of mediumship are entirely different from those designed to develop ordinary psychic powers.

In the case of development for ordinary psychic power, the person must acquire the power of concentration in the direction of sensing in his inner consciousness the impressions coming to him from the outside world, such impressions not being consciously directed to him. He must be able to so concentrate that he will be keenly sensitive to these impressions, and to interpret them intelligently. On the contrary, the person wishing to develop the power of mediumship must learn to develop the power of negative receptivity to the vibrations coming from the spirit planes. As has well been said, he is the acted upon, and not the actor. While he requires concentration, patience, and perseverance in developing the power to raise himself to the proper vibratory key, when the actual work of communication begins he must passively allow himself to speak and act, more or less unconsciously, under the guidance, direction, and control of the communicating spirit.

Unconscious Mediumship

The student will do well, however, to remember that as a popular writer has said: "It must not, however, be supposed that spirit influence is limited to, and exerted solely upon, those who are known to be mediums; or that the spirits do not assist those who use their own psychic faculties. It is probable that all people who are psychically sensitive and open to impressions are indebted to spirit helpers, whether they are conscious of the fact or not. There is undoubtedly a greater degree of influx from the spirit side than even spiritualists are aware. Many persons are indebted to spirit friends for spontaneous impulses, which, while those persons act upon them and reap the consequences, they can neither explain nor trace to their source. Spirits frequently associate with and serve their earth friends, although the recipients of their benefactions are unaware of the fact. There would be very much more of this kind of guidance from the unseen, if, instead of being frightened, or repellant in their mental attitude toward the spirits, the great bulk of people were prepared to accept such assistance from the other side as perfectly natural and to be expected."

Mediumship and Individuality

The student will find it desirable to acquaint himself with the best opinions concerning the possible or probable effects of the practice of mediumistic powers upon the medium himself. There is evidenced a disposition in certain quarters to hold to the idea that mediumship, or control by spirits, is more or less injurious, mentally or physically or both, to the medium. It is also frequently asserted that the medium tends to lose his individuality and personal strength of character. Again, there are some who would teach that the medium should be of a low order of intelligence, and should beware of exercising his intellect, the idea seeming to be that under these conditions the mental path will be freer and clearer for the spirit control. All of the aforesaid notions are erroneous, as will appear as we progress in the statements in this book concerning true and efficient mediumship.

Co-operation of Medium and Spirits

The medium who observes certain simple and plain rules and habits of conduct will not suffer any loss of strength of character or individuality from his exercise of his mediumistic power; on the contrary, an intelligent exercise of the power of mediumship often tends to develop the intellectual power of the medium. As to the idea that the medium must be ignorant, we have but to call your attention to the fact that many of the most efficient mediums are intelligent and even brilliant individuals.

As a writer has said: "There may be some mediums who are ignoramuses, but it is doubtful if there will be any great degree of intelligence or great spiritual illumination presented through their agency. It is possible that some mediums act foolishly when in their normal state, for the purpose of accentuating the difference between their ordinary and supernormal conditions of mental activity; but there is a more rational, intelligent, and, indeed, a more spiritual conception of the relations which should exist between mediums and their spirit guides, which is rapidly finding favor with thoughtful mediums and spiritualists alike. The proper method of communing with the spirits of the unseen realm is conducive to good, and not evil, to the medium. The co-operative association of medium and spirit on the plane of thought and purpose, emotion and motive, ethics and inspiration, results in the education and elevation of the medium."

Mediumship Not Dangerous

The following additional quotations from spiritualistic writers on this point, serve to throw important light on this subject. J. J. Morse says: "Andrew Jackson Davis, Hudson Tuttle, and other writers, if I correctly understand them, claim that mediumship is a constitutional condition, and depends upon nervous adaptation, i.e., 'sensitiveness' and the quickening of the subjective (psychical) faculties; and, personally, my own firm conviction is that there is nothing dangerous in mediumship. The mere dabbling in mediumship, as either the means of a new sensation, or for the gratification of personal vanity, is to be thoroughly deprecated, as a perversion of some of the most wonderful possibilities of our natures; while the prosecution of mediumship, or anything else, to the detriment of mind, nerves, or health, in any direction, is a sin against oneself, and will inevitably call down the resultant penalties of physical and mental deterioration. I have many times advised inquirers who wished to know how to develop mediumship, unless they desired to do so for serious use, and within proper limits, not to seek its development at all. And in cases where I could see it would prove personally detrimental, I have strongly advised the inquirer to let the matter entirely alone."

Wallis says: "Very much depends upon the objects entertained by the medium and the sitters, as also upon the character and intentions of the spirit who seeks to manifest his presence; but, on general lines, where people of average intelligence and rectitude seek communion with those they have known and esteemed, or loved, the results are almost invariably beneficial. There is every reason why this should be so if the common-sense precautions are observed of keeping a level head, exercising patience, exhibiting unselfishness and sincerity, and desiring good spiritual counsel and fellowship."

A. Morton says: "Elevated spirits do not require mediums to surrender their reason; on the contrary, they advise that every new thought should be tested in the crucible of reason, and that it be rejected if not in accordance therewith; but the control of domineering spirits, claiming the name of celebrities, who present unreasonable theories, and in a dictatorial 'thus saith the spirit' manner, demanding unquestioning compliance with their commands, must be rejected by all mediums as debasing and inconsistent with self respect. Any associations or concessions which have a tendency to lower the spiritual standard must be carefully avoided, for there is no growth in any relations which can only be maintained by the sacrifice of self-respect and self-justice."

Rational Mediumship

Wallis says: "The rational course for mediums and inquirers to follow is assuredly that of avoiding the extremes alike of credulity and sceptical incredulity, by letting the spirits do their best and then collating the facts observed and drawing conclusions. Care, patience, and perseverance will save both mediums and inquirers from many misconceptions and enable them to avoid the errors of others. Above all, mediums should observe their own feelings, study their own experiences, try to understand and co-operate with the spirits, but never yield servile or slavish service, nor permit themselves to be swayed by flattery nor dominated by any spirit (in the circle or on the spirit side) who claims obedience, poses as an 'authority,' or refuses to recognize the rights of others.

No medium should remain ignorant, or refrain from giving effect to his (or her) natural desire for knowledge and self-improvement under the erroneous idea that he does not need to think, study, or learn, because he is a medium; and that the spirits will provide and teach through him all that is required. On the other hand, while thoughtfully observant of favorable conditions, and intelligent in self-study and culture, the medium should avoid 'getting up' certain subjects, or thinking along certain lines with the purpose and expectation that such information will be employed while under control. Such action, proceeding from a wrong motive, cannot fail to injure the psychic relations between the spirit and the medium, and will render the work of control doubly hard, because such thoughts will have to be cleared away before those of the spirit can be transferred to, and have free course through, the medium."

Mediums are born or made. That is to say, many persons are born with the gift of mediumship, while others, lacking this natural power, are able to develop the power by practice and gradual unfoldment. Some of the world's best mediums have been developed, while others in the same class have been born with the gift. At the same time, it must be remembered that there is a wide range of power existing between different individual mediums of both of these classes. In the opinion of the present writer, perhaps the very best way of developing mediumistic powers is that of actually participating in "circle work." The wonderful results of earlier spiritualism in America and in Europe were undoubtedly due to the casual and general practice of holding "home circles." These home circles were the nursery of some of the world's greatest mediums. Here the born medium was made aware of his or her natural powers; and, likewise, here others were enabled to gradually unfold and develop their latent mediumistic power.

The Cure for Fraudulent Mediumship

At the present time we have too few mediums, and this fact is attributable largely to the gradual discontinuance of the home circles. Present time folks are too fond of having everything worked out and presented to them, and they flock to the sensational public demonstrations, some of which are undoubtedly "faked" in order to meet the public demand for sensational features; and at the same time the honest, careful, conscientious mediums are often overlooked, and the home circles almost unknown. Many so-called investigators of spiritualism are feverishly anxious to "see something," and are impatient and the comparatively slow order of developments at the home circle or at the careful mediumistic circles. Many earnest spiritualists lament the present tendency, and predict that in time there will be an almost complete dearth of honest, careful mediums, owing to the demand for "quick action" and the temptation to furnish fraudulent counterfeits of the genuine phenomena resulting from this feverish public demand.

Warning to Young Mediums

Wallis says concerning this point: "After a time, as the development progresses, the medium and his spirit friends may be strong enough to undertake public work without the assistance

175

and protection of a circle, in the same manner as did D. Home, Slade, Eglinton, and other noted public mediums; but they should be in no hurry about doing so, and they need to be very self-possessed and level-headed to hold their own against the 'phenomena hunters' on the one side (who sap the very life of the sensitive), and the know-all, conceited skeptics on the other side (who freeze up all the psychic conditions), and before whom it is worse than foolish to cast these pearls of great price.

"The lot of the public 'physical,' 'test,' and 'clairvoyant' medium is not to be envied or lightly chosen. Such sensitives frequently suffer a martyrdom that none but sensitives can realize. What with foolish flatterers; the sitters who are never content, but cry 'give, give, give;' the injudicious friends, who seeing the exhaustion of the worn-out mediums, in mistaken sympathy urge them to take stimulants (instead of securing them rest and change of surroundings), they have a hard road to travel, and our sincerest sympathy goes out to them all. We plead for them. We bespeak kindly and human consideration. Too frequently they are tried and condemned unheard. They are expected to prove that they are not frauds, instead of, as in other cases, being accepted as reputable people. So much has this been the case that some mediums of unquestioned power have retired into private life and business pursuits, where they meet with the respect and recognition which were denied them while they were public workers in the ranks of spiritualism.

"Let us not be misunderstood. In saying this we are not apologizing for, or palliating fraud or wrong doing, but merely asking for fair and considerate treatment—not hasty, unreasoning condemnation. The kindly and appreciative treatment which he receives from some sitters is a welcome stimulus, and affords good conditions for the spirits, who are thus enabled to operate to the best advantage."

Spiritualism is the belief that not only does ones soul survive death, but that these departed spirits are able and willing to communicate with those of us who are still here on the earthly sphere.

PART VII

MEDIUMISTIC CONDITIONS

MEDIUMISTIC phenomena, i.e., the phenomena by and through which spirits manifest their presence and demonstrate their power, may be broadly classified under two heads, as follows, (1) physical phenomena, and (2) mental phenomena.

Physical Phenomena

Physical Phenomena cover a wide range of mediumistic manifestations, among which are movements of tables, the production of "raps," the manifestation of spirit lights, freedom from the effects of fire, the passage of matter through matter, direct writing upon paper or upon slates, direct voices, levitation of the medium, spirit photographs, and the production of the materialized form of the spirit. While in rare cases the spirits may manifest these forms of physical phenomena without the assistance of the medium and the circle, nevertheless as a rule such phenomena are produced by the spirits only through the assistance of a medium, and usually only when there is gathered together a circle.

"Psychic Force"

Various explanations of the power employed by the spirits, assisted by the medium and by the circle, have been offered by the scientific investigators of the subject. The most generally accepted

178

theory of the western scientists is that the spirits employ what is called the "psychic force" of the medium, often assisted by that drawn from the circle and focused in the medium. The medium is regarded as a psychic storage battery which is freely drawn upon by the manifesting spirit. The degree and character of the manifestations are determined largely by the peculiar quality of the psychic force, the capabilities of the medium, the knowledge and powers of the spirits, and the influence of the sitters.

Human Magnetism

Dr. Dean Clarke says: "Human magnetism, or nerve aura, is probably the most sublimated form of ethereal matter, hence nearest in refinement to spirit substance, and therefore spirits use it as the vehicle of their vibrating forces. Those persons who have an excess of magnetism, of the proper quality to unite with both the psychic force of spirits and the forces inherent in natural objects, and thus form an electro-magnetic connection of spirits with the objects they wish to act upon, are the persons chosen by the spirits for physical mediums. The mind and brain of the medium are not often nor necessarily controlled, and only his magnetism and psychic forces are used, through which the spirits transmit the vibrations of their own power to mechanically produce concussions, or movements of material objects."

"Zoether"

Hudson Tuttle (writing under control) gives the following statement of a spirit concerning the manner in which physical phenomena are produced: "Zoether (psychic force) emanating from the medium charges the object to be moved, and a band of spirits directs a current of their own zoethic emanation in the direction they desire the article to move, and it passes along the current thus produced. The charging of the object by the medium is necessary in order that it may be in a state of vibration harmonious to the spirit current. If this current be directed against the table or other charged body, raps or concussions are produced, as a positive and negative relation exists between the spirits and the medium's zoether. One spirit alone cannot produce physical manifestations. If one purports to communicate, assistance will be rendered by many others, who combine their influence."

"Prana"

The orientals account for physical mediumistic phenomena in a similar way, though their terms are different. Instead of speaking of zoether, or psychic force, they always employ the term "prana." In the oriental philosophies "prana" is explained as a subtle form of energy permeating the universe, but manifesting in a special form in the organism of the human being. This subtle force, or prana, is held to be capable of being transmitted from one organism to another, and is held to be the energizing power by means of which many forms of occult or magic phenomena are produced. Prana is very much akin to the "human magnetism" of the western occultists, and the properties attributed to the latter are really those which Eastern Masters for centuries past have held to be among the essential properties of prana; so, at the last, there is found to be a practical agreement here between the oriental and the western schools of occultism, respectively, in spite of their differing terminology.

Mental Phenomena

Mental Phenomena cover another wide range of mediumistic phenomena, among which may be mentioned the following, viz., involuntary or automatic writing and drawing, writing by means of the planchette or "ouija" board or similar mechanical aid to writing, clairvoyant perception of spirits, clairaudient hearing of spirit voices, prophetic utterances of spirits, impersonating and inspirational control of the medium. Mediums are frequently so thoroughly "under the influence or control," especially in private circle seances, that they seem to have been transformed into another personality. Sometimes the medium through which the spirit is manifesting will have his facial appearance changed so completely that persons present will recognize in the changed appearance the looks of the spirit as known when it was in earth life.

The Value of Phenomena

The chief value of physical mediumistic manifestations is not, as generally supposed, that of affording entertainment or food for thought for those witnessing them, but rather that of affording proof of the possibility of spirit communication, particularly when spirit identity is established through the 157manifestation of the phenomena. A writer says of this class of phenomena: "A good psychographic medium will usually obtain writing between closed slates, which may be brought by the investigator, who can insist upon their not leaving his sight, and not even leaving his hand. We have obtained writing on paper that we had previously marked, which was then covered by our own hand, and a friend's and was untouched by the medium. On another occasion, a slate which we had personally cleaned was laid on the floor (fully six feet from the medium) with a small piece of pencil under it (in broad daylight), and on taking it up shortly afterwards there was found written on the underside a long message of a private nature from a deceased friend, of whom we were not thinking. Such phenomena as these are still good and impressive, they cannot be counterfeited under like conditions, and even when no proof of identity is given in connection with the writings, they point so distinctly to the action of a discrete, disembodied intelligence as to compel the recognition of their spiritual origin. The evidential utility of physical phenomena lies in their being inimitable by fraud. Imitations can of course be made which might satisfy the credible and the gullible, but the conditions for testing the phenomena we have specially referred to are so simple that no rational investigator need be deceived; first, to be sure that the slate, paper, or panel to be used is perfectly blank; second, that it does not leave the hand of the inquirer, or if it does, that it is marked in such a way that there can be no doubt of its identification when it is returned to him; and thirdly (with paintings), to observe if the paint be wet, and note the time occupied in their production."

Trance Condition Not Essential

Many persons are under the impression that it is necessary for a medium to go into the trance condition in order to manifest physical mediumistic phenomena, but such is not the case. While many mediums do lapse into the trance conditions at such time, it is equally true that many others do not do so. Some of the very best mediums produce some of the most striking manifestations while in a perfectly normal, waking condition. A writer says of a well-known medium: "She constantly receives evidences of the presence of her spirit friends while she is perfectly normal. We have heard rappings and witnessed movements of physical objects in her presence, while holding friendly conversation with her, when we have been in a good light. Frequently, at meal times, the spirits announce their presence by raps, and respond to the salutations and questions of their medium and other members of the family."

Professor Loveland says: "Many of the best mediums in the world were never entranced in the sense of being in an unconscious sleep. And it is doubted whether that condition is desirable. The Fox girls, and most, if not all of the original rapping mediums, were never in the deep sleep trance. It is not necessary for any of the physical manifestations, and that includes a very large percentage of all the spirit phenomena. The rappings, tippings, movings, slate writings, automatic writings, paintings, telegraphing, voices, materializing, etc., can all occur without the sleep trance, the reason for which is very apparent, as in the production of such phenomena the spirits simply use the surplus radiated nerve-force of the medium."

Scientific Reports on Phenomena

Sir William Crookes, in speaking of D. D. Home and Euspasia Paladino, said: "Most, if not all, of the occurrences with Euspasia seem to have taken place when she was in a trance, and the more complete the trance the more striking the phenomena. This was not always so with Home. Certainly the two most striking things I ever saw with him, the fire test and the visible forms, were to be observed while he was entranced, but it was not always easy to tell when he was in that state, for he spoke and moved about almost as if he were in his normal condition; the chief differences being that his actions were more deliberate, and his manner and expressions more solemn, and he always spoke of himself in the third person, as 'Dan.'

"When he was not in a trance we frequently had movements of objects in different parts of the room, with visible hands carrying flowers about and playing the accordion. On one occasion I was asked by Home to look at the accordion as it was playing in the semi-darkness beneath the table. I saw a delicate looking female hand holding it by the handle, and the keys at the lower end rising and falling as if fingers were playing on them, although I could not see them. So lifelike was the hand that at first I said it was my sister-in-law's, but was assured by all present that both her hands were on the table, a fact which I then verified for myself."

Phenomena Without Darkness

"Home always refused to sit in the dark. He said that, with firmness and perseverance, the phenomena could be got just as well in the light, and even if some of the things were not so strong, the evidence of one's eyesight was worth making same sacrifices for. In almost all the séances I had with Home there was plenty of light to see all that occurred, and not only to enable me to write down notes of what was taking place, but to read my notes without difficulty. Home was very anxious to let everyone present be satisfied that he was not doing any of the things himself—too anxious, I sometimes thought, for frequently he would interfere with the progress and development of what was going on by insisting that some skeptic or other should come around and take hold of his hands and feet to be sure he was not doing anything himself.

"At times, he would push his chair back and move right away from the table when things were moving on it, and ask those furthest from him to come round and satisfy themselves that he had nothing to do with the movements. I used frequently to beg him to be quiet, knowing that, if he would not move about in his eagerness to convince us of his genuineness, the strength of the phenomena would probably increase to such a degree that no further evidence would be needed that their production was beyond the powers of the medium.

"During the whole of my knowledge of D. D. Home, extending for several years, I never once saw the slightest occurrence that would make me suspicious that he was attempting to play tricks. He was scrupulously sensitive on this point, and never felt hurt at anyone taking precautions against deception. He sometimes, in the early days of our acquaintance, used to say to me before a séance, 'Now, William, I want you to act as if I were a recognized conjurer, and was going to cheat you and play all the tricks I could. Take every precaution you can devise against me, and move about and look under the table or where else you like. Don't consider my feelings. I shall not be offended. I know that the more carefully I am tested the more convinced will everyone be that these abnormal occurrences are not of my own doings.' Latterly, I used jokingly to say to him, 'Let us sit round the fire and have a quiet chat, and see if our friends are here and will do anything for us. We won't have any tests or precautions.' On these occasions, when only my family was present with him, some of the most convincing phenomena took place."

Is Darkness Necessary?

From the above it is seen that not only is the trance condition not absolutely necessary for the production of striking mediumistic phenomena, but that, also, there is no absolute necessity for the condition of darkness to be maintained as an essential feature of such phenomena. While many mediums insist upon the condition of darkness at séances, it is thought by some careful thinkers that this arises from the fact that such mediums have been accustomed to such conditions from their earliest days of mediumship, and have grown to believe that the same are absolutely necessary. It is thought that if such mediums would begin over again, practicing in full light in the company of a few sympathetic friends, they would before long grow accustomed to the new conditions, and would then be able to reproduce all of their most important phenomena in full light. Using the terms of modern psychology, it would seem that such mediums are the victims of their own "auto-suggestion," and fixed beliefs; and, as all students of the subject well know, the mental states of the medium have a most important bearing of the quality of the phenomena produced, and form a very important factor of the conditions governing the success of the séance.

Developing Circles

The person who is developing mediumship will do well to surround himself with persons of a certain type of psychical power, and to form circles of such persons. Such persons are invaluable in constituting a "developing circle." Such persons need not be mediumistic themselves, nor are they required to actually do anything. Instead, their service is that of being present as psychical reservoirs of force upon which the spirits can draw for manifesting power. The medium, being sensitive to helpful influences, and the reverse, will recognize such persons by the congenial and harmonious influence they exercise upon him; and he will do well to encourage such persons to sit in his developing circles.

Impersonating Mediumship

What is known as "impersonating mediumship" occurs where the medium is so completely under the control of the manifesting spirit that he will exhibit, often in a marvelously accurate manner, the personal characteristics and mannerisms of the spirit, and which are readily recognized as such by the spirit's surviving friends in earth-life. Sometimes the medium will actually re-enact the dying moments of the controlling spirit. In many cases such impersonations have been so nearly photographically and phonographically correct that they have afforded the most convincing proof to investigators, and in other cases have been a great consolation to relatives of the spirit who have been thus assured that their loved one was still in actual existence on a higher plane of being. These results, however, are possible only when a very close rapport condition has been established between the spirit and the medium. In cases in which such a close rapport condition is obtained, and a high degree of harmony developed, the spirit will be able to positively establish his identity by causing the medium to utter his exact words, and to give names, dates, and close details of incidents occurring in his earth life, and often to employ his exact set phrases and verbal tricks of speech, so as to bring to the consciousness of the sitters the realization that they are in the actual presence of the discarnate spirit friend.

The Proper Mental Condition

The young medium, however, should beware against striving too hard to be the instrument of the phenomena of spirit impersonation. For a too intense anxiety, and desire to please sitters, frequently tends to produce a cloudy mental state in which the ideas in the mind of the medium blend with the spirit communication, and thus produces a most unsatisfactory result, and one which is apt to confuse the minds of the sitters and sometimes actual arouse suspicion that the medium is trying to practice deception. For this reason the young medium should not seek the attendance of persons desiring "test séances;" at least, such should be his course until he has learned not to be carried away with his desire to please or to satisfy such persons attending 164his circles. He should endeavor to cultivate a mental condition of calmness, and a determination not to influence or to interfere with the spirit communications in any way whatsoever, but, instead, to allow himself to become a passive instrument for the communication. The medium should remember that he is not a dealer in merchandise "warranted to please," but is, instead, a medium of communication between the spirit and those still in earth-life.

Demand Proof of Spirit Identity

A certain degree of care and caution, and the employment of honest powers of discrimination, is necessary on the part of the sitters in cases of spirit impersonation. This not because of any lack of honesty on the part of the medium, but because of the habit of a mischievous class of dwellers on the planes of spirit life to falsely impersonate other spirits as such séances. As all investigators of the subject know very well, it is not an infrequent thing for such mischievous and meddlesome spirits to endeavor to pass themselves off as the relative or friends of those in the circle, or even to falsely impersonate some great historical personages.

In such cases the sitters should insist upon the spirit positively identifying himself, just as they would in case of doubt regarding a person speaking to them over the telephone and claiming to be such-and-such a person. And the proof demanded should be similar to that which would be sought from the suspected telephone talker. An honest spirit communicator does not object to such demands, and is only too ready to do his best to furnish the right kind of proofs concerning his identity.

The "Trance Condition"

The psychic condition frequently attending the demonstration of mediumship powers is usually spoken of as a "trance," but this term is quite misleading, for it carries with it the suggestion of an entire loss of consciousness and of a condition of more or less deep sleep. But the mediumistic trance is seldom a deep sleep condition. Instead, it is the condition similar to that of a profound "day dream," in which the person is fully awake but in which the consciousness has been almost entirely taken off the sights and sounds of the outside world. As a writer has well said: "What is called 'trance mediumship' is seldom of the nature of the deep sleep of entire unconsciousness. It is more frequently the suspension of the ordinary consciousness of external surroundings, a temporary oblivion on the outer plane—a semi-conscious state, in fact—in which the subject does not retain the volitional ability to employ his thinking powers, the latter having been 'switched off,' so to speak, and the subject responds to the will of the spirit control."

Spirit Inspiration

Wallis says, concerning the nature of a certain phase of spirit control: "In the case of speaking mediumship, where general and philosophical ideas are to be transmitted, the control is of a different order from that exercised for test manifestations. It is more frequently of the nature of 'suggestion.' The spirit suggestionist suggests to the medium a certain train of ideas, and then stimulates the brain and the organs of expression to do the work of dressing up the thoughts and giving them utterance. Unless the subject is a scientific or a biographical one, in which specific terms are required and accurate data are to be imparted, the relationship between the 'inspired' speaker and the spirit control partakes more of the character of the engineer who feeds the fire and directs the movements of his engine, while the machine does the work, than it does of the actual voicing of the exact words, embodying in a full and complete fashion the ideas the spirit wishes to have expressed.

"At first the operator may succeed by very imperfectly stimulating the brain of the sensitive and causing the cerebration and expression of his thoughts. The utterances may bear but a slight resemblance to what the spirit intended to express. The vocabulary is that of the medium, and the form in which the speech is cast of necessity partakes of the mold familiar to the sensitive—but, by continued close association and frequent control of the medium, the operator gains experience which enables him to exert a more decided influence; and the sensitive, becoming attuned, responds to and expresses the thoughts of the spirit with greater clearness and precision. Just as those who dwell together unconsciously approach nearer to each other and acquire a similarity in their mode of thought and of expressing their ideas (the more dominant personality impressing itself upon the less positive), so the medium imperceptibly, and very often unconsciously, acquires facility and proficiency in thought and elocutionary expression as the result of the co-operation between himself and his spirit guide."

Psychic Attunement

Those who have read the above carefully stated opinion, will begin to see the reason why certain mediums who have attained the greatest proficiency in certain forms of mediumship, and who have become what are known as "reliable mediums," almost always have some particular spirit guide or guides with whom they have become in almost perfect psychic harmony and attunement. These harmonious spirits are not only enabled to express themselves with a high degree of clearness and power through their favorite medium, but are also enabled to assist in the production of the best rapport conditions between other spirits wishing to communicate and the said medium. There is a certain amount of spiritual and psychic co-operation between spirit and medium which is attained only by practice and continued association, which results in a psychic attunement between them. The closer and more harmonious the relationship existing between a spirit and his medium, the thinner is the veil separating the two planes upon which they dwell.

Automatic Writing

In that phase of mediumship known as "automatic or inspirational writing," there is manifested two distinct forms of spirit control of the organism of the medium. In cases of pure automatic writing the spirit controls the arm and hand muscles of the medium, and uses them to write out the message under the direct and absolute control of the mind and will of the spirit. Cases have been known in which both hands of the medium have been so used by the spirit control, each hand writing a distinct and separate message, and both being performed without any consciousness of the nature of the message on the part of the medium. In some cases of automatic writing the medium was engaged in thought about other subjects, or even in reading or study from a book. This is true not only in cases of automatic writing in which the hand is directly employed, but also in those in which some mechanical device such as the planchette or the ouija board intervenes.

Inspirational Writing

In inspirational writing, on the other hand, the spirit impresses the message upon the mind of the medium, either as a whole, or else sentence by sentence or even word by word—in all of such cases, be it noted, the medium is aware of the substance of what he is about to write, either the word, the sentence, or perhaps the entire message. In such cases, of course, the medium retains control of his writing muscles and their action, and the spirit control is merely a phase of higher telepathy, as it were. When the message is impressed upon the mind of the medium word by word, or sentence by sentence, the style is of course that of the spirit exerting the control; but where the entire message is impressed upon the mind of the medium, the style is usually a blending of that of the spirit and that of the medium, for the medium is not likely to remember the literal message as given him, but merely is conscious of the general purport and meaning thereof, together with a few phrases or expressions formed by the spirit mind. In such cases, of course, the personality of the medium enters largely into the message, while in the case of pure automatic writing the personality of the medium plays no part whatsoever, and the personality of the spirit is present in its entirety. This important distinction should be noted and remembered.

Gradual Development of Powers

Most mediums develop their powers of mediumship gradually, and pass through a number of stages in their development of power. At first they may obtain only raps, or possibly the tilting or movement of tables. Then, very likely, they are moved to write, either automatically or else inspirationally. Later they experience the impulse to allow the spirit control to speak through their vocal organism, but it is seldom that the spirit is able to do this at first trial, as the medium is not as yet sufficiently sensitized or attuned to the spirit, and, instead, they can but gurgle, gasp, and make inarticulate sounds, or else shout, laugh, cry, or sing, and possibly jabber some strange jargon or unknown tongue, or else simply utter a series of sounds lacking in definite meaning. Later, the inarticulate sound is succeeded by definite sentences—perhaps a message, or a short address. Sometimes the spirit control will endeavor to relate some of his earth-life experiences, or perhaps even to give an impersonation manifestation. Often several different spirits strive to manifest through the developing medium, taking turns as manifestation, holding the control for only a few minutes and then giving place to his successor.

Spirit Guides

As the development proceeds, it will be found that one or two particular spirits will manifest a greater power than the others, and after establishing a strong degree of harmony and attunement they will assume the position of "guides" to the medium, and will accordingly begin to work in his interests on their side of life, and to accept or reject other spirits who seek to manifest through their medium. At this stage, the medium is often sufficiently advanced to be used as the channel for fuller and more complete manifestations, particularly in the direction of inspirational speaking. Often the medium in this stage of development is also able to manifest psychic powers which were formerly beyond his ability, as for instance psychometry, clairvoyance, etc. Then if his spirit guides be sufficiently advanced and powerful, and the medium be sufficiently receptive and harmonious to their influences, they will educate him to such an extent that he will be able, with their assistance, to become an instrument for the production of still higher forms of mediumistic phenomena. But the development is almost always gradual and proceeds by successive and well-defined steps and stages.

No Loss of Individuality

In concluding this part of our book, we would call your attention to the following statements made by writers along the lines of spiritualism in the leading journals of that school of modern thought. The first writer says: "There is no need for the medium to decline to be influenced or controlled, by spirit friends for fear of losing his 'individuality,' any more than he should insist upon asserting his freedom and refuse the aid of tutors, lest they should infringe upon his sacred 'individuality.' What are called the unconscious phases of mediumship generally lead up to loving co-operation with the wise and kindly souls of the higher life in efforts to establish the fellowship of man; to bring knowledge where ignorance now reigns; to banish the darkness by the light of that spiritual communion which shall yet be a blessing to the race; and reliance upon higher powers in or out of the body does not mean that we sacrifice our own abilities, nor do we thus become exempt from responsibility. Quite the reverse. It is the arrogance of individualism against which we protest. In fact, there is no abiding strength of purpose apart from the dependence every well-ordered mind should accord to the Infinite Light and Wisdom and the beneficial services which His wise and loving ministering spirits can render to us if we are desirous and responsive."

Mediumship Beneficial

A second writer says: "There is no reason why the reactive consequences of frequent control by enlightened and earnest spirits, even in the case of the 'trance' medium, should not prove extremely beneficial to the sensitive, and this, we believe, has been the case with many of the speakers in the spiritualistic movement. Where the medium is inspirational and ready to respond to the thought impulsations of the control, it stands to reason that the transmitted ideas, and the stimulation of the thought-faculties caused by the transference and expression of the spirits' opinions, will not be lost to the medium. 'If you will take one step we can more easily help you to take a second than we could compel you to take the first if you were unprepared,' said a spirit teacher to Mrs. Emma Hardinge Britten, and there need be no loss of dignity or individuality, no injury to body or mind, but a gain of strength and spiritual vigor, education of mind and stimulation of moral purpose, by intelligent co-operation and temporary surrender on the part of the medium to wise and loving spirit helpers and teachers."

Mediumship and The Bible

A third writer, Rev. H. E. Haweis, says in connection with the relation of spiritualism with religion: "People now believe in the Bible because of spiritualism; they do not believe in spiritualism because of the Bible. Take up your Bible and you will find that there is not a single phenomenon which is recorded there which does not occur at séances today. Whether it be lights, sounds, the shaking of the house, the coming through closed doors, the mighty rushing winds, levitation, automatic writing, the speaking in tongues, we are acquainted with all these phenomena; they occur every day in London as well as in the Acts of the Apostles. It is incontestable that such things do occur, that in the main the phenomena of spiritualism are reliable, and happen over and over again, under test conditions, in the presence of witnesses; and that similar phenomena are recorded in the Bible, which is written for our learning. It is not an opinion, not a theory, but a fact. There is chapter and verse for it, and this is what has rehabilitated the Bible. The clergy ought to be very grateful to spiritualism for this, for they could not have done it themselves. They tried, but they failed."

PART VIII
HOW TO DEVELOP MEDIUMSHIP

ANYONE is entitled to be considered a "medium" if he or she is psychically sensitive and capable of receiving and responding to spirit control or influence. Likewise, anyone is entitled to the designation who is capable of so generating freely a sufficient quantity of "psychic force," magnetism, prana, or whatever other name we may choose to apply to the force which is generated in the human organism and is capable of being employed by the spirits in order to produce mediumistic phenomena of the class usually referred to as "physical phenomena." As we have seen, the spirits themselves are not usually able to manufacture or generate by themselves this psychic required to produce the said phenomena, but, on the contrary, must depend upon mediumistic individuals for such force.

Who Are Mediumistic?

Many persons are more or less naturally sensitive to spirit influence, and therefore mediumistic. In many cases these persons tend to take on the psychic conditions of others, both those in earth life and those on the spirit plane of existence, without realizing the nature of the influence operating on them. Such persons are frequently more or less erratic, and are considered as "flighty" by their friends. They need instruction on the subject of psychic laws and self-control, so that they may intelligently guard themselves against undesirable influences, and at the same time cultivate the power of mediumship of the desirable kind. It has been asserted that "everyone is a medium," and in a way this is true, for practically every person is more or less sensitive to spirit influence, and is capable of being developed into an efficient medium of communication with the spirit world. But it is equally true that only a certain percentage of persons possess the true spiritual qualities requisite for the highest phases of true mediumship. That is to say, but few persons are fitted temperamentally and spiritually for the higher tasks of mediumship. We think it safe to say, however, that where a person is filled with a burning desire to become a true medium, and feels within himself or herself a craving of the soul for development along these lines, then that person may feel assured that he or she has within his or her soul the basic qualities required for true mediumship, and that these may be developed by the proper methods.

The Mediumistic Temperament

A leading writer on the subject of mediumship has said: "It is a fundamental proposition that sensitiveness, or the capability of mediumship, is a faculty common to mankind, differing in degree—as hearing and sight are common heritages, but keener in some individuals than in others; or, under certain conditions, it may disappear."

What is called "the mediumistic temperament" is frequently marked self-consciousness and shrinking from public criticism, and a diffidence which causes the person to wish to be out of the range of the observation of strangers and those not sympathetic to them; on the other hand, however, there are other forms of the "mediumship temperament" which is marked by a nervous, almost hysterical, self assertiveness and desire for public notice and attention. Persons of either of these phases of this temperament, however, have the common quality of being extremely sensitive to sneers and slights, adverse criticism and oppositions, while ridicule drives them almost beside themselves. Likewise they are nearly always found to be enthusiastic and earnest workers when their interests and sympathies are aroused; as a writer has said "they are almost invariably emotional, enthusiastic, spontaneous, and ardent." And, as another writer has said they are usually "generous and impulsive, hot-headed and independent, close friends with warm hearts; too sensitive to criticism of an unkind nature, too easily pleased by praise; without malice, without revengeful thoughts." A striking feature of this temperament may be summed up in the phrase, "hungry for sympathy and understanding."

Is Mediumship Desirable?

While it is true that a vast majority of persons possess the mediumistic power, latent and dormant, and capable of being developed to a greater or less active power, it is but honest to say that in many cases it is a grave question whether the person would be justified in undertaking the hard work, and long time, required to develop himself for the minor success which would attend his efforts. As well, once begun, mediumship is a life-long commitment that is never to be taken lightly. There are times when mediums have wished to have never taken on the task.

As a writer has said: "Does the prospective result justify the labor involved to bring these powers into efflorescence? My impression is, that in at least three cases out of four, the time and labor it would take to develop this latent quality to its greatest efficacy would be far in excess of its value when so developed." But, as we have already said, the best indication is found in the "call" to develop his or her latent powers which the true medium always experiences.

Developing the Natural Power

A writer on this subject well says: "Just as a drum or tamborine is incapable of being made to emit a tithe of what can be produced by means of a piano or a violin, in the way of music, so the differences in quality and conditions of the physical organisms, and in the degree of nervous and psychical sensibility of those who desire mediumship, render it improbable that any but a small proportion will develop such extreme susceptibility to spirit influence as will repay them for the time and self-sacrifice involved in the cultivation of their powers. Further, it should be borne in mind that while wise spirits are ever ready to respond to the call of the earnest aspirant for spiritual truth, as wise spirits they are not likely to devote themselves to the preparation of an instrument that would be inefficient for their purpose. The nervous system of the medium, whatever his phase may be, has to be trained to respond to the will and the psychic force of the controlling spirit, just as much as the muscles of the musician or artist, and 'practice makes perfect' in the one case as well in the other. Since mediumship is a strictly natural qualification, depending upon organic fitness and susceptibility, it is not a supernatural power or a special 'gift,' neither does it insure the moral purity nor the intellectual ability of the medium, any more than musical or artistic capabilities are evidences of the special intelligence or the high moral tones of their possessors."

Mediumship and Genius

The spirits controlling the hand of a celebrated writing medium, once delivered through him the following message regarding the nature and development of mediumistic powers: "Mediumship is a development of that which is, in another sort, genius. Genius, the opened and attentive ear to spirit guidance and inspiration, shades away into mediumship, the facile instrument of spirit manifestation. In proportion as the medium becomes open to influence, directly exercised, is he valuable as a means whereby direct messages are conveyed. And in proportion as the individual spirit is lost and merged in the great ocean of spirit, is the result most direct and serviceable. It is when the passive spirit is content to allow us to use the corporeal instrument, as it does when itself operates, that we gain satisfactory results. That can only be when a condition of perfect passivity, as far removed from skepticism as from credulity, has been secured. This opening of the spiritual being to spiritual influences is what you call mediumship. The true and valuable gifts are purely spiritual and must be used for spiritual purposes; not for gain, or for satisfying curiosity, or for base or unworthy ends."

Spontaneous Mediumship.

What may be called "spontaneous mediumship" is experienced by many persons not claiming mediumistic powers, and not understanding the nature of the phenomena manifesting to and through themselves. Such persons at times are conscious of the presence of spirit friends, and may even catch glimpses of them either in the form of a mental image impressed upon their minds by the spirit friends, or else by a more or less clear partial materialization. Sometimes raps manifest themselves in their vicinity, and tables and light articles of furniture may manifest movement at their touch or approach. Such persons, not understanding the laws of spirit manifestation, are frequently greatly distressed, or even frightened, by such manifestations; and in not a few cases they experience considerable annoyance and grief by reason of the attitude of their friends who are apt to consider them "queer," or "spooky," and therefore to be avoided. Moreover, in the case of the physical manifestations such as the movements of tables, furniture, etc., and the production of raps, these persons are frequently accused of deliberate fraud in the production of such phenomena, whereas as a matter of fact they, themselves, are quite in the dark as to the cause and nature of the phenomena in question. It is obvious that the placing of the right information in the hands of such persons, and their instruction in the laws and principles of mediumship would be a blessing to them.

Mediumistic Flashes

A writer has the following to say concerning this class of mediumistic persons: "Those persons who are naturally sensitive sometimes experience strange and sudden impulses. Thoughts come to them 'in a flash,' so to speak. They say things spontaneously which they had not intended to say—the words seem to burst from them and 'say themselves.' Others have equally sudden and fugitive clairvoyant experiences; they see spirits where they least expect, and when they are absorbed in something else; but when they strongly desire to 'see' or to receive guidance, they get nothing. This state of affairs, in all probability, is due to the fact that their susceptibility is not sufficiently developed; their psychical impressibility can only be reached and acted upon under specially favorable conditions, which are disturbed and dissipated when the ordinary intellectual self is aroused.

Systematic Development

"The remedy will be found in the systematic cultivation of interior repose and confidence. The psychic must learn to regard it as a perfectly natural experience that the spiritual states and positive thoughts of incarnate people should impinge upon his spiritual sphere, and while 'attentive to the holy vision,' should calmly accept the fact and maintain the attitude or response; not anxiously nor demandingly, but thankfully enjoying the spiritual communion and illumination thus afforded to him. It is only natural that many people should desire to become mediums, and that they should wish to ascertain what constitutes mediumship, and what is required to secure its development. But those who express these desires should remember that in all probabilities months, if not years, of patient development have been necessary for the success and efficiency of those celebrated mediums whom they admire and probably envy." But, as we have said before, if the "call" to mediumship be felt, then it may be heeded; though the person must be prepared to pay the price of toil and work, patience and perseverance, required to attain the mountain top of mediumship.

The Development Circle

As we have repeatedly stated in the foregoing pages, the actual spirit circle is the best possible means of developing the latent powers of mediumship, and the simplest, readiest, and most effective method of discovering the presence of such latent powers in the individual. As a leading medium has told us, it is "the primary school for the study of spiritual facts, and for the training of mediums."

The "spirit circle," as most of you know, is a company of harmonious, earnest, sympathetic persons joining their psychic powers for the purpose of aiding the medium to establish the lines of psychic communication between the earth plane and the planes of the spiritual world. Within this circle the proper state of mind is produced and a path is cleared to allow proper communications. It must here be stated that by "development" we do not mean the cultivation of the powers of the spirits, but rather the training and unfoldment of the powers of the medium to receive and transmit the power exercised by the spirit controls.

The Aspirational Attitude

To those who purpose to develop their latent mediumistic powers by and through the development circle, we would say that it is of the highest importance that they should cultivate a trustful, hopeful mental attitude, and a willingness to open themselves to the inflow of the spiritual power of their friends of the spiritual planes. As a writer has said, they should "make some mental preparation, such as eliminating from their minds all disturbing or irritating thoughts, and by striving to consciously realize union of purpose with those who may have previously made their presence known or indicated their intention to help in the work of the development of their mediumistic powers, by mentally requesting that the spiritual ties may be strengthened. Even where there has not been any clear indication of the presence of spirit helpers, a generally aspirational and receptive attitude of mind will do much towards providing favorable conditions."

Natural Unfoldment

Again, the person wishing to develop his latent mediumistic powers must exercise patience and perseverance, and must not insist upon a premature attempt at revelation on the part of the spirits. The process of the unfoldment of the mediumistic powers should be akin to that of the unfoldment of the bud of the flower, that is to say, it must be gradual, natural, and unforced. The writer above mentioned, says on this point: "Too many people, instead of waiting until the spirits were ready to communicate with them, have pressed for 'tests' before the connections were properly made. They have complicated matters by their eager questionings, and have worried the operators until everything went wrong; and then, because the answers were incorrect, inconsequent and misleading, or persistently negative, they declared that the spirit was a deceiver, evil, or foolish, and, while having only themselves to blame, gave up the sittings in disgust, whereas, had they been less impetuous, less opinionated, less prejudiced, they would in all probability have eventually obtained satisfactory proofs of the presence of their spirit loved ones."

Persistent Watchful Waiting

Some persons are so disappointed because they have not obtained results after two or three sittings that they give up further efforts. It would perhaps amaze such persons to know that many of the world's most celebrated mediums have, in the beginning of their development circle work, sat for several weeks, or even several months, at frequent intervals, without obtaining more than the most meager results; but they afterwards developed the most marvelous power. An extreme case is cited in the history of spiritualism, in which a couple sat night after night for six months, without missing a sitting and without being rewarded by a single physical result; but after this tedious and discouraging wait, all at once, as it were, the spirits secured the most perfect kind of communication through them, and difficult table tippings and levitation, convincing raps, messages, writings, and finally materializations follows, until their fame spread all over the world of spiritualism.

Building Lines of Communication

Just how long it will require obtaining convincing results at the development circle is a matter largely dependent upon certain conditions. Much, of course, depends upon the faculty of the medium to adjust and harmonize himself with the spirits, so as to furnish a "clear wire" for them to operate over. Again, much depends upon the character of the persons constituting the circle. A circle composed of harmonious, helpful persons will do much to hasten the coming of the manifestation, whereas one composed of inharmonious, skeptical, impatient, and materialistic persons will do much to retard the progress and development of the mediumistic powers.

Developing Concentration

The following advice on this particular subject will be found helpful to those contemplating the formation of development circles, and the unfoldment of their latent powers of mediumship; it is from the pen of an earnest student of this subject, and one who is himself a competent medium.

This person says: "One of the most important prerequisites for success in the development of mediumship along spiritual lines is the cultivation of the power of concentration. In the early days of the movement the would-be medium was advised to be 'passive,' and passivity was often construed into self-effacement. We are now learning to distinguish between receptivity and docility, between apathy and aspiration. A medium is not, and should not be willing to become a mere irresponsible tool. For intelligent and beneficial association with, and inspiration from, the people of the higher life, a certain degree of abstraction is necessary.

"To cut one's self off from ordinary conditions, to retire into the sanctuary of one's own inner consciousness, to 'enter the silence' as it is sometimes called, is helpful training for the preparation of conditions favorable for the manifestation of spirit-power. The Quakers were true spiritualists in this sense, and evidently realized the need for the concentration of the soul's forces and their withdrawal from the outer plane, preparatory to the descent of the spiritual influence that moved them to speak. The outer world is full of distractions that can cause the medium to lose focus and cut-off any ability to sense higher worlds.

The Call for Illumination

"The sincere supplication for illumination and guidance is never in vain. The spirit breathes a serener air, and is calmed, strengthened, and comforted by the subsequent reaction. It is harmonized thereby, and thus becomes accordant to the psychic forces which, like the ocean's tides, ebb and flow throughout the universe, and bathe every soul that lies open to their vivifying and quickening influence. Still more, there are those who dwell in the Light, whose thoughts and love go out to all such as truly call upon God; and these, the ministering messenger spirits, often pour their libations of sympathy into the sad hearts of the sorrowful ones on earth, even though they remain unknown and their interposition is unrecognized by those to whom they have given their loving and helpful thoughts.

The Jacob's Ladder of Communion

"By the earnest study of the conditions requisite for the development of body, mind, and psychic sense, the intelligent medium will endeavor to meet the friends who inspire him at least half way on the Jacob's ladder of communion. The medium can then easily and gladly enter into reciprocal and conscious fellowship with them on the thought plane, so that their inspirations may freely flow through his instrumentality to others, unobstructed by his personality and the all too common worries of the material world.

"Classes for the development of mediumship along these lines are very much needed; classes in which the members are expected to take an active part, not merely to sit and sit, and let the spirits do all the work, but by systematic preparation and spiritual aspiration and cultivated receptivity prepare themselves to become lucid and capable instruments for the transmission of information and helpful influences from the other side.

The Attainment of Excellence

"There is but one course of procedure for the successful attainment of excellence in any field of labor or thought, and that is by study and training, by observation, by persevering application and determined effort, by readiness to learn, and responsiveness to every influence which will help to smooth the pathway to the desired success. The intelligent medium who follows this course will not go blindly on groping in the obscurity of the psychic realm, and becoming the tool for unseen and unknown agents, but he will unfold his powers, and by co-operating with them will learn to know and trust his preceptors, until he may possibly become as a spirit among spirits, the conscious possessor of such knowledge regarding his own spiritual nature and powers that he will be a ready instrument in the hands of enlightened spirit people, with whom he can knowingly work for human good."

What a Development Circle Is

Now then, with the above advice and admonitions in mind, the persons who desire to develop and unfold their mediumistic powers will do well to take the necessary steps to form a development circle. The "circle" it must be remembered, is not merely a crowd of persons gathered together for the purpose of witnessing spiritualistic manifestations or phenomena. Instead, it is a gathering of persons who desire to co-operate in establishing relations with the world of spirits, and to receive communications there from.

In the case of the development circle, the purpose is to demonstrate that well established spiritualistic principle that the mediumistic faculty in all of its forms is best developed and unfolded, cultivated and strengthened, by an actual sitting in the circle, in such a way as to perfect and spiritualize the magnetism of the sitters by their mutual action on each other, and by the influence and power of the spirits employing such magnetic and psychic forces so furnished them by the circle of harmonious sitters. Or, as a writer has well expressed it: "The purpose for which a spirit circle is held is that by the blending of the aura, psychic force, or magnetic emanations of the sitters, the attention of disembodied spirits may be attracted and a battery be formed by means of which they can communicate with the circle. The focalization of this force rests with the unseen operator, and if they are skilled in the 'modus operana,' they know where, how, and in what way to use it to the best advantage."

Forming the Development Circle

The circle should be composed of not less than four persons, and not more than twelve. It is well to have an equal number of persons of each sex, if this be possible; if not possible to obtain an equality of the sexes, the effort should be made to come as near to that equality as is possible. The members of the circle should seat themselves around a table, and as nearly as is possible the sexes should be alternated in this grouping, that is to say, a man should sit next to a woman, and so on. It will be found well to have the same persons regularly attend the circles, so far as is possible. This creates a special rapport between members.

Likewise, it will be found advantageous to always use the same table, and to hold the circle in the same room—but these things are not absolutely essential, and very good results may often be obtained by having the members of the circle gather at the different homes of its respective members. While cheerfulness is well on the part of the sitters, there should be no indulgence in levity and joking during the sitting. The room should be comfortably warmed and lighted in the ordinary way.

The Sitters in the Circle

The sitters will do well to occupy their same places at each sitting, unless the spirits indicate otherwise. The medium, or in the absence of a recognized medium the most sensitive person in the circle, should sit in the circle at a place mentally recognized as the "head of the table," even though the table be circular in form. It will be well for the sitters to hold each others' hands at the beginning of the circle, in order to generate the necessary magnetism. But after the circle is actually formed, the sitters should place their hands on the top of the table, close to its edge; the small fingers of the hands of each sitter touching those of the sitter on either side of him—in this way there is a psychic and magnetic battery formed of the sitters, providing perfect connection is maintained.

The Spirit Communication Code

At the beginning, the leader should plainly announce the signaling conditions, so as to avoid confusion on the part of the sitters and the visiting spirits (for there are several codes in use, and confusion sometimes occurs). The most general used and approved code is as follows: "Three indicates Yes; One indicates No; Two indicates 'doubtful'; Four indicates 'don't know'; and Five indicates 'call the alphabet.'" The numbers refer to the number of raps or table-tilts, etc., given by the spirits in answer to questions asked them. When the alphabet is called for, some one of the circle slowly calls out each letter of the alphabet, in regular order, until a rap or table-tilt indicate that the right letter has been indicated; this letter should then be written down, and the alphabet again called, until the next letter is indicated; and so on until the message is completed. For instance, the name "John" would be spelt out as J-O-H-N, four callings of the alphabet being necessary to obtain the same.

The Matter of Time Conditions

The time at which the séances are held is not in itself important, but it will be found best to fix such time at such an hour that will be most convenient for the sitters, and at which their minds will not be distracted by thoughts that they should return home, or should be attending to certain household or business duties, etc. The séances should be held not oftener than, say, twice a week, or at the most three times a week. Each séance should be continued for about an hour or a little over—certainly not over two hours at a time. The sitters should be punctual in attendance, so that no time may be lost or wasted. The idea should be that the spirit friends are awaiting your coming to fulfill your engagement with them, and one should be as careful to keep such an engagement as he would were the engagement with his most valued friend or esteemed acquaintance. Regularity in attendance is also important, as it is important that so far as possible the same general conditions be maintained at each and every séance. The séance should be started at the same hour on each occasion, at least so far as is possible, so as to preserve the same time rhythm.

Opening of the Séance

It will be well to open the séance with a few moments of earnest, silent meditation—a few moments of dwelling "in the silence," as some have well called it; and these moments should be observed in a religious and devotional state of mind, all frivolity and flippancy being carefully avoided. If some present feel moved to prayer, then by all means let the prayer be made, for there can scarcely be a more fitting occasion for reverent prayer than a properly conducted séance. A few moments of hymn-singing may also be found advantageous in the direction of producing the devotional state of mind on the part of the sitters. The sitters should preserve a solemn frame of mind and reverent general demeanor during the séance—perhaps the best model is that of an old time Quaker Meeting in which the silent devout spiritual feeling was so plainly manifest that it could almost be felt physically. Patience is necessary in conducting a séance, and perseverance is essential. The manifestations cannot be unduly forced, and there is often required a great deal of psychical adjustment before the lines of the spiritual communication between the two great planes of life are fully established.

Developing a Medium

If the circle be one devoted chiefly to the development of mediumistic powers in some one of its members, then it will perhaps be best to have only that particular medium present. The remainder of the sitters should be highly sympathetic toward the developing medium, and should assume the mental attitude of help and aid toward him. While the early results of such a circle may not be so interesting as those at which a fully developed medium is present, nevertheless the gradual unfoldment of the powers of the medium will be found highly interesting, and the gradual evolution of the character of the phenomena produced will be a liberal education in itself.

In case that in the circle there are no particular persons regarded as being mediums, and where there is a general desire to develop mediumistic powers among many or all of the sitters, there must be carefully avoided anything approaching a rivalry between the members of the circle; and at the same time a strong desire and perfect willingness for the spirit power to manifest through whomsoever it may prefer, without regard to the personal ambitions of the individual sitters. Most certainly there must be no spirit of "competition" among the sitters in the circle as this will cause a state of undesirable vibrations that could quickly bring to end the session.

The Personnel of the Circle

The personal composition of the spiritualistic circle is a very important matter, and those entering into circle work should pay careful attention to the personal and psychical character of those composing the circle; and it may be added here that such work requires very nice powers of discrimination, and a great degree of tact, in order to preserve the proper character of the circle, and at the same time to avoid wounding the pride of those who are to be rejected. Regarding the character of those composing the circle, the following statement of a practical medium will be found of importance.

"There are some people who are so sensitive that they should not sit in circles, because they are liable to become charged with the psychic emanations from, and dominated by the expectancy of, the sitters, but who are not influenced by spirit power to any great extent. Or probably there may be 'cross magnetism,' that is to say the inharmonious magnetism of different members who are antagonistic to each other. Some sitters may be sarcastic, merely curious, or selfish, or mercenary, or not over clean, sober or scrupulous, and all such surroundings act and react upon the highly sensitive organization of the undeveloped medium, and, above all, provide conditions favorable for the manifestations of mischievous or malicious spirits, unless the medium is sufficiently developed, or is protected by wise spirits powerful enough to resist or control such influences. Like attracts like, as a general rule; but there are exceptions to this, as to most rules, as, for instance, where unfortunate or unhappy spirits are permitted to manifest, and are even brought to the séance by other and more experienced spirit people, so that they may be helped. The influence of the sitters in molding the conditions is too little realized. If they introduce an atmosphere of suspicion, doubt, distrust, or detraction, they break the continuity of the flow of psychic energy that has to be employed. By thus severing the current and dissipating the power, they mar the conditions essential to success; and, as all such disturbances of necessity center upon and injuriously affect the sensitive medium, they render soul-satisfying and uplifting communion impossible. To all sitters, we would say, 'You get to a very great extent what you make conditions for, therefore open the doors of the heavens by love and purity.'"

Changing the Sitters

Changes in the membership of a circle is sometimes found to be quite beneficial. If a circle meets night after night with the same membership, but without obtaining any perceptible results, then it may be well to consider the desirability of adding some new elements to the membership in the hope of improving the conditions. Sometimes the addition of a new sitter of the right physical and psychical temperament works a most remarkable improvement, and in many of such cases noteworthy phenomena are then produced almost from the time of the change. We have seen circles in which the condition of non-success was changed in a few moments to one of great and marked success by the introduction of a new element among the sitters.

Adding a Medium

Sometimes there may result certain physical phenomena such as table tippings and movements of furniture, in cases in which there is a sufficient amount of psychic force generated among the sitters; but in such cases there may be an absolute failure to produce some of the higher forms of mediumistic phenomena, 193such as, for instance, clear spirit messages by raps or otherwise, the failure being caused by the fact that the circle did not include in its membership any person of sufficiently developed mediumistic powers to be considered a "medium." In such cases the introduction into the circle of a person possessing fairly developed mediumistic powers of the higher order may change the condition of affairs at once, and almost immediately the higher manifestations may present themselves. In such cases the soil is richly fertilized and highly cultivated, and all that has been lacking is the strong, vigorous seed of true mediumship. In such cases when a true medium is discovered by means of his or her introduction into the circle (for such discovery is often made in this way), it may be well for the circle afterwards to devote itself to the development of that particular medium. And it must not be forgotten that such development of the particular medium frequently also results in the development of the other members sitting in the circle.

Reasons for Changes

In cases in which the spirits suggest changes in the order of sitting of the members of the circle, or suggest other changes in the personnel of the circle, such suggestions should be heeded, and those who are asked to withdraw from the table should not feel hurt or offended, for there is usually nothing personal in the matter, and no personal reflection intended by the spirits; the whole matter is one connected with psychical or magnetic requirements, and all should so accept it.

A writer on this subject has well said: "If you are requested, either by the controlling intelligence or by the manager of the circle, to take another place, or even if your room is desired for some unknown cause, do not get angry and create a disturbance, but get with those with whom you are in spiritual harmony and try it again. All who have succeeded have passed through great trials and failures, and when success is gained, think of what you have gained. A knowledge of immortality, possibly, or you have assisted in producing an instrument through which proofs of immortality may be given."

Psychic Attunement

One of the most common faults of the sitters at a circle is to become unduly impatient, and to try to force matters to a clear manifestation of phenomena almost from the moment of the start. This is all wrong, and is frequently the cause of many failures to obtain the higher phases of mediumistic phenomena. Sitters should remember this important point, i.e., that the first requisite of the circle should be to secure perfect and free communication and flow of spiritual power—after this the more elaborate phases of phenomena may be obtained with comparative ease.

One should hold in mind the illustration of a great wireless telegraph system, in which the sending and receiving instruments have not as yet been placed in perfect attunement. In such a case it is of course necessary for the two respective sets of instruments to be adjusted so that they may be in perfect attunement with each other; and until this is accomplished, there can be messages sent or received properly—certainly none received in this way. If this idea be held in mind, their circle will probably secure the psychic attunement in a much shorter time than otherwise.

Pre-Test Manifestations

Do not be in too much of a hurry to obtain "test" messages. Let the communications flow on in a somewhat rambling manner at first, until the lines of communication are fully and firmly established, and then you may begin to think about asking test questions of the spirits in order to establish their identity. A writer says on this point: "Should table movements occur, or raps be heard, let them go on for a little. Do not ask test questions just yet. Request repetitions, or ask for them to be clearer or louder, so that they may be sharp and decisive. You may also ask for a certain number of movements or raps. After that, you may proceed to ask questions as to whether the circle is sitting in the best arrangement for success. If changes are desired, these should be made as suggested. It may happen that one or more of the sitters may be requested to change places, or to withdraw from the table altogether. In such a case the sitter should not take umbrage for it merely means that their psychical conditions do not blend with those of the rest of the circle."

Premature Tests

Regarding the matter of premature tests, or unreasonable demands, the same writer further says: "Remember that the first requisite is to establish the channel of communication; and all personal questions as to who and what the spirit is should be reserved until the initial difficulties are overcome. It is at first most probable that the spirit operators will not be fully aware just what effect they are producing, and the mind of the medium may not as yet be sufficiently passive, in fact it may be in a sort of state of protest against being acted upon in this particular way; accordingly, it is extremely unwise to attempt to obtain responses to test questions or to secure evidences of the identity of the spirit under these imperfect conditions.

"Many mediums and inquirers have been deterred from further development or investigation because such questions have been prematurely put and the answers pressed for, with the result that confusing and contradictory responses were given, and the conclusion was hastily drawn that it was all fraud, delusion, of the devil. Nevertheless, these sorts of hasty conclusions should be avoided as well as all types of negative thinking. The state of one's mind is extremely important during these sessions."

Forcing Tests

Another writer has said on this point: "I then, in my anxiety, made a mistake which anxious inquirers sometimes make. I wanted more—I pressed for another test, forgetting the difficulties of mediumship, and the supreme effort which must have been made to give me what I had obtained. And this resulted in failure after remarkable tests had been given." Another writer, commenting upon the last quoted statement, says: "This is exactly how mediums are used; they give test after test, not to satisfy, but only to produce the desire for more. Then when the power is weakened, comes the inability—or 'fraud,' as the imperfection in mediumship is often called. This will be the case until they can have the only condition which is suitable for spiritual communion—passive trust and confidence. Real tests cannot come when sought with materialistic conditions. The tests come unsought, unasked for."

Spirit Directions

Another point which should be borne in mind by the sitters in the circle is that the spirits should be consulted as to just what they wish to manifest at the séance. They should be asked to state plainly just what order of phenomena they desire to manifest and demonstrate, and just what they wish the circle to do in order to create the best conditions for the manifestation. And it will be found advisable to heed the wishes and instructions of the spirits in such cases, and to conform as far as possible with the same. In this way the intelligent co-operation of spirits and the circle may be obtained and the most desirable results be obtained. However, there is a limit to this acceptance and course, and in no case should the limits of reasonableness be exceeded in the matter. As a writer has well said: "It may happen that the conditions asked for by the communicating intelligence may seem to be ludicrous or impracticable; and in such case representations to that effect should be made to the spirit, and if such instructions are persisted in, except where, through long association, confidence is felt in the spirit, or very clear evidence of knowledge has been manifested, the medium and sitters, exercising their own reasoning powers, should quietly and firmly decline to do what is asked of them, and some other course should be suggested. We do not advise either medium or sitters to blindly accept or follow what is given to or through them. Reason should ever reign, but even reason will show that in experimental work it is sometimes advisable to tentatively adopt and follow some course that may not, at first sight, appear quite reasonable."

Questioning the Spirits

After a satisfactory arrangement of the sitters is obtained, and the table tiltings or rappings have assumed a clear, definite character, then the sitters may proceed to ascertain the identity of the spirit seeking to communicate to the circle; or else to ascertain whether the spirit wishes to deliver a message directed specially to some particular one of the sitters. In the latter case, the person indicated should prepare to question the spirit direct, either verbally or else silently and mentally. In either case the question should be stated clearly and to the point, so that the spirit may give a simple definite answer. Questions which may be answered by a simple "Yes" or "No" are of course preferable. If the spirit agrees to move the table, or else produce raps, as the alphabet is called over letter by letter, the communication and answers may of course be given in much fuller detail. In such case the spirit may be called on to spell out its name, and to designate its relationship to any of the sitters; or even to spell out a complete message. In addressing the spirit one should pursue the same general course employed in addressing questions to a friend in the flesh; and care should be taken to address the spirit politely and in a kindly tone. Some spirits are very sensitive concerning these details, and will resent any impoliteness or discourtesy, or flippancy from strangers.

Substance and Shadow

Moreover, the earnest investigator of spiritualistic phenomena must always bear in mind that the mere production of mediumistic phenomena of the physical phase is not the real object of the investigation and sittings. These things, interesting as they may be in themselves, should be regarded as merely the incidents of the intelligent communication and reception of messages from the inhabitants of the higher planes of life and existence. The spiritualistic circle should be more than a mere "wonder shop" in which are exhibited strange and unusual physical phenomena; rather should it be regarded as the receiving end of the wireless system over which we may and do receive valuable communications from those who have passed on before us.

As a writer has said: "It is not so much that the table moves with or without contact, or that strange rappings are heard, that is of paramount importance, but that by these means of communication actual and intelligent communication can be obtained and maintained with so-called dead people; and evidences of spirit identity, as well as loving and cheering messages may be obtained in that way from loved ones who were supposed to be gone forever. This is the important point to be established beyond all peradventure."

PART IX
MEDIUMISTIC PHENOMENA

SOME students of this book who have noted in the foregoing pages certain references to the conduct of the sitters in the circle may ask themselves the question: "Why are the sitters so important, when the power is really exerted by the spirits through the medium?" In fact, such questions, often uttered in the spirit of adverse criticism, are frequently propounded by skeptics to spiritualists, and it is well that the answer should be correctly given. As a matter of fact the understanding of such answer will mean the possession of some important facts concerning the phenomena of mediumship, and without which the investigator will possibly wander far astray from the main road of truth concerning such phenomena.

The Part Played by the Sitters

All of the best authorities on the subject of spiritualism are practically agreed concerning the important part played by the sitters in the circle in all manifestations of spirit power. As J. J. Morse says: "There are three factors concerned in mediumship: (1) the spirit controlling; (2) the mental atmosphere of the medium controlled; and (3) the mental atmosphere of the people surrounding the medium." And as A. Morton has said: "The requirements for honesty on the part of mediums are equally binding upon investigators; they must have honesty of purpose if they expect to attract honest spirits."

Result of Bad Sitters

And Wallis has said: "Although the spirits may be intensely anxious to demonstrate their power, they are sometimes repelled from those whom they seek to approach by the bristling and discordant conditions of mind that prevail among the sitters, who disperse with a feeling of dissatisfaction and disappointment. If the sitters only knew it, the so-called failure was directly traceable to the destructive thought-atmosphere with which they surround themselves and the medium. Too frequently they do not prepare themselves for 'the hour's communion with the dead,' and their mental attitude is anything but conductive to success. They do not put away the thronging thoughts, anxieties, and worries of their busy lives, but carry them right into the séance chamber, yet expect good spiritual results. Both sitter and medium may very easily destroy the indispensable conditions of spirit-manifestation, and the medium's honesty, not his want of growth, or of knowledge, is called in question by the investigator who knows, and perhaps cares, nothing for the occult laws he has violated, not obeyed."

Mental Atmosphere of the Medium

Likewise, it must not be forgotten that an important factor in the production of mediumistic phenomena is that which Morse, in the above quotation, has called "the mental atmosphere of the medium controlled." In many cases the spirit powers are present and ready to manifest freely, and the mental atmosphere of the sitters is likewise desirable and sympathetic, but still the manifestations are but faint, irregular, and generally unsatisfying—the weak link of the chain being found in the mental state of the medium, and consequently in the mental atmosphere arising from the same. Such undesirable mental states and atmospheres may be said to arise principally from two general causes, as follows: (1) Desire on the part of the medium to produce sensational or brilliant results, and (2) Doubt on the part of the medium concerning the genuineness and validity of the communications. Let us consider each of these in further detail.

The Mediumistic Mind

If the medium is filled with the idea or notion of producing brilliant or sensational results, he will in all probability so disturb the placidity of the receiving surface of his mind that the latter will fail to register or record the impressions being made upon it by the spirit vibrations. It is similar to the case of a placid bosom of a deep lake which, normally, will reflect clearly and distinctly the images of the surrounding scenery cast upon it from the light waves; but which, if disturbed by strong breezes, will exhibit merely a distorted, disturbed, incomplete, and untrue reflection of the surrounding scenery cast upon its surface. A strong desire of the kind mentioned will tend to agitate and disturb the normal placid condition of the mental reflecting surface of the mediumistic mind.

Mediumistic "Stage Fright"

In the same way the placid reflecting surface of the mediumistic mind may become disturbed by the presence of fear, doubt, and distrust in the mind of the medium. It may at first seem strange that the medium should doubt the manifestations being made through his mentality, provided that he be honest and genuine. But the answer and explanation is very simple. The medium (particularly the young medium) may become panic-stricken by the thought that "perhaps this is merely the result of my own imagination or fancy, instead of spirit power," and the result will be that he will begin to halt and stumble, stammer and stutter, instead of allowing the message to flow through him uninterrupted. This is particularly true when the message is of the nature of a test of identity, and where the vocal organs of the medium are being employed in the manifestation. It occurs far more frequently than the public suppose, that the medium is stricken by stage-fright or the panic of fear, arising from the causes above given, i.e. the sudden fear that he is allowing his fanciful imagination to run away with him instead of his being under genuine control.

The Psychic Telephone System

The medium should ever strive to guard against this harmful mental state, and should open himself completely to the spirit influence, casting aside all fear and doubt, and placing all responsibility upon the controlling spirit or band of helpers. The medium should remember that he is merely the "medium" or psychic telephone system, and is not an active party to the process of spirit communication. He should, therefore, never either unduly strive to please, nor be fearful or distrustful concerning the validity of the manifestation being made through him. Let the spirits attend to their end of the line, and the sitters to the other end—the medium is on neither end of the line, but is the line itself.

Interrupted Communications

It should not be forgotten, in this connection, that the spirits have their own difficulties to contend with. In the current slang phrase, they "have troubles of their own" to overcome in the production of mediumistic phenomena. Not only does the spirit wishing to communicate have to draw sufficient psychic power from the medium and the sitters, not only has he to scientifically adjust the apparatus at the sending end of the psychic telephonic line, but he has also to be sure that he is actually communicating the message so that it may be received by the sitters. In such cases the spirit is placed in a position similar to that of a person at one end of a telephone line, who after had an answer to his opening "Hello!" talks away, thinking that the person at the other end is hearing every word he utters, perfectly unconscious that the communication has been interrupted from some cause or other common to telephone lines. How often do we, in our telephone conversations, interrupt our flow of talk to anxiously inquire, "Are you still there?" or "Do you hear me?"

Some Difficulties of the Spirits

A writer on the subject has well said regarding this difficulty on the part of the communicating spirit: "Spirits have many difficulties to overcome." On one occasion, a medium felt the influence of an arisen friend very strongly. It was accompanied by an intense desire to speak, and yet the medium was unable to give utterance to that which the spirit wished to have said. In answer to an inquiry that was subsequently made as to why the spirit had been unable to communicate with his dear ones, one of the familiar controls of the medium explained that he thought that he had actually spoken. His feeling of nearness to them was so vivid, and his wish to express himself through the lips of the medium had been so intense, that it was only after he had ceased his efforts to control that he realized that he had only thought and intended, but had not succeeded in compelling the sensitive to utter his message. This will perhaps explain why mediums sometimes rise to their feet and act as if they were about to speak, but get no further—they do not receive the impression, or the right mental impulse; they feel as if they could speak and yet they have nothing to say. At such times a few words of sympathy and inquiry from the conductor of the circle may assist the control to realize the situation and succeed in his endeavors to communicate.

Difficulties Overcome

"Even on this side, when we send telegraphic messages or use the telephone, mistakes and misunderstandings are by no means uncommon occurrences, and our letters sometimes create an impression in the mind of the reader which we did not intend to convey. Is it any wonder, then, that messages from the other side are imperfectly impressed upon, and incorrectly rendered by, the medium? Most persons who have attempted to transfer thoughts to mesmerized sensitives have realized that general ideas can be transmitted much more easily than names, dates, or specific words can be impressed upon or expressed by the subject. The wonder is, not that so few names, ages, and special details are given by spirits to and through mediums, but that, considering all the attendant circumstances, so many 'test' messages are continually being given, both privately and in public."

The Psychic Triangle

In considering the question of the requisites of the mediumistic circle, the student should remember always that there is a psychic triangle in all such circles, viz., a triangle of which the spirit constitutes one side, the medium a second side, and the sitters a third side. And it is essential that a harmony and sympathy between all three sides of the triangle should be preserved and maintained. Therefore, sitters at the circle should endeavor to do their part in producing and maintaining such harmony with both the medium, the spirits, and finally with each other—and this last is not the least, by any means. Unless there be at least a very fair degree of harmony between the several members constituting the

225

circle, there will be something important lacking in their harmony of the circle as a whole toward the other two sides of the psychical triangle.

Harmonious Relationship

The sitters composing the circle should always remember that mutual harmony is a most important factor contributing to the success of the manifestations sought to be secured. Accordingly, each sitter should strive to bring himself or herself into a sympathetic and harmonious relationship with each and every other sitter, so far as is possible. To accomplish this result the sitters should endeavor, so far as is possible, to lay aside their respective prejudices, jealousies, and differences of opinion. These incidents of their personality should be left, together with their hats and outer wraps, in the outer hall of the house in which the séance is held. Differences of religion, politics, race and creed, all should be cast aside at least temporarily, in order that the greatest amount of harmony should be manifested by the group. It is difficult to maintain harmony during these types of sessions because of the strong emotions that are generated.

A safe rule to follow is this: seek to find the largest number of points of mutual agreement, and to set aside all the rest of the items of personal tastes, customs and habits of feeling and thought. Dwell together on the plane of common agreement, shutting out the planes of respective disagreements. In this connection we should state that the customary attitude of cold reserve, blended and colored by suspicion, which too often is found between comparative strangers, is far from being helpful in producing the best conditions for the séance. For the time being, at least, the sitters should try to remember that they are all members of one great human family, and united by the bonds of common origin and nature.

The Discordant Note

A writer recites an incident in a circle which he once attended, which so thoroughly illustrates the point just made, that we think it worthwhile to reproduce it here. He says: "On one occasion in particular, we had a remarkable illustration of the detrimental influence of one or two sitters. It occurred at a séance at which a number of mediums were present, and, under ordinary circumstances, successful results would have been practically certain; but this was not an ordinary séance—at least, not in the opinion of one lady who apparently imagined that she had been invited to discover fraud, and that the rest of us were suspicious characters. Up to the moment of her appearance in the circle we were a happy family of sociable folk, and enjoyed a very pleasant season of conversational interchange. When, however, the said lady, accompanied by a friend, joined the company, there was a silence that could be felt. The social temperature fell rapidly— people visibly stiffened and became constrained. The two ladies appeared to feel afraid to speak lest they should say anything that might be used by the mediums, and spoke in monosyllables. Sitting bolt upright, grim and silent, they drew up to the table, and when the phenomena began they displayed no signs of interest. Their 'detective' attitude was so objectionable that even those who had endeavored to thaw out these self-constituted Sherlock Holmeses, gave up the attempt, and, in consequence, what had promised to be a really enjoyable evening, proved one of the most uncomfortable it has been our lot to experience."

Antagonistic Elements

Another incident of the kind is related by a writer, as follows: "On one occasion, when some experiments were being made by a medium, under control, in the direction of psychometry and clairvoyance, a lady expressed a desire to be the subject for delineation. After one or two efforts the medium exclaimed, 'I am very sorry, but for some reason I am quite unable to get anything from you, or for you.' Shortly afterwards the lady in question remarked to one of the sitters, 'I knew he would not be able to give me anything. That is the third medium that I have knocked out.' The failure to obtain results under such impossible conditions is a proof of the genuine psychic nature of the powers of the mediums. If they were pretenders they would succeed in doing something under any circumstances and in spite of such adverse psychic conditions." While we are far from holding that the sitters in a circle should lay aside all ordinary caution and good judgment, and instead to assume the mental attitude of utter and unquestioning credulity and acceptance, we do positively declare that the mental state of preconceived distrust and suspicion is often almost fatal to the production and demonstration of the highest manifestations of spirit phenomena.

The Open Mind

The proper mental state of the scientific investigator of spiritualistic phenomena is that of "the open mind." The sitters should endeavor to lay aside all prejudices and preconceived conceptions, and in place thereof should endeavor to hold a fair, impartial mental attitude—and this accompanied by a desire to have the manifestations proceed naturally, freely and fully. The results should be sympathetically awaited and received, and the judgment of careful reasoning withheld until afterward when the whole proceedings may be recalled and considered in the light of cold reason.

One has but to consider the extremely sensitive psychical condition of the mentality of the medium, and the nicely balanced mental atmosphere of the circle, to realize how easily this sensitiveness may be affected, and the nice balance be disturbed, by the projection of strong mental waves of distrust, suspicion, and antagonism into the atmosphere of the circle. The attitude of the intelligent scientific investigator should be that of a calm and observant soul. Such an investigator should have what Sir William Crookes once called "a mind to let," i.e., a mind from which all prejudices and preconceived theories and notions have been ejected for the time being, and into which Truth, from any source, should always be welcomed as a tenant. Instead of seeking to throw obstacles in the way of the medium, one should endeavor to assist by mental attitude and demeanor, and by observance of the necessary conditions, in the production of the spirit manifestations and in the demonstration of spirit identity.

Spirits and the Sense of Humor

It is not necessary for the sitters to assume an attitude of preternatural gravity and solemnity. Instead, they should be natural and cheerful, though of course not flippant or trifling, or indulging in an exhibition of the cheap remarks which by so many is mistaken for wit. The sense of humor, however, need not be thrown aside or discarded, for as all investigators know many of the spirit visitors have a very highly developed sense of humor, and sometimes even go so far as to seemingly endeavor to shock some of the melancholy, over-serious, "prunes and prism" type of sitters. As a writer well says: "Spirits are human still, and a good, breezy laugh, a hearty, joyous, kindly sympathetic disposition, goes a long way to open the avenues by which they can approach us." Another has said: "Experience has taught that the spiritual circle should be presided over by 'a pure heart and a strong head'—to which qualities might well be added a well-ordered development of the sense of humor, for the absence of humor often tends to make philosophy grotesquely ill-proportioned."

Rhythmic Harmony

The manifestation of rhythmic harmony often materially aids in the generation of psychic power, and the consequent production of advantageous conditions at the circle. Many circles are opened by having the several sitters indulge in harmonious rhythmic breathing for a few minutes—all breathing in unison—in order to produce this condition of rhythm. Those who have never practiced this unison of rhythmic breathing will be surprised at the consciousness of psychical harmony which may be produced in this way among a number of persons gathered together in a circle.

This principle of rhythm is what is really involved in the call of many spirits for singing at the beginning of a séance. In singing there is a certain unison and rhythm unconsciously observed, and it is this rather than the air or words of the songs which produces the desire conditions. A writer states that upon one occasion a manifesting spirit said: "It isn't noise that I want; it's harmony! If you cannot sing, you can at least count out loud, and count altogether—that may give us the right vibrations." That spirit had the right idea, and one which it would be well for all sitters to remember and put into effect. Vibration is the secret of all things, and rhythm is the measure and spirit of all vibrations; therefore, the very harmony of a circle may be said to be rhythmic. There is a great truth involved in these statements, and you will do well to ponder over them.

Retarding Factors

It should be almost unnecessary to state that haste, hurry and impatience are retarding factors in a spiritualistic séance; but, alas, too many persons seem to be totally unaware of this important fact. We call your attention to the following remarks concerning this point, the same having been made by a writer on the subject who himself is a medium of extended experience. He says: "Impatience and anxiety are disintegrating mental conditions. People who are all the time looking at their watches and thinking, 'Oh! I wish they would hurry up.' 'Oh! do be quick, don't keep us here all night, we shall surely miss our train,' etc., are disturbers of the peace, and break the conditions which require harmony and repose. 'We have found out that we cannot hurry them,' said a lady who had enjoyed much experience in circles; and consequently, when you are sitting for different phenomena, you need to have plenty of time and be prepared to sit good humoredly for hours, if need be, to see it through; and then results are likely to speedily ensue; whereas the more you try to hurry, the more anxious you become, the less likelihood is there that you will secure results at all. You can surely realize that hurry, impatience, anxiety, intense expectancy, fear and suspicion must of necessity disturb the conditions and prove inimical to the efforts of the spirit operators to present clear and convincing demonstrations of their power and identity."

Reasonable Demands of Spirits

In the above stated instance, and others similar to it, it at first seems as if the spirits were over particular, and "finicky" about the conditions, but a little careful thought will show you that this is not the real state of affairs at all. The spirits are not "finicky," but are merely desirous of securing the conditions necessary to a successful manifestation, and all their efforts are bent toward that end. Also, it must be considered that there is a "natural law" that comes in play here. Things will work only a certain way. This and this alone, is the cause of their so-called "finickiness." Surely they are justified in this—would not any and all of us feel the same way if we were trying to establish communications with another plane, where such communication largely dependent upon the production and maintenance of certain conditions? I think so.

Harmonious Conditions

It is not an easy task to give specific directions for development of mediumistic power for the guidance of one who is desirous of unfolding such powers after they have first manifested their presence in him. In fact, as many of the best authorities on the subject agree, it is practically impossible to lay out a course of cut-and-dried directions of this kind. This arises logically from the conditions present in such cases, and from the special circumstances surrounding the subject of mediumship. In fact, it may be broadly stated that at the beginning the medium can do but little in the direction of such development, other than to present harmonious conditions through which the spirits may be able to manifest their presence and their power.

The Channel of Communication

It must be always remembered that the medium is not the active agent in the production of mediumistic phenomena—he is not called to do anything except to passively act as the medium or channel of communication between the two planes of existence. He is always the intermediary between the two planes, and is not the active agent on either plane. The active agents are the spirits on the one plane, and the sitters in the circle on the other plane. The sitters must supply much of the actual operative power from the one plane, and the spirits must do all of the communication from the other plane. The medium serves to connect the two opposite ends of the psychic telephone system so that the messages may pass through and over the mediumistic channel, secure and maintain the best psychic conditions.o

It must not be supposed for a moment that every spirit is possessed of the necessary knowledge enabling it to communicate easily through a medium, or even to develop the medium so that he may become an efficient channel of communication. Spirits are

232

frequently found to be sadly deficient in such knowledge and experience, and the development of the medium as well as the production of satisfactory phenomena, suffer from this lack. The spirits who seek to use a medium may or may not be fitted for such task. Many spirits are utterly unable to properly develop a medium; some fail by reason of their lack of knowledge, and others fail because of their lack of special aptitude for the task.

A writer on this subject well says regarding this particular point: "Some spirits may lack both knowledge and aptitude; others may have the knowledge, but yet fail from want of the power to control. They may be able to affect one mediumistic person and not another. Likewise, they may be able to use a sensitive medium for one phase of mediumship, and yet be unable to succeed in any other direction. A spirit may be in such conditions that he can produce good physical phenomena; he may, however, try to do so through a sensitive who is fitted only for trance or clairvoyant mediumship, but who does not possess the quality or psychic force for sensuous manifestations. A medium who is naturally qualified for physical demonstrations may persist in desiring trance or inspirational mediumship, and be determined to become a speaker or nothing.

Disturbing Elements

"Frequently at the outset both spirits and sitters are ignorant of their powers, of the conditions necessary for success, and the association that exists between them being affectional rather than intellectual or spiritual, they have to grope their way towards each other. It follows, therefore, that experiments have to be made on both sides. Sitters and young mediums often spoil the séances by over-anxiety. There would not be half so much heard of 'evil spirits' (so-called) if more regard were paid to the necessity of maintaining a calm, patient, and serene frame of mind. Some people become excited as soon as phenomena commences; mediums not infrequently get nervous or timid when they feel that they are being affected, and, although they desire to be controlled, they are afraid to submit to the influences when they are likely to lose consciousness. All these are disturbing elements, and naturally interfere with the flow of the forces that are to be utilized, and prevent the success that is desired. A spirit without any very definite purpose, finding himself in the presence of a mediumistic person, may seek to influence him, and spasmodic actions may result. Unless the control should soon give evidence of clear thought and definite purpose, he should be requested, in a kindly and courteous manner, to seek the assistance of some spirit who understands the methods to be employed, and induce him to exert his power for the benefit of the medium and the circle."

Impersonation Mediumship

One of the most interesting phases of mediumship, and the one perhaps most sought after by earnest seekers of the truth concerning those who have passed over to a higher plane of existence, is that commonly known as "impersonation mediumship," or perhaps "impersonating test mediumship," in which the vocal organs of the medium are employed by the communicating spirit in order to speak directly to those in the circle, or to the visiting friend of the discarnate spirit who comes into the presence of the medium. Many mediums devote their entire time and attention to this phase of mediumship, and place themselves at the service of those on the earth plane who wish to converse directly with their spirit friends or relatives who have passed on. This is by far the most satisfying phase of mediumship to those on the earth plane who are thus enabled to receive communications, and perhaps even direct answers to specific questions made to them.

The most convincing evidences of the identity of the communicating spirit are also obtained through this particular form of mediumship. And this affording of comfort to those still on the earth plane is one of the most satisfying features of mediumship, and one which will do more than aught else to reconcile the medium to annoyances and to the personal sacrifices so often made by the medium.

The True Purpose of Mediumship

A writer has well given to mediums the following inspiring message concerning the nature, purpose and aims of their work: "The modes of spirit manifestation are many, the phases wonderfully varied, but, like a golden cord running through them all, there is a distinct purpose of bringing to those on earth the glad tidings and proof positive of continued conscious personal experience in the life after death. The process of psychic development is usually slow, and the medium will be likely to grow disheartened; but by looking back over the ground already traversed, and by comparing the faint efforts made at the commencement with the later and fuller indications of spirit power, he should feel encouraged, and proceed with renewed vigor."

Gradual Development

The best authorities constantly impress upon young mediums the fact that they should develop their mediumistic powers to a considerable degree before they venture to give public séances or exhibitions of their power. As Dr. Dean Clarke well says: "Novices in mediumship have no business to assume obligations they are not fully qualified to fulfill. Let them take the counsel metaphorically given by Jesus, to 'tarry in Jerusalem till their beards are grown.'" They should by all means wait until the spirits are strong enough to control and guard them from the meddlesome interferences of other persons, both those in the flesh and those out of it. Many spirits will overwork the medium, and the latter not knowing enough to protect himself will often suffer by reason thereof. On the other hand, young mediums often yield to the importunities of friends and other sitters, and will try to oblige and satisfy them, even often at the expense of their own powers and forces.

Public Séances

A writer, himself a successful medium, gives the following good advice to young mediums: "I strongly advise all mediums to wait and serve out their apprenticeship thoroughly before they undertake to sit for skeptics or perform public work, either as test, impersonating, speaking, seeing, or healing mediums; and the best place to secure the necessary experience, training and unfolding is in the home circle. After a certain stage has been reached, however, the medium who has been used for impersonations will in all probability begin to display the powers of clairvoyance and to receive vivid impressions. Then will come, or they will be accompanied by, the efforts of the spirits to pass beyond the purely personal and limited forms of expression associated with the affectionate messages and greetings, to the consideration and explanation of the conditions and experiences of life on the other side. Spirits who can teach and give more sequential and sustained addresses will in all likelihood assume control, and under such conditions it will be found necessary to enlarge the circle and introduce fresh sitters. The clairvoyant, or psychometrist, needs new subjects with whom to experiment, and the speaking medium requires an audience to listen to his discourses, so that the next step beyond the small private circle may well be a semi-public one, or an 'after circle' such as is frequently held at the close of the public Sunday services in many towns, at which mediums who have reached this stage are afforded the opportunities they need.

Home Circle Development

"Around the family table, where those who are united in affection meet to hold joyous communion with their spirit friends, where the blended desire ascends to the spiritual plane, and becomes the potent magnetic attraction, by which those friends can establish harmonious relations with the sitters—in such a circle and under such conditions even a weak degree of mediumistic responsiveness to the outpouring from the spirit side will become intensified and exalted, until rhythmic vibrations are established and thought and emotion will readily pass from one to another, and all will be attuned.

"The best method of cultivation is to regard the mediumistic sensitiveness as a natural and desirable quality, to be evolved by training and experiments, under the direction of the reason and the conscience. In this manner the tribunal which decides the conduct of life is ever present, and no matter what influences are brought to bear on the sensitive he remains steadfast, realizing that the responsibility for use or abuse rests upon himself."

Undue Prolongation of Séances

There is a great temptation to young mediums to allow their enthusiasm, and desire to aid in demonstrating spiritualistic phenomena, to cause them to prolong their séances far beyond the limits which prudence and regard for the medium's physical well-being would dictate. There is a certain stimulation and excitement arising from the manifestation of phenomena through the medium, and this in itself is helpful rather than hurtful—a tonic rather than a depressant; but like all other forms of overindulgence, and excessive yielding to this excitement tends to bring on a reaction and a swing to the opposite emotional extreme, and the medium suffers thereby in many cases.

There comes a time in all séances when the high-water mark of psychic power is reached, and this is a good time for the medium to bring the séance to a close—in fact, experienced mediums do precisely this very thing at this particular time. But this point once passed, there is experienced a peculiar weakening and depressing feeling, this often being accompanied by a physical weariness and a feeling of chilliness in the extremities, or even a slight chilly feeling over the whole body. When these feelings are experienced, the medium should remember that the limit of reason has been passed, and he should bring matters to a close without further loss of time.

Experienced spirits will usually detect the approach of the reaction time, and will, themselves, bring the séance to a close, independent of any action on the part of the medium. But when the spirits are not experienced, they fail to notice this, or even may become careless about such things in their desire to communicate to the circle. In the latter cases, the medium must take care of himself.

A mediumistic writer gives the following advice on this subject to young mediums: "Never forget that your nerve-vital energy is used and expended in the exercise of your mediumship, and that the supply is limited, hence the necessity for care and moderation. Too frequent, prolonged, or discordant séances; inharmonious conditions and sittings, when you are already jaded and exhausted, are therefore to be avoided. If you make excessive demands upon your energies, nervous prostrations and derangements are an almost inevitable consequence. It is not the use of mediumship, but its abuse that is dangerous—perversion and excess are as injurious in this direction as they are in others, whereas temperate and healthful exercises are strengthening and exhilarating. If you feel 'run down,' decline to act. If you feel that the circle is inharmonious, or that the sitters are depleted and exacting, refuse to sit. If you feel that you are tired, and feel weary and debilitated on the day following your séances, you may be sure that you are sitting too long, or that you require the help of a larger circle of congenial friends to supply the requisite psychic force for your further development."

Self-Protection for Mediums

Another writer says on this subject: "Mediumship occasionally acts in such a manner that it becomes a stimulant to every organ and function of the system, and the individual becomes excited, nervous, and irritable; hence, the greater the acceleration of physiological functions as the result of psychical influences upon the human body, the more need of caution and restraint in every department of physiological life." But it must not be understood that the proper practice of mediumship is harmful and not conducive to good health. On the contrary, as a writer has said: "We consider the highest degree of physical health perfectly compatible with the best manifestation of mediumship." Another writer has well said: "If you are not robust enough, if you have not sufficient knowledge and self-mastery to use your will and maintain control over your psychic self; if you are unable to guard against the adverse emanations or the drawing power of others, you had better take lessons in concentration and psychic self-protection; and until you understand the art of self-possession, refrain from attempting to cultivate your sensitiveness. It will never do for you to be 'too sensitive'—be natural, sensible, and strong."

Danger in Indiscriminate Magnetizing

Another point against which the medium should guard himself, is that of allowing others, indiscriminately, to "magnetize" him to "aid his development" or to "increase his power." Mediums, particularly while in the psychic condition, are very sensitive and susceptible to outside mental influences. And for this reason they should be particularly on guard against allowing themselves to be "magnetized" or influenced psychically by persons of whom they know nothing. Otherwise, the medium not only places himself under subjection to the mentality and emotionality of strangers and undesirable persons, just as would a hypnotic subject if he placed himself under the control of such persons. Moreover, in the case of the medium, there is a danger of his being so influenced in this way that thereafter he may attract to himself a class of undesirable spirit influences who would otherwise never have come into his psychic aura or world. We call attention to the following advice on this point given by an experienced mediumistic writer: "No sensible person should surrender himself to the magnetic influence of a human being of whom he knew nothing; he should need to know and have confidence in him before doing so; yet we find many who, impelled by a desire to be a medium, without understanding how much the word implies, sit down and invite any magnetizer who comes along to experiment upon him. Under such circumstances, nothing but a high motive and a pure purpose will protect them from the operations of unwise or mischievous intelligences.

"As well might they go and sit in a public place with their eyes blindfolded, and with an inscription on their breasts, 'Who will come and magnetize me?' Mesmeric influence from an experienced operator, for the purpose of inducing susceptibility, is sometimes helpful to a sensitive. If the mesmerist can put you in the trance condition and then hand you over to trustworthy spirits to control you, well and good. In the same way, mesmeric passes may be helpful in the liberation of your clairvoyant powers. The operator may succeed in throwing you into the deep trance state, in which you may travel or become clairvoyant, but we would not recommend you to submit to mesmeric influence or hypnotic suggestions from anyone, unless you know that he is experienced and a thoroughly honorable and trustworthy individual. In circles for development one member is frequently impressed, or controlled to make magnetic passes over another to aid in his unfoldment; and if such a thing should happen to you, and the influence is congenial, there need be no objection raised by you; but beware of those people who claim to be able, by mesmerism, to develop you into a medium in a given period of time."

Mediumistic Auto-Suggestion

Other authorities have pointed out the fact that in some cases hypnotism has resulted in a sort of pseudo-mediumship, or bogus mediumship, in which the control is not that of a real spirit, but is merely the result of the suggestion of the hypnotizer, or else the auto-suggestion of the would-be medium himself. A writer on the subject has said of this: "In too many cases, only the power of auto-hypnotism is manifested, and we have obsession, fraud and folly as the result. There is one sure method of detecting the auto-hypnotic trance, and showing the difference between that and the genuine spirit trance. Any competent magnetist or hypnotist can throw off the spell in all cases of self-induced trance, unless it has reached the condition of complete catalepsy. But if a spirit has induced the trance and controls the medium, it will laugh at the hypnotist's efforts to restore him to the ordinary condition. The most unfortunate feature of this sorry business is that the poor subject is self-deceived, and imagines that he is a full-fledged medium; and when he has made some terrible break on the platform or elsewhere he shields himself by laying all the responsibility upon some supposed spirit guide."

"Psychic Sponges"

A writer has also called the attention of young mediums to another undesirable class of psychic hangers-on at séances, as follows: "There are some people who, when they sit in a circle, are extremely helpful, and give off the right kind of force that readily blends with that of the sensitive; but there are others who draw upon and appropriate the psychic forces which are needed by the medium, or by the spirits through the medium. While they mean well, enjoy the séances, and feel 'so much better' after them, the success of the circle is endangered so far as the object for which it was formed is concerned. Such persons are 'psychic sponges,' and should be requested to sit outside the circle, or be asked kindly to refrain from attending."

Finally, the young medium should understand the true nature of the spirits, and just how far he may be safely guided by their advice and wishes. The instructions given by an intelligent spirit of good character may be safely followed as a rule, but the character and general intelligence of a particular spirit must first be ascertained through acquaintance with him. Until the character of a spirit has been fully established, and his claim to intelligence well supported by his messages, the medium will do well to rely on his or her own good judgment and intuition. As a writer has well said: "The medium must keep a level head and proceed cautiously. He should never allow any spirit, in or out of the body, to usurp his right of private judgment or exercise any undue authority over him. Eternal vigilance is the price of liberty; you must use your own discretion and try the spirits before you trust to them."

Spirits Are Still Human Beings

Many persons seem to be under the impression that because a spirit happens to have passed out of the body he will, of necessity, know the truth about every subject in the range of human thought, and can make no mistakes, and can always work miracles. But this is a grave mistake; it should always be remembered that a discarnate spirit is as much a human being as is an incarnate spirit such as yourself; and not any better or worse, on the average, than yourself or other incarnate spirits.

One needs but to remember that all sorts and conditions of people are constantly passing out on to the spirit plane, and that, at least for some time, they continue to be practically the same kind of persons that they were on the earth plane. This being so, it will be seen that it would be very unwise to surrender oneself indiscriminately to each and every kind of spirit who happens to manifest his presence at a séance.

Persons in the flesh should talk and reason with those out of the flesh just as they would were the latter still on the earth-plane of life. A writer well says: "In a developing circle many things can be tolerated, because both sides are experimenting and 'feeling their way towards each other,' and it is difficult at first to know just what is necessary or possible. But it is a safe rule to follow for one to refuse to be dictated to by the spirits and to decline to go on blindly."

Beware of Domineering Spirits

A writer has given the following good advice to young mediums, which such will do well to heed: "Do not always be ready to be controlled, or to drop into a trance just because you 'feel the influence,' and 'a spirit wants to say something,' or to oblige injudicious friends who 'wish you would let him come.' Many people are very inconsiderate, and although they do not say so, they think (and the sensitive feels their thought) 'I do wish he would go under control and tell me something.'

You should decline to be controlled except at the times when you voluntarily and with set purpose lay yourself open to the influence of the spirits, in a properly constituted circle, or when you are prepared for it. If the spirits cause you to do foolish or ridiculous things, gently but firmly refuse to again submit. Do not be induced to yield by promise of future greatness and success. Not a few people have had their vanity tickled and their ambitions aroused by the flattery of crafty and domineering spirits, and in consequence they have been misled into doing and saying very absurd and foolish things."

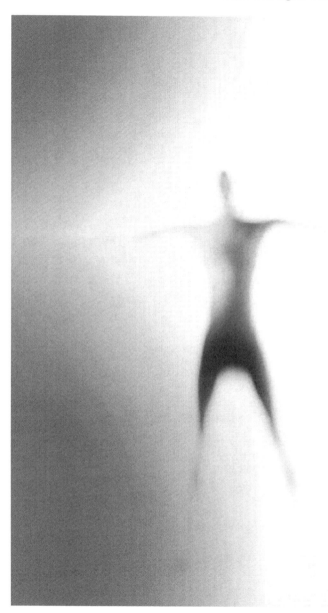

It should always be remembered that a discarnate spirit is as much a human being as is an incarnate spirit such as yourself; and not any better or worse, on the average, than yourself or other incarnate spirits.

PART X
EXPERIENCES IN THE CIRCLE

WHEN a circle of sensitive people has been formed, and the necessary preliminaries of the first sitting have been completed, it is not at all infrequent that even at the first sitting there should be more or less manifestation of spirit power. In many cases the sensitives among the sitters begin to experience a peculiar sensation in their arms and hands, the latter being placed on the table in front of them.

Signs of Spirit Presence

There will be manifested in most cases a peculiar sense of heaviness or weight in the hands on the table, and an impression that the hands are being held to the table as if by glue or other adhesive material. In the arms are manifested peculiar tingling, pricking sensations, or a "needles and pins" feeling, something akin to a gentle current of electricity passing along them. Sometimes there is experienced the sensation of a gentle cool breeze passing over the sitters—particularly over the backs of their hands. In other cases there may be a sense of numbness or partial loss of sensation, something akin to that experienced when a hand or arm "goes to sleep," as the popular phrase expresses it. In other cases there is manifested a peculiar jerking, twitching, or vibration of the hands and arms, sometimes extending to the whole body of some of the sitters. Sometimes the hand of the medium will begin to make motions as if he were trying to write, and a pencil placed in his hands may trace crude figures or attempts at letters. At this stage it will be found that the singing of hymns or similar music will tend to have a quieting, soothing, harmonizing effect.

Spirit Rappings

At the first sitting, or one shortly following after the first, it is likely that raps will be produced, and communication established in this way. In such case the leader of the circle (not the medium) should be sure to inform the spirits just what communicating code is to be used in the circle, so that there may be no misunderstanding concerning the same. In such case he should address the spirits as if there were several present, for such will most likely be the case. It must be remembered, however, that the raps will not always come from the table. They may also, for that matter, come from the wall, the ceiling, or from some of the furniture in the room. The table raps come from the top of the table or under the table. Sometimes they sound like ordinary raps, and then again they may give forth a peculiar hollow sound which is difficult to describe or to definitely locate. The appearances of these raps give positive proof that the conditions are being established more or less fully, and the success of the circle is almost sure to follow.

Table Tippings

Sometimes, however, in place of the raps being manifested by the spirit forces, there will instead be manifested that peculiar tipping of the table which was the distinguishing characteristic of early spiritualistic phenomena in the western countries. In this case the tipping of the table will proceed just as in the case of the raps, so far as the transmission of messages is concerned. That is to say, the table will tilt three times, one time, etc., in accordance with the code, just as in the case of communication by means of the raps. In addition to this, however, the table may begin to manifest strange motions; it may begin to raise itself, jump around, spin around on one leg, slide across the rooms, etc. In such cases the hands of the sitters should be kept on the table, or if they slip off they should be at once replaced thereupon. Sometimes heavy tables will manifest more activity than the lighter ones.

The Spirit Signals

When these rappings or table-tiltings begin to be manifested, all in the circle should keep cool and calm, and should refuse to become agitated or excited. If the phenomena should be apparently meaningless and disconnected, and resulting in no definite communication from the other side, do not jump to the conclusion that the meaningless rapping or senseless table tipping is the work of foolish spirits or flippant discarnate entities. On the contrary, you must remember that not only is your circle experimenting, but that the spirits on the other side are also experimenting in hopes of securing proper conditions for intelligent communications and definite messages. As we have said before, the spirits have their own troubles, as well as the sitters, and both sides are really engaged in an effort to "find each other." As a writer has said: "Remember also that you are merely experimenting, and that the spirit people are also, perhaps for the first time, trying to penetrate the veil and utilize powers and agencies of which, in all probability, they know as little as do you. So many disturbing factors exist—weather, varying psychical conditions of the sitters, agitated mental states, too great expectancy, or anxiety for successful demonstrations—that the true disposition to be maintained by the inquirer is that of the scientific student, who carefully watches what transpires, and endeavors to discover the causes of failure as well as the conditions which favor success."

Flashes of Communication

In some cases the circle will have to sit several times before the persistent though disconnected and apparently meaningless raps or table-tilts will begin to show positive signs of intelligent signaling. The same thing would probably occur were the inhabitants of the planet Mars to find themselves able to flash signals to our earth—for a long time the flashes would seem meaningless to us, until at last they would seem to manifest a definite intelligent purpose and rhythm. When this stage of the raps or table-tilts has been reached, then the leader of the circle should acquaint the spirits with the code used, and ask definite questions concerning the future conduct of the séance, the answers to which the spirits are requested to give through the signal code of raps or tilts. When these answers begin to "come through" plainly and definitely, then the séance enters a new phase.

Spirit Code Signals

In this new phase, when once entered into, the formal set procedure to be followed will be about as follows: The leader of the circle, recognizing the signs of the presence of spirits in the circle, will address them and ask them whether or not there is a spirit present who wishes to convey a message to the circle, or to any one present. Then the spirits signal back in the affirmative or the negative.

If the answer be in the affirmative, the circle leader asks the spirits to indicate by the affirmative signal when the name of the right person present is named—and he then proceeds to slowly and plainly name each person present, in succession, until the affirmative signal is received. Or, he may ask the spirits to indicate the identity of the spirit friends present, when their names are called; and he then proceeds to call over the names of the departed friends of those present, as the same are requested by the sitters or visitors to the circle. When the right name is reached, the spirits signal in the affirmative, either by raps of table-tilts, etc.

After the question-and-answer line of communication has been firmly and strongly established, more definite information may be obtained by the instruction of the system of "alphabet calling," as described in a preceding portion of this book. In this system, the letters of the alphabet are slowly and clearly called off, in succession, until the affirmative signal is given regarding the letter just called, which indicates that that letter is to be marked down as a part of the sentence. Wonderful messages have been received in this way, although the process is very slow and somewhat tedious in the case of long messages.

Ouija Boards

For a number of years, sitters at circles have found a quicker method of obtaining "letter by letter" messages by means of the "the Ouija Board," which consists of a moving "Planchette" with an indicator which moves over the letters marked on a board, the hands of the sitters (or certain of their number) being placed on the table of the "Planchette." The indicator moves over the line of letters, and indicates the letters of the message, one by one.

Ouija Boards can be found in almost every store as well as Amazon.com. They are a valuable adjunct to any spiritualistic circle with public attention being strongly directed to this manner of obtaining spirit communications. The Ouija Board has received a lot of bad press over the years by those who say that using the boards is a gateway to evil spirits, demons and even Satan himself. However, by properly preparing before a session with meditation and prayer, there is no reason to fear using the Ouija Board. Any session to contact spirits can draw unwanted attention from less than friendly entities. Caution is always the best approach.

A Home-Made Ouija Board

A writer has given the following directions for making a "home-made Ouija Board," viz., "A Planchette may be used as an 'Ouija' by laying down a sheet of paper upon which the letters of the alphabet have been written or printed in a fairly large semi-circle, the words 'Yes' or 'No' being written at either end, and figures from 1 to 9 written straight across a little lower down. Now remove the pencil and insert a small moderately sharpened stick as a pointer, and the Planchette may run about, point to letters or numbers, answers your questions at 'Yes' or 'No,' or messages may be spelt out as you watch its movements."

Trance or Inspirational Mediumship

Through the development and unfoldment afforded by the development circle, the mediumistic persons in that circle, particularly the medium who is "sitting for development" in the circle, will in all probability develop that phase of mediumship caller "Trance Mediumship," or "Inspirational Mediumship." Of this phase of mediumship a writer has said: "This mental phase of mediumship involves the development of a degree of impressibility which may range from the conscious reception of suggestion, or impulses, or thoughts from other intelligences, to the lucidity on the spiritual plane which is displayed by conscious clear-seeing, or spirit-sight. The phenomena of super-sensuous reception due to spirit influence are elicited in much the same way as a mesmerist arouses the clairvoyant powers of his subject. The somnambulic sleep, or trance, is induced in the subject whose voluntary powers are no longer under his control, and the involuntary processes are well-nigh suspended. In this state his spirit sometimes gains a larger degree of freedom, and is able to perceive on the inner or spiritual plane.

Symptoms of Trance Condition

"If you are likely to become a trance-speaking medium, you will probably experience a sensation as a falling or dizziness, as if you were going to faint; this may continue until you become entirely unconscious on the external plane, and you will know no more until you regain your normal condition, although, while under the influence of the operator, you may have been speaking more or less coherently. He may not, at first, be able to convey the exact impression he wishes to produce. His 'suggestion' is not strong enough to set your involuntary nerves vibrating in just the way he desires; consequently his thought is not transferred to you in a manner which insures faithful reproduction, and you should not be disappointed because of such imperfect results at the outset. If your mind is filled with the desire to succeed, you will become too self-conscious, and will thus destroy the very condition upon which success depends."

The Entranced State

Another mediumistic writer says: "The entrancement usually takes place all at once, and the entranced one passes into the realm of communication with the spirits without much warning of any kind. When the medium is entranced it is highly essential that there be no commotion or fear expressed in thought or action in the circle. It must be remembered that the welfare of the medium depends a great deal on the conditions of the others present, and purity of thought and pleasant expectation should be the first thing looked after when the entrancement occurs. In passing into the trance, the medium usually grows very pale and acts not unlike a person going into a faint. But he or she must be allowed to pass behind the veil without any commotion. When the entrancement is accomplished, the manifestations may take place in different ways. There are, in fact, many forms of manifestation belonging to this particular phase of mediumship, but they all come under the general rule and conditions."

Trance Phenomena

Another writer has said: "In entering the trance condition of mediumship, you will probably become semi-conscious, or perhaps almost completely unconscious. The influence will stimulate your breathing, which will become rapid and irregular; your eyes will close and you will be unable to open them, and your hands and body may twitch and jerk as if you were being subjected to a series of galvanic shocks. The sitters should keep calm and sympathetic, but they should check any tendency on the part of the medium to undue noise, or violence, or absurdity. You will be aware of what you are doing, but will be unable to fully exercise the will to interfere or try to stop. You will most likely become conscious of an impulse to do something, or to blurt out certain words. If you resist, you will only make the task more difficult and hinder the attainment of the end you have in view. Your best course is to hold your judgment in suspense; so do not be hostile or critical, but act out your impressions.

Entering the Trance

"Let the influence have its course—say what you feel you must say, and never mind about your own state of consciousness. You will be much more likely to pass into the unconsciousness of the trance (if you desire to do so) if you say, 'Now, spirit friend, I trust myself to you, and will yield my body and brain to your control, for you to do the best you can with and through me. I am willing to co-operate with you for the time being, and trust you to do your utmost for the good of others.' It is not necessary that you should be utterly unconscious, although you may think it is, to prove that another intelligence is operating upon and through you. The evidence of that fact will be displayed in the nature of the message and the unusual ability displayed by you when under the stimulating influence of the operator.

Advice to Trance Mediums

"Most mediums find that their powers vary. Sometimes there seems to be a high degree of lucidity. The impressions which they receive are clear and strong; and the ideas seem to flow through them freely, and the quality of the inspirations is exhilarating, and they feel strengthened and uplifted. But there are other days when they feel very much alone. The influence that affects them is weak; they get only hazy impressions, and there is a woeful lack of ideas. It seems as if the heavens were brass, or that they themselves were unresponsive. They know not why, but whatever they can 'lay hold of' to speak, or whatever the spirit people can project into their sphere seems forced and incomplete. If you should ever have these experiences, turn your attention to something else. Do not 'harp on one string' too much. Physical exercise, change of scene, social company, and rest, will soon restore your tone and renew your powers."

Speaking Mediumship

In that form of Trance or Inspirational Mediumship generally known as "Speaking Mediumship," the communicating spirit assumes partial or complete control of the vocal organs of the medium, and the spirit then directly addresses the circle or audience of listeners, just as he would do were he, himself, actually in the flesh confronting them and using his own vocal organs. In such addressing the spirit manifests many of the characteristics which distinguished him during his earth life. The medium's voice is changed, and his manner takes on a quite different form, i.e., that of the spirit which he possessed in his own earth life. In fact, in some cases, it has actually been observed that the very body of the medium seemed to either shrink, or else enlarge, as if taking the form of the etheric framework of the controlling spirit.

Public Speaking Under Control

A writer gives the following advice concerning Speaking Mediumship: "Should you be controlled to give public addresses, it will be best to withhold the name of the spirit who prompts or controls your utterances. Most intelligent spirits prefer to be known by their teachings, rather than by the names they bore when on earth. If the addresses are eloquent and beautiful, and the thoughts presented are good and true, they will be acceptable on their own merits, and would not be one bit more valuable because they were inspired by some well-known historical persons. Whereas, if you announce the name of a spirit, your hearers may consider that the address does not come up to the standard of the ability displayed by that individual before he dies, and may discredit and discard the good that they might otherwise have found in your utterances."

Spirit Advice and Counsel

If spirits voluntarily tender you their advice upon business matters, especially if they are friends or relatives whom you know and trust, and who, when here, were capable and experienced business people, you may well give heed to their counsel, even though you may not feel it wise to follow it; but do not make a practice of going to the spirits for information concerning trade or finance. Why should you expect that wise and enlightened spirits should concern themselves about stocks and shares, commerce, or manufacturing? Probably they knew but little about these things when they were here, and have no heed for such knowledge over there; and it will be well for you to learn to live your own life, do your business, and accept the ordinary duties and responsibilities which naturally devolve upon you. Let mediumship be a part of your education and development, not the whole.

Impersonating Manifestations

It will often happen that some spirit will take control of the medium for the purpose of communicating with a friend present in the circle or audience, and for the purpose of positively identifying himself to that friend; he may deem it necessary to cause you to impersonate himself as he was during his earth life. At first this may seem odd, but there are reasons why this happens.

In such cases you will experience a peculiar feeling of undergoing a complete transformation of personality, and often a dual-personality for the time being. Another instance of this kind is where a spirit wishing to communicate with friends, and this being his first opportunity to manifest in the impersonating phase, he may yield to that peculiar psychic law which seems to operate in the direction of causing a spirit, manifesting for the first time, to enact his dying experiences, and to manifest a pantomimic reproduction of his last hours preceding death.

In such cases, the medium reproduces, in a most startlingly real manner, the movements, ways of breathing, coughing, gestures, ejaculations, and may even go so far as to utter the "last words" of the dying man whose spirit now controls the medium. Every medium should be prepared for an experience of this kind, for it will sometimes completely upset a medium unfamiliar with it, and not knowing just what it all means.

Incidents of Impersonations

In a case such as stated above, the medium will probably find himself either partially or completely conscious of what is being said and done by the spirit through his body or vocal organs. He will naturally strive to escape the utterance of the strange cries, moans, vocal gasps and efforts, and the dead cries and farewell words of the dying man or woman. Some mediums have felt at such times as if they were losing their reason, and they have struggled to throw off the spirit control and influence in order to regain their mental balance. The best mediums advise the young mediums to keep as cool, calm, and collected as possible in such cases, and not to allow themselves to become panic-stricken. A writer on the subject has said: "Trust to the sincerity of the spirit and the good sense of the sitters, and throw off your fear. Yield obedience to your control, and neither help nor hinder it. Just do and say what you feel you have to do or say, and leave the results. You cannot, or should not, be held responsible for failure by the sitters, if there is no recognition; and by responding and giving free course to the suggestion, which reaches you as an impulse or mental impression, greater success will follow, and the development you seek will be promoted. If, however, you find that the impersonations are untrue, and the sitters are unable to interpret or recognize what you do or say after you have followed out your impressions a number of times, then resist them with all your strength of will, and require from the spirit the proof of his identity in some other way."

Incidents of Inspirational Mediumship

Another writer speaking concerning inspirational mediumship, has said: "In inspirational speaking it will be noted that the medium often gives a really wonderful speech, although he may naturally be a very poor conversationalist. These speeches are often preserved and some of them form exceptionally interesting literature. These speeches are generally given when the medium is seated, but sometimes he loses balance and falls to the floor. Still, as long as the spirit control has anything to say, he will say it through the vocal organs of the medium. But it must always be borne in mind that a medium does not, as a general rule, become an inspirational speaker all at once. There is a stage of development through which he must pass in which the spirit control assumes charge of the body of the medium, and this takes some time and is usually accomplished in steps. First, the medium gives evidence of inspirational speaking by uttering guttural sounds, and very often his mouth merely moves without giving forth any sound whatever. Little by little the control gains access to the inner atmosphere of the medium, and when he has broken the final barriers, he can speak and act and deliver what he has to say. But it must be remembered that the mind of the medium is not to be left out of the question entirely. He is often called upon to aid in the interpretation of the speeches the spirit delivers, and these he may misinterpret and lend to them color of his own mentality, without his conscious intention to do so, however."

Value of Identification

In impersonation mediumship, however, no matter how interesting the manifestation may be, it is of prime importance that the identity of the spirit should be clearly established, providing that the spirit himself claims positively to be some particular individual; this, of course, does not apply to instances in which the spirit does not claim identity with any particular departed person, and where the communications are given anonymously. It is this feature of identification that renders this phase of mediumship so valuable and important. A well-known 244medium, in a trance state, once delivered the following message from a spirit: "Impersonation mediumship is the most valuable that the world can possibly have today. When by the aid of the impersonating medium, the inquirer is enabled to converse with his beloved deceased friends, and they make themselves actually visible in the personality of the medium, plain to consciousness and understanding, and tell him specifically points and facts of identity and experience that are utterly beyond the power of any other intelligence to tell, then he has something borne in upon him through the senses of sight, of hearing and understanding that appeals to him. Therefore, the impersonating medium is the most valuable medium you can present to inquirers." Another mediumistic writer has said: "This kind of mediumship carries conviction of the real presence of the so-called dead, and your aim should be to get into communication with the intelligent operator at the other end of the line, and elicit from him evidences of his identity and purpose. Table movements, raps, materializations, writings, messages, or controls, are of comparatively little value unless by their agency you can secure proofs of the personal identity and survival after death of your departed friends, or some indications of a rational purpose on the part of the operator."

Fraudulent Claims of Identity

We would be lacking in our sense of duty and obligation toward our readers, however, were we to refrain from calling their attention to the fact that positive and strict identification of the spirits, in cases where identity is claimed, is a duty on the part of investigators, particularly on the part of those who happen to be relatives or friends of the deceased person whose presence and identity are being claimed by the controlling spirit who is manifesting the impersonation. As we have said, elsewhere, we must remember that there are all kinds of discarnate spirits, just as there are all kinds of incarnate spirits; and that the nature of a spirit is not greatly changed by passing out of the body. Just as there are imposters on the earth plane, so are there imposters on the spirit plane. And, accordingly, caution is to be exercised on both planes. The following quotations from mediumistic writers will serve to illustrate this point, and to show that the best mediumistic authorities themselves insist upon this precaution being taken.

Guarding Against Fraudulent Spirits

One writer says: "While most mediums seek for some guide or control of prominence, it must not be always taken for granted that the controlling spirit during a séance is always just what he claims to be. For instance, a spirit control might give his name as Henry Clay, and he might deliver a spirited talk or oration, which, however, would be reeking with grammatical errors. Even though he insists that he is Henry Clay, our reason will tell us that he is not what he pretends to be. The change which we call death cannot lead all spirits to reform, and there are many who, as in earth life, are unworthy of our association, and should be gotten rid of as soon as they appear. When these fraudulent spirits appear, the atmosphere of the circle should be made very sacred and high in character. Evil spirits, and those of low characters, cannot endure the presence of elevated and high thoughts, and by the holding of thoughts of this character the circle can soon rid itself for good of these troublesome entities—and it should do so without fail."

Spirit Jokers

Another writer says, on this point: "That there are spirits who sometimes impersonate, and seek to pass themselves off as friends of the sitters, cannot be denied; in fact, we have had personal proof of the same on several occasions. But these troublesome and vexatious visitors invariably get 'bowled out' if the investigators are observant and careful. In fact, such entities are neither as numerous, or as evilly disposed, as many persons imagine them to be. There are spirits who 'play up to' the weaknesses and flatter the vanity of those to whom they communicate. And it is equally true that there are spirits who give glowing assurances of the good things that they will perform by-and-by, and profess to be some of the 'great ones' of the past, is equally true. It is a well-known saying that 'people love a lord,' and this amiable weakness is fully realized by the jokers on the other side—but the fault does not wholly rest with them! Their too confiding and credulous mediums are too often in the main responsible for their own mystification and misleading. They are often so anxious to be guided by some 'eminent' person who will be to them an 'authority,' that they practically invite spirit pretenders to fool them to the top of their bent. This does not apply to all cases of real or supposed deception, but it does cover a large proportion of such experiences. In many instances there is an element of self-deception—or auto-suggestion—and the 'wish becomes father to the thought,' and the sensitive medium's unrestrained imaginative powers do the rest."

A Typical Case of Identification

The following typical case of undoubted identification of a visiting spirit is related by Smedley in his work concerning spiritualistic experiences, and may be taken as a pattern to be followed by investigators in demanding and obtaining proofs of identity in cases where same is asserted. The medium in this case was a woman of high standing in spiritualistic circles, and the séance took place in Mr. Smedley's own home. The medium was at that time a perfect stranger to the Smedley family, and to their little circle of invited friends. The séance was opened by the singing of hymns, and before long the medium went under control. Mr. Smedley says: "She passed under the control of an intelligent being, opened her eyes, and manifested the greatest amazement." He then relates the subsequent experience as follows: "After looking around the room very deliberately at various objects, then at one person after another, and fixing her eyes on my wife, she ran across the room, and throwing her arms around my wife's neck, she kissed her most affectionately, addressing her as 'My dear sister.' After speaking with my wife in endearing terms, she came across the room to me, and placing her right hand on my shoulder, said: 'Well, my dear brother.' (This was exactly as a deceased sister of my wife had been in the habit of doing.) 'How unspeakingly glad I am for such a privilege as this! When we used to sit by the hearth at night, conversing on various topics that used to interest us so much, we little expected we should ever have such a privilege. You know we used to sit up at night discussing theological questions till the embers in the grate died out, and sometimes a chiding voice from upstairs cried out: "Alfred, Alfred, do come to bed. Do you know what time it is? You know Charlotte is not fit to sit up so late."' This was precisely what had taken place, the exact words being used.

Identifying Property

"She referred to a number of incidents known only to her and ourselves. She asked for an album in which she had written the dedication, pointing this out, and also various pieces of poetry she had written in it. She asked for a hymn-book, and desired us to sing what had been her favorite hymn, which at my request she instantly found. She next asked for a Bible, and asked me to read her favorite Psalm. I requested her to find it, although I knew well which it was. She turned to it instantly, and I read: 'The Lord is my shepherd,' etc. When the Psalm was finished, the medium stood transfigured before us; her countenance was radiant and her eyes bright with a heavenly light. Turning to my wife, she said: 'Sister, dear, by inviting strangers to your house tonight you have entertained angels unawares!' After the meeting, the medium remarked: 'When under control I was strongly influenced to look around for a picture, but could not find it. I do not know what it meant, but the control was anxious to find a picture.' My wife replied: 'My sister painted a picture of the Saviour bearing His cross, many years ago, and it now hangs in our dining room.' The above incidents, combined with her mannerisms, and bearing in mind that the medium was an entire stranger to us, and uneducated, were sufficient evidence of the presence and influence of her deceased sister to cause my wife to exclaim, 'Of a truth, that was my sister Charlotte!'"

Identifying Historical Personages

Of course, a close, personal identification, similar to that stated in the above recital, is impossible in cases when the spirit claims to be some well-known historical personage. But in the last named class of cases it will be found possible to ask questions concerning the life and career of the supposed celebrity and to form a general idea of the correctness of the claim by the quality and general character of the answers given. It will be found that genuine spirits are nearly always anxious to definitely establish the truth of their claims to identity, and will often go to great pains to do so. In short, treat the spirit just as you would were he in the flesh, speaking to you over a telephone, and endeavoring to establish his identity; this will always be a safe and just rule to employ and follow.

PART XI

HIGHER SPIRIT MANIFESTATIONS

WE frequently hear of, and witness manifestations of, what is called "spirit psychometry," "spirit clairvoyance," and "spirit clairaudience." In the earlier chapters of the present book we have spoken of the psychic principles and laws underlying psychometry, clairvoyance, and clairaudience. We have seen that all of these forms and phases of psychic phenomena are capable of being produced independent of spirit guidance, control, or influence. In fact, most of such manifestations are so produced, even when they are considered to be phases of spirit mediumship. But, outside of these manifestations, there are found cases in which such phenomena are produced by the aid, influence, and assistance, if not indeed the direct power of, the controlling spirits of the medium.

Spirit Psychometry and Clairvoyance

In those instances in which the controlling influence of such phenomena is clearly that of disembodied spirits, we find two distinct classes of the same, as follows: (1) cases in which the spirits aided in the establishing of the psychic rapport, and thus rendered more efficient, clear, and strong; (2) cases in which the spirits exerted their own psychometric, clairvoyant or clairaudient power, and then communicated the result through their mediums to the circle. In the first of above classes, the psychic faculties of the medium really perform the work, although greatly aided by the addition of the psychic power of the spirit. In the second of the above classes, the work is performed solely by the psychic powers of the spirits, and the medium acts merely as the line of communication between spirit and the circle. It must be remembered that the spirits who have passed out of the body are possessed of the same order of psychic faculties as are those still in the body, and that, likewise, on both planes there is a great variation of the degree of such powers between different individuals.

Spirit Psychic Assistance

From the above, it will be seen that a mediumistic person may practice in psychometry, clairvoyance, and clairaudience, either with or without the assistance of the spirits. In case the spirits are assisting in the direction of performing the psychic work themselves, and then communicating the result to the medium, the medium of course has but to remain passive and receive the communication. In cases, however, in which the spirits assist merely by strengthening the psychic power of the medium by aiding in the production of the rapport conditions, or by lending the psychic power to add to that of the medium, then the medium has but to proceed just as we have pointed out in the earlier portions of this book devoted to the subjects of psychometry, clairvoyance, etc.

Writing Mediumship

In what is known as "writing mediumship" the medium's hand is controlled by the spirit, and is caused to write messages to those present, or to answer questions propounded by some of those present at the circle. In some quarters such writing is called "automatic writing," but inasmuch as this last term is also applied to cases in which the hand of the person writes a message telepathed by a living person, it would seem that the old term "writing mediumship" is still the best one to use in the cases in which the spirit control is using the hand of the medium for the purpose of communication. The following statements made by different mediumistic writers on this particular subject will prove interesting and instructive to the young mediums seeking development along the lines of this special phase of mediumship.

Incidents of Writing Mediumship

One writer says: "If the medium reaches the writing stage, he generally passes into it in much the same manner that he does into the inspirational speaking. That is, he becomes entranced, and in entrancement of this kind he usually loses his conscious self, although it is not essential that he should do so. He may remain partially conscious, but he will be very pale and will have no control whatever over the hand which does the writing. When the hand that writes is generally the only part of him that becomes numb, one entire side may become limp and inactive, and it is at this stage that a pencil must be placed in his hand all ready for writing, and a large sheet of heavy paper be put on the table before him. It is urged that the pencil be a heavy one, and the paper tough and coarse, for the first writing of a writing medium is not even a fair specimen of penmanship, being heavy and very difficult to decipher. As his hand wanders here and there, his body may sway and the pencil be brought in contact with the paper. When he begins to write, the strokes are crude and jerky and uncertain. The first notes that he delivers to the sitters are very often difficult to make out, and sometimes it is impossible to tell what they are. But this condition will be gradually overcome until the writing is very fair, and finally it can be written on much finer paper and with an ordinary pencil. When questions are to be asked, they may be put direct to the medium, and the answers will be written out and signed by the spirit sending them. As the medium develops, it will not be necessary for him to have the questions put to him verbally. Write the questions on a little slip of paper, and place these slips in his hands. The spirit will read them, and then use his arm as before in writing out answers. But this stage cannot be attained in a day or a week, and it is a sign of the higher forms of development, and should be looked upon by the members of the circle as evidence of the highest order establishing the great success they have attained."

Developing Writing Mediumship

Another writer on the subject of writing mediumship says to those developing this phase of mediumship: "Your hands may be caused to shake and move about as if you desired to write. You may be quite conscious, or only semi-conscious, but you will feel that you are unable to prevent the movements. In such a case, the sitters should provide pencil and paper and await results. They should speak to the control and request him to work quietly, and in all probability the rapid preliminary scrawls will soon give place to slower and more legible writing. Many persons have developed as writing mediums who have never sat in a circle, and without being entranced. We should advise you, if you decide to sit alone and make experiments in this direction, to avoid excitement, expectancy, and preconceptions. Proceed as though you were speaking to a visible friend, and request that someone will move your hands to write. Provide yourself with a writing pad, or several sheets of paper, and while holding a pencil in readiness, withdraw your thoughts from your hand and arm, and assume a passive condition. If you are strongly mediumistic, words and sentences may be written, but you need hardly expect such results at first."

Stead's Method and Results

W. T. Stead, the eminent English investigator, said: "I hold my pen in the ordinary way, but when the writing is beginning I do not rest my wrist or arm upon the paper, so as to avoid the friction, and to give the influence, whatever it may be, more complete control of the pen. At first, the pen is apt to wander into mere scrawling, but after a time it writes legibly. Unlike many automatic writers who write as well blindfolded as when they read what they write as they are writing it, I can never write so well as when I see the words as they come. There is danger in this, which is most clearly illustrated When my hand writes verse—especially rhymed verse—for the last word in each line suggests to my conscious mind a possible rhyme for the ending of the following line; this rouses up my mind, my own ideas get mixed with those of the communicating intelligence, and confusion is the result." The above statement of Mr. Stead becomes doubly interesting and valuable when we remember that through his hand, controlled by a spirit intelligence, came that wonderful series of messages afterward published under the title of "Letters from Julia," which book excited the attention and interest of the civilized world at the time of its publication, and even to this day enjoys a great popularity.

Automatic Writing vs. Inspirational Writing

Another writer says: "Inspirational or impressional writing is frequently mistaken for that which is more purely passive or automatic. The medium or sensitive person experiences a strong impulse to write, but does not receive any clear or consecutive train of thought. He sets down one word, and then others follow as fast as he can indicate them, but he must begin to write before the complete sentence is given to him. In other cases, the thoughts flow into his consciousness faster than his pen can record them;

but in the truly 'automatic' form of communication the mind of the sensitive is not consciously affected. He can read and think about other and entirely different subjects, and need take no more interest in the work than he would if his hand did not belong to him nor than if a spirit laid hold of and guided the pencil. Some mediums who write automatically have to be mentally quiet; they find that if the mind is preoccupied the hand will not write, although, even in such cases, it frequently happens that the amanuensis is ignorant of the communication until he reads it afterwards."

Use and Abuse of Automatic Writing

J. A. White, a trance and clairvoyant medium himself, says of the phase of writing mediumship: "There is a great tendency, particularly in cases of automatic writing, to do too much of it. No sooner do some people find that the pencil will move, than they spend all their spare time in this fascinating pursuit, which, in their undeveloped state, I believe to be a dangerous and unwise practice. They are apt to exclaim, when any question arises during the day: 'Let us see what the spirits have to say.' This, carried to extremes, leads to one thing and one thing only—obsession. I believe in fixing a time, and, unless in exceptional cases, refusing to sit at any other.

"Of course I am speaking of mediumship when it is in its budding stage. A developed medium can judge for himself, and knows from experience how far to go. It is a favorite trick of a certain class of spirits when they find they have a sensitive who can 'feel' them, to give them that pricking sensation in the arm which denotes their presence. 'So-and-so wants to write,' and away rushes the medium for the pencil, and sits down. This I do not believe in. I have seen far more harm than good come from it. The proper way to develop, in my opinion, is to sit at home in a small, carefully selected circle, two or three times a week, at stated hours, and with a competent conductor who knows what he is doing."

Advice to Writing Mediums

A French medium says: "We urge beginners in their own interest not to take up the pencil for automatic writing, or to sit at a table for communications at any free moment, without rhyme or reason, for disorder in experiment is one of the first and most serious dangers to be avoided. An absolutely strict rule should be made not to attempt the effort more than once every other day."

Another writer says: "The communications that are received by the various forms of passive, impressional, automatic, and inspirational writing must not be regarded as valuable merely because of the conditions under which they were obtained, nor because of their spirit origin, real or supposed. Under all circumstances receive with the utmost reserve and caution long-winded communications from notable characters who claim to be 'Napoleon Bonaparte,' 'Lord Bacon,' 'Socrates,' or other great personages; for in the majority of cases, the value of the communication is exactly the reverse of the importance of the name attached.

"This applies to automatic writings quite as much as to spoken messages. Judge the statement made by the ordinary standards, apart from their claimed exalted origin. If rational, beautiful, and spiritually helpful and enlightening, they are worth having on their own merits; but if they are unreasonable, wild or dogmatic, or pretentious and flattering, they should be discarded. All conversations must be immediately brought to a halt. Much like an unwelcome telephone call, no attention should be given. As well, it is unlikely that their character can be changed by you... attention then should be turned in some other direction."

Drawing Mediumship

What is known as "drawing mediumship" is but a variation of writing mediumship, at least so far as is concerned the nature of the manifestation. In both cases the spirit control moves the hand of the medium, in one case forming letters and words, and in the other case forming figures, designs, etc. In some rare instances, the spirit control operating through the hand of the medium has produced crayon drawings, water color sketches, and even oil paintings, although the medium himself or herself, was unable to even draw a straight line, much less to execute a finished drawing or painting. The principle governing such mediumship, and the development, thereof, is precisely the same as that governing the phase of writing mediumship previously described.

The Planchette

From time to time, during the past fifty years, there have been invented or arranged various forms of mechanical contrivances designed to assist in the development of writing mediumship. The most popular of these has been the Planchette, which has enjoyed great popularity for many years past. The Planchette is a little heart-shaped board, having two legs, with tiny wheels at the end, attached to the board. Near the pointed end of the heart-shaped board is a hole, into which a pencil is inserted. A sheet of paper of good size is spread upon a table, and the Planchette is placed thereupon. Then the sitter, or two sitters, place their hand or hands upon the board—generally resting only the tips of their fingers lightly upon it. The sitter or sitters then await results.

How to Use the Planchette

If the sitter is mediumistic the Planchette will begin to move about slowly at first, gradually gathering force and definite direction.

After a few preliminary strokes, circles, or lines having been drawn, the Planchette will seem to have been firmly taken hold of by some spirit hand, and will begin to write words and sentences in a more or less 'scrawly' fashion. When the writing once begins, questions may be asked of and answered by the spirits. Some persons report that to them the Planchette seems to move by itself, pulling their hands with it; but others report that they feel the movement of their arms and hands, as the spirit propels the machine in the work of waiting. Some know what is being written during the process, while others do not know what has been written until they afterwards read it. Sometimes the writing begins Boon after the sitting is commenced, while in other cases the sitters have to wait a long time, or even to sit several times before the writing actually begins. Sometimes the Planchette will refuse to write for certain persons, but will write freely for others. The general advice is to exercise patience in the Planchette sittings, and not to expect to get the best results at once; and, particularly, not to begin asking questions immediately after the writing begins.

Healing Mediumship

Some mediums seem to be particularly adapted to the work of healing by psychic force, and this phase of mediumship is known as "healing mediumship." The healing medium is guided principally by the spirit influence, so far as is concerned the choice of methods of procedure in his healing work. The following directions, however, given by a mediumistic writer, will give the young medium a very good, practical general idea of the procedure to be followed in case his spirit control does not indicate some other method. This writer says: "If you are impressed with the idea that you possess healing power, you can easily experiment upon your suffering friends or acquaintances. If you are mediumistic, and spirits desire to develop you for the healing work, you will readily feel that you are impressed what to do. Your hands will be guided to the proper position, and you will spontaneously make the requisite passes. Magnetic healing has really nothing to do with massage, the induction of sleep, or with any form of mesmerism or hypnotism. The healing medium should centre his thought and interest solely and wholly with the idea of creating a cure. He will need to be sympathetic, but hopeful. Do not let your patient think about his ailments, but arouse his thought and engage his attention upon some outside subject. Make him feel comfortable, and lead him to expect good results; to do this you must be affirmative and confident. Unless you are impressed, or are controlled, to do otherwise, sit in front and take hold of the hands of the sufferer for a time, then make gentle, short, downward passes over the part affected, and conclude with long sweeping passes from head to foot without contact.

"For local affections, point your hands at or just touch the spot with your finger tips, or make direct horizontal or slightly downward movements, as if you were throwing something at him. A warm, comfortable room is favorable to magnetizing, and a genial mental atmosphere, created by cheerful and kindly minds in the operator and persons present, will contribute largely to the success of the treatment. You will do well to act upon your impressions and make the passes in whatever way you feel impelled or compelled.

"If you operate under spirit guidance, you will be impressed more or less clearly how to proceed in each case. In all probability you may sympathetically 'take on,' and be affected by, the symptoms of the disease from which the patient suffers, and in that way be able to form an accurate diagnosis of the case; but you must guard against exhaustion, and should always 'throw off' from yourself the influence that you have received, and wash your hands thoroughly after each treatment."

Materialization Mediumship

One of the rarest, and at the same time the most eagerly sought after phase of mediumship, is that known as "materialization mediumship." In this phase of mediumship the discarnate spirit is able to draw upon the vital forces of the medium, and those present at the seance, to such effect that it may clothe itself with a tenuous, subtle form of matter, and then exhibit itself to the sitters in the same form and appearance that it had previously presented in its earth life. Many of the most remarkable testimonies to the truth and validity of spiritualism have been obtained through this phase of mediumship, and it is the aim of all investigators to witness, and of most mediums to be the channel of the production of, this remarkable phase of mediumistic phenomena.

In almost all instances of materialization phenomena in the record of modern spiritualism we find that a cabinet was employed. There are two main reasons advanced for the necessity of the cabinet in this phase of mediumistic phenomena. The first of said reasons is that in many cases darkness has been found necessary for the preliminary work of the materialization, although absolute darkness is not necessary in the general room in which the materialized spirit forms afterward appear. The second of the said reasons is that there seems to be a psychic atmosphere created by the blending of the spirit forces with those of the medium, which atmosphere must be kept apart from and unmixed with the auras of the members of the outside circle or the general visitors at the séance.

Why the Cabinet Is Necessary

Just what is the technical reason for this necessity is a source of argument and dispute among the different authorities on the subject, and it may be said that the matter is not as yet definitely settled. But whatever may be such technical explanation, the fact remains that the seclusion of the medium has been found almost absolutely necessary for the production of the phenomena of spirit materialization. The few exceptions noted in the history of modern spiritualism only go to establish the general rule. For the purpose of a general study of the subject, it may be accepted as a general fact that the production of spirit materialization has as one of its necessary conditions the presence and use of a dark cabinet in which the medium is secluded from the circle or assemblage of persons attending the séance.

How to Make the Spirit Cabinet

One of the best kinds of cabinets for this purpose is a small alcove room, or other small room adjoining the room in which the visitors sit at the séance. A large closet will also answer the purpose very well; in fact many mediums prefer the closet to any other form of cabinet. If neither a small room nor closet is available, then it becomes necessary to build or erect a cabinet for the medium. One of the simplest and least expensive methods of building or erecting a cabinet for the medium is as follows: Take a large piece of dark cloth, cotton or woolen, or else a large shawl, and fasten it by stout twine or cord across a corner of the room. It will be better if the curtain is made in two pieces, so as to allow it to part in the middle for the purpose of the entry and exit of the medium, and for the purpose of allowing the materialized spirit form to show itself to the circle. It is not necessary that all light be excluded from the cabinet, and therefore it need cause no worriment if a little light filters in over the top of the curtain; but the lights in the main room should be kept burning "dim and low," not only for the purpose of aiding in the actual work or materialization, but also in order to preserve the proper conditions when the materialized spirit presents itself between the opened curtains.

How to Use the Spirit Cabinet

When the cabinet is properly arranged the medium enters it and sits down on a chair provided for that purpose. He should not be disturbed thereafter, but should be encouraged and aided in his work by the maintenance of a quite, reverent mental attitude on the part of the members of the circle. It will be found helpful if a few hymns are sung while waiting for manifestations from the cabinet. The best way to encourage materialization at a regular circle is for gradual steps to be taken leading up to this high phase of phenomena. For example, the circle should sit in the ordinary way at its regular meetings, and devote itself to the production of the lesser forms of phenomena. Then, before adjournment, the medium may go into the cabinet while the circle sits for materialization phenomena. This practice may be made to form a regular part of the proceedings of the circle. But the circle must be very patient concerning the production of this class of phenomena, for the necessary conditions are very difficult to develop, even when aided by the most powerful spirits. Many sittings may be required before even the slightest sign of materialization is obtained—but the final result will repay much waiting and watching, much patience and much perseverance. But sooner or later the phenomena will come if the proper conditions are provided for them.

Spirit Phosphorescence

The first evidence of the presence and activity of the spirit forces striving to produce the phenomena and materialization will probably be the appearance of peculiar hazy phosphorescent lights playing in front of the curtain forming the front of the cabinet. These lights will consist of small globules or balls of phosphorescent light that will dance about, like the familiar will-o'-the-wisp seen over swamps and in damp, woody places. These lights will flit here and there, will alternately appear and disappear. Sometimes they will appear as if a multitude of fire-flies were clustered in front of the curtain. When these fire balls appear the circle may know that it is well on the way to perfect materializations.

Appearance of Materialized Substance

As the power increases and the conditions become stabilized and perfected, the manifestations will become more pronounced. It often happens that cloudy nebulous bodies of psychic substance are formed and float around in front of the cabinet, like clouds of steam or vapor illumined by a dim phosphorescent light. Sometimes attempts will seem to have been made to form these clouds into the semblance of the human body, and often these bodies are more or less incomplete, as for instance the arms may be missing, or else there may be dark holes where the eyes, nose, and mouth should be.

It may be stated here that the sitters should not be frightened by these sights, nor should mental agitation be permitted to manifest too strongly, as such conditions act to retard further developments. However, it is often difficult to contain such feelings under certain circumstances. No one can be blamed if they are suddenly overtaken by fright during a particularly unnerving situation. The best thing to do is to always be prepared and have a friend close at hand to lend emotional support. Sometimes perfect hands and arms materialize, but apparently not attached to a body. These hands may float out over the circle, and may touch the members thereof. In rare cases these hands take articles handed them by members of the circle, which articles are then "dematerialized" and vanish from sight, afterward appearing in other parts of the house. Large articles of furniture have been known to be dematerialized in this way.

277

Materialized Spirit Forms

Later on, the nebulous spirit forms will take on more definite lines and form, and will become more plainly visible, and will also assume a far more "solid" appearance. When the phenomenon reaches its highest phases, the materialized spirit forms can be plainly seen and actually recognized by their friends in earth life. In some cases they will actually leave the front of the curtain and will walk down among the sitters, shaking hands with them, touching them on the cheek, or even embracing some loved one. In rare cases these materialized forms are able to converse with the sitters in the circle, just as plainly as when in earth life. There have been numerous well documented accounts of full-body apparitions appearing during certain séances with photos and even video taken of the events.

Scientific Proof of Materialization

It is not the purpose of this book to prove the existence of mediumistic phenomena—rather it points out the means and methods whereby the student may obtain such proof for himself or herself. But it may be suggested here that the skeptic may find an abundance of proof of the genuineness of materialization phenomena in the records and reports made by eminent scientists, statesmen, and others. Particularly, the report of Sir William Crookes, the eminent English scientist, will furnish such proof to the inquirer who demands "scientific proof" before he will believe anything out of the usual.

Sir William Crookes has given convincing evidence of the genuineness of spirit materialization, even going so far to offer records of the weight of materialized spirits, and their photographs taken by him—in some instances the photographs showing the forms of both medium and spirit materialization.

How to Conduct a Materializing Séance

In sitting for materialization, the circle should maintain the same general demeanor that it observes at other times. Silence or dignified conversation may be indulged in, but joking or levity should be forbidden. Hands should be held, and reverent singing indulged in. It should be remembered that this phase of mediumistic phenomena is not something apart and distinct from the lesser phases which have been described in detail in this book. On the contrary, it is simply a matter of degree, and the same general principles underlie all phases of mediumistic phenomena. Therefore, it is not necessary to repeat the instructions regarding the conduct of the circle, or the rules for the development of the medium. Read the earlier chapters for the same, which are equally applicable in this place as in the places in which they originally appeared.

Trumpet Mediumship

In what is known as "trumpet mediumship," the sound of the voice of the communicating spirit is increased in power by the use of a trumpet shaped arrangement of paper, card-board, tin, or aluminum. There is no particular virtue in the material used, and anyone may make a serviceable trumpet out of heavy paper or thin card-board. The principle of the use of the "spirit trumpet" is precisely that of the well-known megaphone, i.e., it magnifies the sound, and increases its carrying power. A spirit speaking in the faintest whisper through the trumpet is enabled to have its voice heard plainly by those present in the circle, where otherwise nothing would be heard. This method is often superior to the use of electronics that have become so popular recently. This is because electronics are often plagued by outside interference

Often the spirit force is so strong that it will pick up the trumpet and carry it around the circle, tapping the various members thereof, and whispering through it into the ear of some particular members. Weak spirits, therefore, who are unable to make themselves heard in the ordinary way, often employ the trumpet with effect in séances. When the trumpet is used, it should be placed on the table, awaiting the use of the spirits.

Spirit Playing on Musical Instruments, Etc.

The spirit forces also sometimes will see fit to play upon musical instruments placed in the cabinet with the medium, the guitar, mandolin, concertina, accordion, etc., being the instruments preferred in such cases. Of course the skeptics will claim that the medium may play the instruments himself or herself, and thus give ground for the claim of fraud; consequently in the case of public seances, and many private ones as well, the medium will insist upon having his or her hands tied, and other precautions taken to eliminate the possibility of fraud and deception. Such precautions are in no way a reflection upon the medium, and are, in fact, demanded by many mediums as a matter of self-respect, self-protection, and the cause of truth. In many cases in which the mediums were entirely lacking in musical education, knowledge, or training, the spirits have performed skilled selections of music upon the instruments in the cabinet.

Independent Slate Writing

Even though it has gone somewhat out of fashion, what is generally known as "independent slate writing" is a very interesting phase of mediumship, and one of the peculiarities thereof is that such phenomena is sometimes produced through mediums who seem to possess little or no mediumistic powers in other directions. In independent slate writing there is no employment of the hands of the medium by the spirit to form the letters, words, and sentences of the communication. On the contrary, the writing is done directly by the spirit forces, independent of the organism of the medium. Of course the psychic power of the medium and his vital energy as well is drawn upon by the spirits in producing this form of manifestation, but the medium is sometimes seated out of reach of the slates and in no case actually touches the pencil.

The Slate Writing Circle

Independent slate writing is performed as follows: The circle selects two common slates, or else one folding slate. A small bit of chalk or a tiny piece of slate pencil is placed between the two slates, the latter being then placed tightly together, and then bound with thick, strong twine—in some cases the ends of the twine are fastened with sealing wax. This trying and sealing is for the purpose of eliminating the suspicion of fraud or deceit, and for the purpose of scientifically establishing the genuineness of the phenomena. The bound slates are then placed on the table in the middle of the circle. In some cases the medium rests his hands on the slate, and in other cases he keeps his hands entirely away from them—the phenomena itself evidently being produced with equal facility in either case. A written question may be placed inside the slate on a small bit of paper, or else sealed and placed on top of the tied slates.

In some cases the scratching sound of the pencil may be heard proceeding from the tied slates, while on others no sound is heard while the writing is being done. When the slates are opened, at the end of the séance, the slates will be found to contain writing—the answer to the question, or else a general message to the circle—the writing sometimes consisting of but a word or two, while in other cases both of the inside surfaces of the slate will be found to be covered with writing. It often requires quite a number of sittings before this phase of phenomena is secured; in many cases it is never actually secured in a satisfactory form.

Spirit Paintings

There are cases of record in which crayon drawings have been produced on the slates by enclosing small bits of various colored crayons therein when the slates are tied together. Again, oil paintings have been secured on the slates, after small dabs of oil paint of various colors have been placed on the inside surface of the slates, a little linseed oil being poured on each.

Fraudulent Slate Writing

Slate phenomena have been brought into some degree of discredit and disrepute during the past ten years or more, by reason of the fact that a number of unscrupulous "fakers," or bogus-mediums, employed a system where this class of phenomena was counterfeited by trick methods. But, as all careful investigators of mediumistic phenomena well know, some wonderful results are still obtained, quietly and without publicity or notoriety, in many family or private circles. In this case, and in many others, the very best mediumistic phenomena is often produced in those family or private circles, where mutual sympathy, harmony, and spiritual understanding prevail, and where there is an absence of the skeptical, caviling, negative mental attitudes, which tend to interfere with the free flow of spirit power and the degree of manifestation. The tiny flame burning on the family altars and in the private shrines serve to keep alive the Light of the Spirit, which is too often dimmed by the public glare of counterfeit and sensational exhibitions of so-called spirit power.

Practical Advice to Developing Mediums

The young developing medium who has read the foregoing pages of this book will in all probability soon discover just what phase of mediumship is best suited for his natural powers, temperament and psychic constitution. As his innate psychic powers unfold and develop he will be almost instinctively led in the particular directions in which these powers may find the opportunity for the best form of expression and manifestation. And, at the same time, the spirit friends which the young medium will have drawn to himself will have discovered, by means of experimentation, just what phase of mediumship the young medium would best develop in order to convey the messages and communications from the spirit side of life. The following bits of advice from mediumistic writers of good standing will, however, perhaps serve to make the path clearer for the young medium who is reaching out toward the best and most efficient form of manifestation of the powers which he has found are within himself.

Need of Special Development

A writer says: "As a general rule, the best results of mediumship are secured by special development along the lines of natural aptitude. A 'Jack of all trades is master of none,' and such a one is a failure in mediumship as in anything else. You may find it helpful to visit a public medium who is already developed, and who can examine you and give you insight into your natural psychic powers, and counsel you regarding your qualifications and aptitudes, and tell you what to do. But do not attach too much importance to directions received in that way, because so much depends upon the knowledge and power of the operator. One spirit might use you with success in one direction, and another in some other phase; just as one mesmerist may make a subject clairvoyant when another has previously attempted to do so and

283

failed. Nothing but actual experience will settle that point. If, however, after a reasonable amount of patient devotion to the experiment you do not succeed, or are disappointed with what has been done, it will be advisable to effect a change in the conditions. A dissatisfied state of mind is a dangerous one. You may, if you choose, sit by yourself, and try to obtain table movements, or to get 'automatic' or passive writing. You can make experiments in psychometry or try crystal gazing, or endeavor to visualize and to become clairaudient, but we should not advise you to sit alone and invite spirits to put you into the trance. It is better to join some good private circle."

Advice to Discouraged Mediums

A writer gives the following excellent advice to young mediums who have become somewhat discouraged at their lack of success, and slowness of progress: "You have been already informed that you are a medium, and that if you sit you will develop special gifts. But you may say: 'I have sat, and have not developed as I was assured I should.' That is quite probable. The medium whom you consulted may have misjudged your capabilities; the spirit may have estimated what he could have done with or through you, and, from his point of view, may have been perfectly accurate; but possibly the spirits who have endeavored to develop you were unable to succeed.

"People often say: 'I have been told many times that I should make a good medium, but I have not had satisfactory results.' When we hear such statements we are prompt to ask: 'Have you sat for development for any length of time in a harmonious and congenial circle? You cannot expect growth unless you give the requisite conditions. You might as well anticipate a harvest without sowing the seed—just because you bought a sack of wheat! The marvelous results achieved by expert acrobats and athletes are due to their indomitable determination to succeed, and their steady and continuous training of eye, and muscle, and nerve. They concentrate their attention and focus all their powers, and are at once temperate, patient, and persevering in their experiments. The same spirit of devotion; the same firm attitude and watchful attention to all the details; and the same observance of the conditions, physical, mental, moral, and spiritual, are needed if you would educate yourself and become a fit and serviceable instrument for exalted spirit intelligence to afford humanity the benefit of their experiences "over there."""

Avoid Cross-Magnetism

A popular mediumistic writer has given the following excellent words of warning to young mediums: "Do not go into public promiscuous 'developing circles.' There is always a danger of 'cross magnetism' and disorderly manifestations in such gatherings. Owing to the mixed and inharmonious mental, moral, and physical conditions which necessarily exist where a number of strangers and curiosity seekers are attracted, you run the risk of being affected by undeveloped, unprincipled, frivolous, mercenary, self-assertive, or even immoral spirits, who, being attracted to such assemblies, seek to influence incautious and susceptible people who ignorantly render themselves liable to their control.

"The people 'on the other side' are human beings of all grades; they are not morally purified by passing through the death-change; and as we are constantly sending into their other state 'all sorts and conditions of people,' you need not be at all surprised if you get into intercourse with the vain and foolish, the unreliable and pretentious, or the selfish and sinful, if you indiscriminately open the doors of your psychic self and give a free invitation to any spirit that is passing by."

Avoid Psychic Absorption

"You can waste your time, and you can sit in circles, absorb all kinds of psychological influences, exhaust your own, and in many cases become so filled up with contending influences that you are in a state of psychological fever all the time, or so exhaust yourself that you will become as limp and useless as a rag. This is not the way to use the opportunities you have; and you should avoid the injudicious, promiscuous, and insane methods of development of many who are extremely anxious to develop you as a medium, and who often bring discredit upon the subject of mediumship, and do no one the slightest practical good—not even themselves.

We admit that the motives of those who conduct public promiscuous developing circles are good in most cases, but their methods are frequently 'injudicious'—to put it mildly. Under ordinary circumstances, your own pure purpose and the spirits who are in sympathy with your exalted desires and intentions, are sufficient safeguards against the intrusion of low, mischievous or malicious spirits, but you should not venture into conditions which require the trained and disciplined will, and the influence of wise and powerful spirits to protect you against danger, until you have acquired the ability to render yourself positive to the psychic spheres of undesirable people, both in or out of the physical body, and can voluntarily become passive and responsive to the true and trustworthy friends whom you know and love."

The Stewardship of Great Powers

We cannot hope to more fitly close this book devoted to the brief presentation of the facts of the psychic world, and the world of spirit, than by quoting the following words uttered by a faithful laborer in the vineyard of spiritualism: "Spiritualism helps us to understand the 'unity of spirit' and 'the brotherhood of man' in the divine relationship wherein the greatest among us is the servant of all. The possession of great gifts is an added responsibility. We are only stewards of our powers on behalf or others, and our desire to gain knowledge and influence should be vitalized and dignified by the intention to use them to help, teach, and serve our fellows, and in such service we shall ourselves be blest."

For your FREE Catalog of Out-Of-This World
Books, DVD's, and Other Items of Interest...
Please Send Your Name and Mailing Address to:

Global Communications
P.O. Box 753
New Brunswick, NJ 08903

Email: mrufo8@hotmail.com

www.conspiracyjournal.com

Made in the USA
Charleston, SC
09 August 2016